NEANDERTHAL

NEANDERTHAL

Douglas Palmer

Foreword by Christopher Stringer

Dedication

To my wife Tamsy for twenty years of stones to bones.

First published in Great Britain in 2000 by Channel 4 Books

an imprint of Macmillan Publishers Ltd
25 Eccleston Place, London, SW1W 9NF
and Basingstoke

Associated companies throughout the world

ISBN 0 7522 7214 4

A CIP catalogue record for this book is available from
the British Library.

Design by DW Design, London.
Colour origination by Speedscan, Basildon, Essex
Printed and bound in Italy by New Interlitho

Cover photographs by Stephen Morley

wall to wall

This book is published to accompany the television series
Neanderthal, produced by Wall to Wall Television for Channel 4.
Executive producer: Alex Graham
Series director: Tony Mitchell

While every effort has been made to trace copyright holders for
illustrations featured in this book, the publishers will be glad to
make proper acknowledgements in future editions in the event
that any regrettable omissions have occurred at the time of
going to press.

contents

Foreword

As the only human species now on Earth, it is difficult for us to imagine that just 1500 generations ago we shared the world with another kind of human – the Neanderthals. For the last few generations of our modern times, these extinct people have intrigued and perplexed scientists in equal measure. As scientific debate about them has developed, so too has public fascination about their fate. I myself first became interested in the Neanderthals as a boy, and vividly remember a schools radio broadcast that reconstructed the burial of a Neanderthal child. If they were so like us, I wondered, why did they die out? A school project on 'Fossil Man' led me to read more on human evolution, visit the Natural History Museum, where I now work, and eventually go on to study anthropology at university.

There have been many attempts at portraying prehistoric times factually and fictionally, in film and on television, but nothing like the Channel 4 series *Neanderthal*. The recent television series *Walking with Dinosaurs* has been an unprecedented international success and set new standards with which it portrayed the environment and creatures of the ancient past. Now, in *Neanderthal*, the bones and stones that represent the only direct evidence we have of *human* life in Ice Age Europe 35,000 years ago have been brought to life, in the most scientifically accurate and detailed manner ever attempted. Being involved as a consultant to the programmes was a new and challenging experience for me.

Scientifically, I have always shied away from areas where we have little or no data on the Neanderthals, such as determining how hairy they were, what colour eyes they had, or what clothing they wore. But for this series, even though all such evidence perished long ago, an imaginative leap had to be taken. Sometimes this was informed, where data from our closest relatives, the apes, or from modern hunter–gatherers could be used. But in other cases, a sheer guess had to be made.

The world of the Neanderthals was also the world of our ancestors. A world unlike anything we know today, when having to face dangerous animals was an everyday event, and the Earth's fluctuating climate caused mayhem for its human inhabitants. In *Neanderthal* we are back in those dangerous times, in a vanished landscape alongside a vanished people. Douglas Palmer's book shows how that world has been reconstructed from many pieces of a scientific jigsaw, but one where many more are missing, and some will never be found.

The century and a half since the discovery of a strange fossil skeleton in the Neander Valley, Germany, has seen many pendulum swings of scientific opinion between the extremes: Neanderthals as subhuman primitives, or as a slightly different form of modern human. Were they bestial 'ape-men', or just *Homo sapiens* without the benefits of an education, a wash, a shave and decent clothing? The public view of the Neanderthals is still inclined to the former, with the term applied as an insult to any kind of loutish behaviour. But some scientists have claimed that the Neanderthals played music on bone flutes, and buried their dead under garlands of flowers, painting a much more sympathetic and sensitive portrait of these extinct people.

Recent scientific research is perhaps finally stabilizing the pendulum around the view that the Neanderthals were fully human, but were also quite different from us. From their fossil remains, it seems justified to regard them as belonging to a different species from us, *Homo neanderthalensis*. There is now even DNA data to support the view that Neanderthals lay on a different evolutionary line from modern humans. But recognizing the Neanderthals as a different species does not mean we should dehumanize them. Comparing them with us should help to define what it means to be human (what we share with them) and what it means to be a modern human (how we are different).

Research has now also highlighted the complexity of the overlap in time between the last Neanderthals and the first modern humans (Cro-Magnons) in Europe. Although we still cannot date events very precisely, it seems that the Neanderthals survived late (until about 30,000 years ago) in regions such as Spain, Croatia and the Caucasus. There is also some evidence of 'advanced' behaviour by late Neanderthals, behaviour that has sometimes been thought exclusive to modern humans – such as the exploitation of marine resources (excavations in Gibraltar show that over 50,000 years ago their diet included baked mussels, as well as birds, wild goat, deer and rabbit), and the working of bone and mammoth ivory to make jewellery. A fierce scientific debate has developed about whether they did this independently, or only under the influence of neighbouring Cro-Magnons.

While most researchers now agree that the fossil record shows no evidence of evolution from Neanderthals to modern humans, and only hotly disputed evidence of interbreeding between them, it does seem that the supposed behavioural gap between 'them' and 'us' has narrowed. This, together with an apparent long period of coexistence in Europe, makes any simple scenario of a massive superiority of *Homo sapiens* much less plausible. So additional or alternative explanations for the extinction of the Neanderthals are required, and these might include the effects of a remarkably unstable climate during the period of overlap in Europe.

The Neanderthals may not have been our ancestors in any meaningful sense of the word, but some of their behaviour seems very familiar – and so it should. Their world was our world, and their origins were ours, too. They took a different human path, a path that eventually led them to extinction, but there was nothing inevitable about their fate. A few different twists and turns in the evolutionary story and they might be here now, not us. So when we look at the world of the Neanderthals we should think about not only how it was, but how else it might have been if fortune had been on their side rather than ours.

Chris Stringer

Introduction

Just 30,000 years ago there were people living in Europe who looked like us, who behaved and walked like us, and yet were not us – nor even our actual ancestors: they were the Neanderthals. In Ice Age Europe, theirs was a dangerous, hand-to-mouth existence. They took shelter in natural caves where these were available; otherwise they lived out in the open. They clothed themselves with skins of the animals they preyed on for food. Neanderthal game hunters were armed only with wooden spears and intelligence. They killed game at close quarters and often suffered the consequences. They were tough survivors who lived through hard times – and thrived despite it for around 200,000 years.

In many ways, their lives were like our own – they had sex, gave birth, looked after their young and sometimes buried their dead. But there were also differences – they grew old quickly and died young, they could not communicate with complex language, nor could they create art. But one thing is clear – the Neanderthals were people, not ape-men.

When modern humans first arrived in Europe, what did they think and feel when they discovered that there were other people in the world apart from their own kind? For years, writers have been trying to imagine what such an alien encounter might be like. We now know what the final outcome was for the Neanderthals: extinction. But the story of these remarkable people is still largely shrouded in the mists of academic language and the niceties of academic argument over the detailed interpretation of the bones and stones.

The Channel 4 television series made by film-makers Wall to Wall seeks to bring the Neanderthals to life. With the help of some of the world experts in Neanderthal studies, they have recreated the Neanderthals' world in the 'Ice Age' landscapes of Glenveagh National Park, County Donegal in the Republic of Ireland, and populated it with a band of 'living Neanderthals'. The life and being of the extinct Neanderthals are resurrected by actors who can reach into their basic humanity and reproduce a convincing portrayal of a lost people and their way of life.

These reconstructions are the source for most of the illustrations in this book. The synthesis and careful re-enactment of the life of these people and their meeting with modern humans is based on the most up-to-date scientific understanding. Inevitably, however, some of the reconstructions are more secure in scientific fact than others, which are much more speculative. *Neanderthal* examines the facts drawn from the stones and bones, and the interpretations based upon them. There are also contemporary sources we can use, such as the study of our nearest living relatives: the primates. We share common ancestors with these primates – ancestors who lived in Africa some 4 million years ago. The chimp, gorilla and orang-utan we know today give some insight into primitive social behaviour and culture.

The aim of this book is to tell the story of the Neanderthals: where they came from, what they looked like, how they behaved and what happened to them; to give a sense of our scientific understanding of the Neanderthals today. However, the great challenge in trying to understand the Neanderthals, as with any approach to history or prehistory, is to get a sense of the original contemporary circumstances and attitudes of these ancient peoples.

Neanderthal begins by placing the discovery of the Neanderthals in its historic nineteenth-century setting. The intellectual climate in which the discoveries were first made was very different from today, and to begin with the finds were dismissed as historical curiosities rather than what they really were – clues to our prehistoric past. The book goes on to recreate the physical world in which the Neanderthals lived – the Ice Age environment, with its extraordinary plants and animal life. Again, what we readily accept today as evidence for a recent Ice Age was scientific news in the nineteenth century. Many people still firmly believed in the biblical Flood as an explanation for fossil remains on dry land. Now we are in a much better position to understand the chronology of events and the details of the constantly changing climates and habitats that the Neanderthals lived through.

To understand what exactly our ancestors saw when they first came across the Neanderthals, we then have to examine the basic anatomical differences between the Neanderthals and modern humans as preserved in the fossil record of the bones. We can flesh out their appearance to a remarkable extent, but when it comes to the subtleties of skin and hair and eye colour, our interpretations have to rely on other biological and anthropological data. Widening the picture, the social aspects of Neanderthal life are more speculative than their anatomy, but nevertheless much can be reliably established about the way they lived from the archaeological evidence.

The beginning of the end for the Neanderthals was marked by the arrival of modern humans in their territory. To appreciate what modern humans were doing in Europe around 40,000 years ago and where they came from, it is necessary to consider the more ancient evolution of the very distant human relatives in Africa and elsewhere in the world. Although much of the evidence is still based on stones and bones, some remarkable advances in modern biomolecular technology are helping to underpin ideas about human evolution. In addition, biomolecular analysis of genetic material, both modern and fossil DNA, is helping resolve one of the outstanding puzzles of the Neanderthals' extinction – did they breed with Cro-Magnons, and therefore leave a trace in our own inheritance?

There is hope that it will be possible to see how fragmentary fossil sequences, such as Neanderthal DNA, compare with the human genome – especially since the first complete sampling of over 3000 million components of the human genome, announced in June 2000. When the human genome is completely sequenced, even fragments of Neanderthal DNA could then be compared with it to see what differences have evolved over the last 30,000 years since the Neanderthals became extinct. The Neanderthals are no longer just a fossil species preserved as bones and stones but a real biological entity.

How do we know what we know?

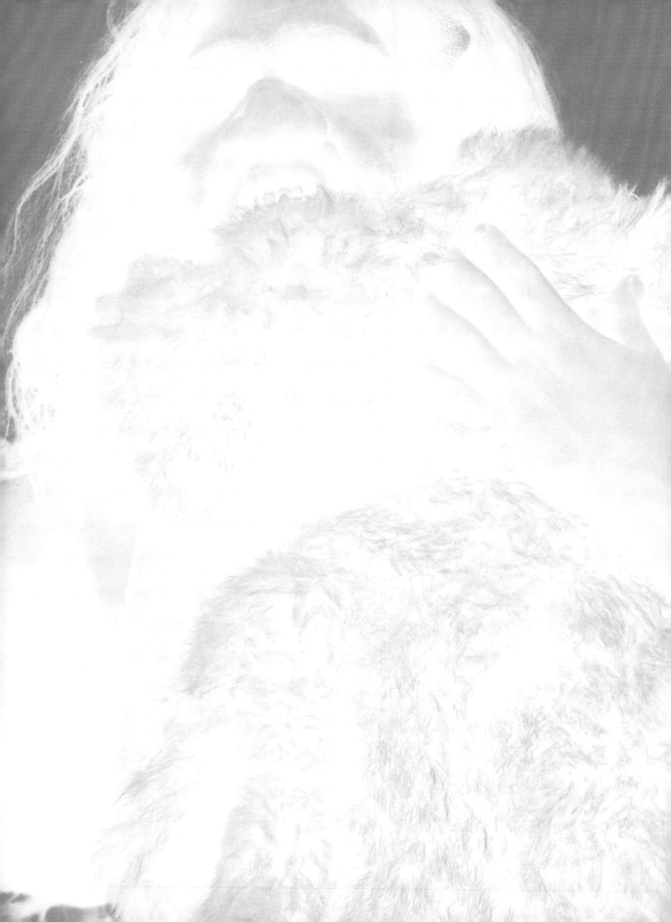

I N THE MIDDLE YEARS OF THE NINETEENTH CENTURY, THE WORLD WAS shaken by conflicts reverberating everywhere from Crimea to China, and civil war was brewing in America and India. The chance discovery in 1856 of a few old bones in a German cave would hardly have seemed significant to many people – yet it was eventually to help bring about a revolution in our understanding of human history.

The small cave, formed by water action in natural limestone, was known locally as the Feldhofer Grotto. Its entrance was high on a rock cliff rising above the Neander valley (or 'Neanderthal' in German), through which the Düssel River meanders on its way to join the Rhine near Düsseldorf. Some lime-workers were digging through deposits blocking the entrance when they came across the very well-preserved bones. The cap of a skull, some limb bones and part of a pelvis were recovered from beneath a layer of mud that formed the grotto floor. The workers were used to finding occasional animal bones in caves and assumed that they belonged to a cave bear. Luckily, however, they told a local schoolteacher, Johann Fuhlrott, of their discovery.

Fuhlrott was also an amateur natural historian. He recognized that the bones were human-like but, more importantly, that there was something special about them. The skull cap had a strangely pronounced brow-ridge and a very low sloping forehead, while the limb bones were curiously curved and thick-walled. Realizing that the skeleton was incomplete, Fuhlrott returned to the find-site with the workmen to see if he could retrieve any more of the bones. Unfortunately, he was too late – the grotto had been emptied of all the remaining deposits and fossils. But he did ascertain the circumstances of the find as best he could from the workmen. Most significantly, he discovered that the bones had been buried beneath at least 1.5 metres (5 feet) of mud. In addition, his detailed examination of the bones revealed that, in places, they were covered with curious little moss-like growths of mineral, similar to those found on cave-bear bones.

This was pretty acute scientific observation. Fuhlrott did not know the significance of what he was seeing but noted it nonetheless. In retrospect these so-called dendritic mineral growths are an important clue to the considerable antiquity of the bones. Dendrites do not form overnight but require prolonged burial in sediment, flushed through with mineral-bearing groundwater, to develop. The fact that the bones were entombed beneath such a thickness of mud is also testament to their antiquity. However, Fuhlrott did not feel confident enough to assess fully what the bones really signified and passed them on to Hermann Schaaffhausen, a professor of anatomy at the University of Bonn.

PREVIOUS SPREAD, INSET The skull cap of the 'original' Neanderthal, found in 1856 buried in a cave above the valley of the river Neander in Germany.

OPPOSITE Slow beginnings. Although Neanderthal remains were first found in the mid-19th century, very few people were prepared to accept that humans had ancient and extinct relatives.

Together, Schaaffhausen and Fuhlrott did what scientists have done for the last 250 years and more when they are on to something new and interesting. They presented their information, ideas and conclusions at the first opportunity to a meeting of a scientific society. In their case it was on 4 February 1857, to the Lower Rhine Medical and Natural History Society in Bonn.

Schaaffhausen gave meticulous details of the bones, describing their heavy build and how this implied a muscular physique and physically demanding lifestyle for their owner. He particularly noted the unusual shape of the skull cap with its prominent bony brow-ridges, sloping back into the low narrow forehead. The features certainly seemed to be natural but Schaaffhausen could not find any previously published record of such anatomically distinct specimens. In their 1861 report on the fossil inhabitant of the Neanderthal, details of the bones were accurately illustrated with beautiful engravings.

When it came to interpreting the find and drawing conclusions, Schaaffhausen and Fuhlrott were faced with considerable problems. They had no idea of the age of the find and the bones were not associated with any other fossils or artefacts. The two scientists were well aware of the active debate going on around them about the nature of the development of organisms through time, and particularly the thorny question of the antiquity of mankind. Indeed, Schaaffhausen had himself written 'On the Constancy and Transformation of Species', in which he tentatively concluded that the fixedness or 'immutability of species', as he referred to it, 'is not proven'. This was a roundabout way of admitting that species may have changed through time.

Without an established prehistoric context for their 'Neanderthaler', Schaaffhausen and Fuhlrott had to fall back on vague chronicles of the past, speculating that 'the human bones from the Neanderthal exceed all the rest in those peculiarities … which lead to the conclusion of their belonging to a barbarous and savage race'. Such races, they thought, might have coexisted with the animals whose fossil remains littered the near-surface deposits of Europe. Such deposits were still regarded by many of the naturalists of the day as having been laid down by the waters of the Flood recorded in the Old Testament of the Bible.

Translating the language and terms of the time into modern usage, we can see that in many ways Schaaffhausen and Fuhlrott were right. The Neanderthaler did indeed belong to an ancient group of humans that lived alongside extinct animals. We now know that these deposits were not laid down by a great deluge but were formed during one of many relatively warm phases throughout the Pleistocene Ice Age of the last 1.8 million years.

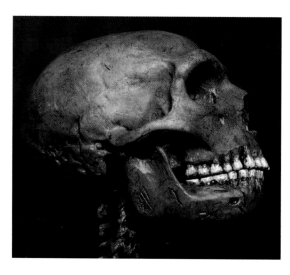

ABOVE Bare bones from the past reveal a glimmer of a lost people we now know as the Neanderthals. The prominent brow-ridge and low forehead of the Neanderthal skull were mistaken as signs of some kind of deficiency.

ABOVE Half a century had to pass before the image of the Neanderthals emerged from obscurity.

In his analysis, Schaaffhausen had not been able to resist the temptation to add a sprinkling of his 'proto-evolutionary' thoughts about the possibility of species improving through time: 'many a barbarous race may ... have disappeared, together with the animals of the ancient world, while the races whose organization is improved have continued the genus'. Again, in modern terms he was not so far off the mark but such comments were extremely controversial at the time and they unleashed a storm of criticism.

August Mayer, one of Schaaffhausen's faculty colleagues in Bonn and a specialist in pathology, also examined the bones. To Mayer, the curvature of the thigh bones seemed to resemble those of a lifelong horseman. He also suggested that the curvature of the limb bones could have been the result of rickets, a chronic nutritional deficiency disease of childhood due to lack of vitamin D or calcium. The condition would have been very familiar to Mayer, as it was common among poor and undernourished children in nineteenth-century Europe. Mayer also noted that the Neanderthaler's left elbow had been fractured during life and had healed badly. He surmised that the prolonged pain of this injury had induced the furrowed brow-ridge – through the victim's constant frowning!

In putting all his observations together in 1864, Mayer attempted to explain away the unusual features of the skeleton within an everyday historic context. Accordingly, the bones belonged to a Cossack cavalryman whose regiment had been pursuing Napoleon's army as it retreated through Prussia. The Cossack had been injured in a skirmish and deserted when his regiment paused near the Rhine before pushing into France in January 1814. On spotting the Feldhofer Grotto as a possible refuge, the cavalryman crawled into it to recover but eventually died there of his wounds.

Professor Mayer's story is good on imagination but not so good in producing a scientific explanation of the Neanderthaler's peculiar osteology. There may well have been a hidden agenda behind Mayer's explanation. The dominant figure in German biological science at the time was Rudolf Virchow, a brilliant scientist who pioneered the study of cellular pathology, first described leukaemia and had an interest in the developing science of archaeology. Perhaps unsurprisingly with his background, Virchow supported Mayer's interpretation of the Neanderthaler's peculiarities as a pathological condition.

Virchow was a politically active liberal, who remarked that 'there can be no scientific dispute with respect to faith, for science and faith exclude one another', but he was also implacably opposed to the idea of evolution. Mayer knew this and may have been keen to counter Schaaffhausen's progressionist ideas in order to get the eminent Virchow's endorsement for his own interpretation of the find – if so, it worked.

The Neanderthal idea goes abroad

While the German scientists became embroiled and bogged down in somewhat fruitless argument, Schaaffhausen's work was receiving a more enthusiastic reception in England. The middle decades of the nineteenth century were the key period for the revolution in the understanding of human prehistory. For the first time, a number of the foremost scientists were recognizing that humans have had a prolonged existence quite different from that represented in documents of the biblical tradition. Researchers such as Charles Lyell, Thomas Henry Huxley and of course Charles Darwin were seriously engaged in the whole problem of the antiquity of 'Mankind' and our relationship to the primates.

This was not a new problem – over the centuries many natural philosophers had given their opinions on the topic – but the time was right for another go at 'cracking' it. At last, important new information, such as the Neanderthal find, was available and relevant to the debate.

Huxley, the renowned biologist and defender of the Darwinian theory of evolution, addressed the issue in his well-known collection of essays entitled *Evidence as to Man's Place in Nature*, published in 1863. He noted how the size of the Neanderthaler's skull cap indicated that he had a relatively large brain. Huxley remarked that it was 'the most pithecoid [ape-like] of known human skulls' and belonged to the 'extreme term of a series leading gradually from it to the highest and best developed of human crania'. But, even so, Huxley proclaimed that the Neanderthals were not the elusive 'missing link' between man and the apes.

The problem of 'missing links' in the evolutionary story was a considerable one for Darwin and his evolutionist supporters such as Huxley. According to the theory of evolution there had been gradual transitions from one species to another through time. And yet the fossil record, as known at the time, seemed to be full of gaps between successive life forms. Darwin had gone to considerable lengths to explain how these gaps were a result of the imperfect nature of the geological rock record. Even so, evolutionists were keen to try and find some of the 'missing fossil links' between major groups in order to deflect some of the criticism pitched at the theory by its numerous detractors.

Huxley went on to speculate:'in still older strata do the fossilized bones of an ape more anthropoid, or a man more pithecoid, than any yet known await the researches of some unborn palaeontologist?' His question was prescient – but it was to take nearly another hundred years for the answer to be discovered and generally accepted.

As an ex-student of Charles Lyell, the geologist William King had been well trained to tackle such 'hot issues'. By the 1860s, King had been appointed professor of geology at Queen's College Galway in Ireland. He grabbed the chance to make something of a stir at the 1863 British Association for the Advancement of Science (BAAS), just as many British scientists still do at these ongoing annual meetings. King argued that the Neanderthaler should be distinguished as a member of a separate biological species from modern humans or *Homo sapiens* as we were named by the Swedish systematist Linnaeus in the eighteenth century (see the box on page 18).

BELOW Human relations. Our closest relatives are extinct humans. Together, humans present and past are classified as hominines and then grouped with the apes as hominoids, with the monkeys as 'higher' primates and with the lemurs as primates. Genetic and fossil evidence suggests an approximate chronology for this evolutionary development.

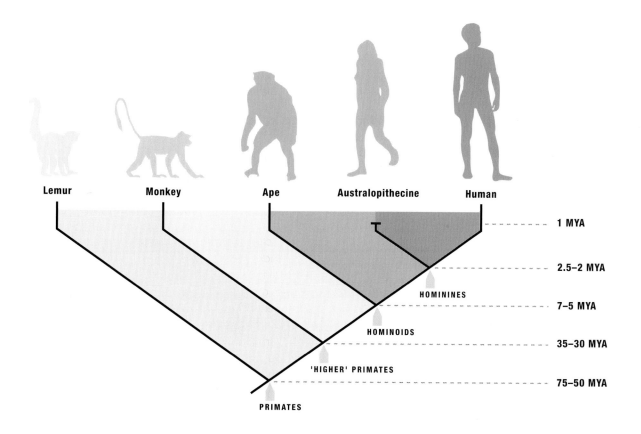

Lemur   Monkey   Ape   Australopithecine   Human

1 MYA

2.5–2 MYA

HOMININES

7–5 MYA

HOMINOIDS

35–30 MYA

'HIGHER' PRIMATES

75–50 MYA

PRIMATES

The scientific identity of humankind

Homo sapiens is our scientific label and means 'wise man'. The human species first acquired this Latin name in 1758, when the Swedish naturalist Carl Linnaeus (1707–78) extended his new system of nature beyond the mineral and vegetable kingdoms to include the animal kingdom. Although Linnaeus was a devout Christian, mankind was still an animal to him and could be fitted into orderly categories within a hierarchical world of classes, orders, genera and species. To Linnaeus, his system of nature merely revealed God's ordering of life.

Linnaeus, in company with many other naturalists working in the cultural and religious climate of Protestant northern Europe of the time, saw it as a moral duty to investigate and interpret the 'munificent' works of the Creator. For naturalists of the eighteenth century there was no question that the Creator would be any other than benevolent and rational. Accordingly, all his creations, the Earth and its inhabitants must have been formed in some meaningful order. And so it was up to sapient man to discover this natural world and its underlying order.

Linnaeus's most important innovation was his consistent use of what are technically known as Latin binomials. For some time organisms had sporadically been given two Latin names by naturalists. For instance, rose plants were all called *Rosa*, signifying that they belonged to the same 'genus'. Then each different kind of rose was specified by a second 'species' name, so that the common dog rose is called *Rosa canina*. All organisms that can interbreed to produce fertile young belong to the same species. All organisms within the same genus are very similar but the evolutionary significance of the hierarchy was not added to the classification until much later. Linnaeus did not invent this way of naming plants and animals but he was the first to attempt its systematic application to all known organisms.

Not until he reached the tenth edition of his *System of Nature* (published in 1758) did Linnaeus get around to classifying mankind. When he did so, *Homo sapiens* was grouped along with another human species, *Homo troglodytes*, and the chimpanzee, which Linnaeus called *Satyrus tulpii* in the order Anthropomorpha. *Homo troglodytes* was a kind of taxonomic 'shaggy dog', a fanciful creature based on rumour and exaggerated travellers' reports. The chimpanzee had been known and scientifically described in the west since 1698, when a young and sickly chimp was shipped to London. The poor beast died and a London physician, Edward Tyson (1650–1708), dissected its corpse and provided the first accurate description of the chimp anatomy and skeleton. Tyson also demonstrated and listed forty-eight features that chimps have in common with humans, compared with twenty-seven for monkeys and humans.

To Linnaeus, this remarkable degree of similarity between the chimp and human fully justified his association of the two in the same order of Anthropomorpha (later changed to Primates, where they still are classified). Although he was severely criticized for doing so, Linnaeus challenged anyone to show him how chimp and human anatomy and structure differed in any significant way. Today we know that basically these anatomists were right in their diagnosis; moreover, we now also know that the genes of chimps and humans are 98 per cent similar – so similar that the two groups must have shared a common ancestor no more than 6 million years ago.

The name *Homo neanderthalensis* was coined by King because he considered that the Feldhofer skull was more like that of a chimpanzee than that of a human, and therefore must belong to a different species. He hinted that the Neanderthal might have been tinged with a shade of chimp-like 'darkness', as he called it, and might even belong in a separate genus from mankind. But King's shot at instant scientific fame fell short, there being no immediate takers for the idea of the Neanderthal as a separate species, let alone a human-like being belonging to a different genus.

So often in science facts become clearer in retrospect, and it was realized much later that the Feldhofer remains were not the first bones of a Neanderthaler to be found. In 1829 two skulls had been found at Engis in Belgium by a naturalist, Dr Philippe-Charles Schmerling, associated with the fossil remains of some extinct animals. The skull that received the most attention was that of a modern human, but the other is now known to be that of a Neanderthal child. The strong brow-ridge and other typical Neanderthal features do not develop in the skull until late childhood, so it was not until 1926 that scientists realized that the skull belonged to a Neanderthal.

More significant was a nearly complete skull found in Forbes Quarry, Gibraltar, in 1848. But it too was not recognized until much later as having any special significance or connection with *Homo neanderthalensis*. In fact, by one of those extraordinary quirks of history, the Forbes skull suffered the same lukewarm reception as King's claim for the taxonomic independence of the Feldhofer find. Clearly the intellectual climate was just not ready to grasp the implications of these finds.

The Forbes skull was also launched at a meeting of the BAAS, at Bath in 1864, as yet another human species, named as *Homo calpicus* by two British fossil experts, George Busk and Hugh Falconer. The Forbes skull is in fact broadly similar to the Feldhofer one but is more lightly built and may be that of a female. Its beauty lies in the survival of its facial bones. The large face shows features that came to characterize the Neanderthal people, such as sharply receding cheekbones and a large opening where the nose would have been. The shape of human noses is maintained by flexible cartilage which does not normally fossilize.

If its importance had been recognized a few years earlier, the Neanderthals might have been known for evermore as 'calpicians' or perhaps 'Gibraltarians' (though possibly the present inhabitants of that rocky portal to the Mediterranean wouldn't be too happy about the association). But as we

ABOVE A better view of the lost people was seen in the female skull from Forbes Quarry, Gibraltar, the first nearly complete skull of a Neanderthal to be found. It is now known to be about 50,000 years old.

shall see, Gibraltar and its limestone caves were to continue to play a role in our subsequent understanding of the Neanderthal people.

Busk confirmed that the Neanderthaler did 'not represent … a mere individual peculiarity' and wryly commented on Mayer's interpretation, 'Even Professor Mayer will hardly suppose that a rickety Cossack engaged in the campaign of 1814 had crept into a sealed fissure in the Rock of Gibraltar.' Unfortunately, Busk and Falconer did not follow up their presentation with a more complete description of the skull – that had to wait another forty years.

Building the evidence

With the benefit of hindsight, it is now evident that a number of significant finds relating to the question of human ancestry had been made in the first half of the nineteenth century or even a little earlier. Curiously fashioned flint stones had been found at Hoxne, in Suffolk, England, at the end of the eighteenth century. A local naturalist and antiquarian, John Frere, published a description and illustration of the flints in 1800. From their well-formed, pointed axe-shape, he felt obliged to conclude that they must be the relics of 'a very remote period indeed; even beyond that of the present world'. Here was the first good evidence for the existence of early humans, capable of making stone tools, but Frere's percipient claim fell on deaf ears: the world was not ready to countenance any such implications for human ancestry.

Some twenty years later a more famous British geologist, the Rev. William Buckland of Oxford University, excavated a partial human skeleton from

RIGHT First sign of the Stone Age. The Hoxne hand-axe from Suffolk was the first stone tool claimed as the work of ancient humans.

Paviland cave on the South Wales coast in 1822–3. The body had been covered in red ochre and was accompanied by carved pieces of mammoth ivory and perforated shells – obviously it had been buried with some ceremony. Buckland was a very astute scientist but even he concluded that the body was that of a Welsh woman who had lived during the Roman occupation of the British Isles. He thought that her kinsfolk had made the artefacts from tusks that they had found in the cave.

We now know that 'she' was a 'he' and is about 28,000 (26,000 radiocarbon) years old. Not until much later in the century was he identified as a Cro-Magnon – and we will meet his people again.

A French connection

Some important discoveries had also been made in France, gradually helping to change ideas of human prehistory. In 1834 a French shepherd found a large tooth on the lower slopes of Sansan Hill in Gascony. He showed it to Edouard Lartet, owner of the local Château d'Ornezan, knowing that he was interested in such things. The shepherd also told Lartet that bones could be collected by the shovelful at the site. Lartet's enthusiasm for natural history had been fed by the great French anatomist Georges Cuvier, whose lectures he had attended in Paris. Lartet recognized that the tooth belonged to a mastodon, a kind of extinct elephant.

With his interest aroused, Lartet energetically excavated the Sansan site and discovered countless remains of fossil mammals. Among these was a single complete jawbone that was distinctly ape-like. Later named as *Pliopithecus antiquus*, it was the first fossil anthropoid to be found. Its discovery revealed for the first time that there was a prehistory of the apes, and perhaps humans, waiting to be uncovered within the Earth's surface deposits.

Another wealthy Frenchman, Jacques Boucher de Perthes (1788–1868), was a great 'amateur' of antiquities. He amassed a collection of more than a thousand worked flints from the Somme River valley deposits around St Acheul in Picardy. In 1847, he published a magnificent volume entitled *Antiquités celtiques et antédiluviennes*. In this work Boucher de Perthes illustrated and described the distinctive, pear-shaped and clearly worked flints which came to be known as Acheulian hand-axes, and the fossil bones they were associated with.

Together, the flint tools and animal bones provided the first convincing evidence that humans had lived alongside the great antediluvian animals, the mammoth, straight-tusked elephant, rhinoceros, bison and so on. The traditional chronology and division of world history into two great epochs separated by the biblical Flood was still present, but the flaws in this story were now very evident. However, this did not make the new evidence immediately or generally acceptable. The old paradigm of the biblical chronology was far too deeply ingrained. It took the discovery of the skeletal remains of human-like bodies associated with those of extinct animals to convince the sceptics that the biblical chronology just did not work.

In 1852 another piece of the puzzle of human prehistory was turned up when a French road worker pulled a human bone out of a hillside rabbit hole near Aurignac in southern France. When a trench was dug into the hill, it revealed a cave entrance blocked by a larger block of limestone. Behind the slab lay seventeen skeletons, so obviously like modern humans that they were duly reburied in the local cemetery. The news of the find attracted the attention of that French pioneer of prehistory, Edouard Lartet. He excavated the floor of the cave in 1860 and found some isolated bones that were also similar to those of modern humans but were associated with those of extinct animals. Most scholars of the time were still unconvinced of the significance of the find but, a few years later, in 1868, Lartet's son Louis made a breakthrough in the prevailing prejudice.

This time, railway workers found human remains buried beneath a rock overhang near the town of Les Eyzies in the Dordogne region of southern

RIGHT A big face, strong brow and low forehead distinguishes a Neanderthal *(left)* from a Cro-Magnon *(right)* which has the smaller face and higher forehead of a modern human.

France. Louis Lartet found that the human bones lay in a layer together with stone artefacts, perforated shells and animal teeth, the bones of lion, reindeer and the extinct mammoth. The bones belonged to at least five modern-looking people, including a baby, a young woman, two young men and an older man. The cliff overhang had formed a natural rock shelter and was known by the local name of Cro-Magnon. The name was subsequently applied to all ancient remains of modern humans in Europe. As we shall see, the Cro-Magnons came to play a highly significant role in the story of the Neanderthals.

Lartet realized that this at last was incontrovertible skeletal evidence for the coexistence of humans with extinct animals. The human remains were therefore of great antiquity, and a 'deep' history and ancestry for humans could no longer be denied. Even so, there were still scholars whose conceptual mindset precluded them from acknowledging what to others was obvious.

The wider time-frame

The whole question of prehistoric time was a major item on the agenda of early-nineteenth-century scientists. Many were convinced that the genealogically derived Judeo-Christian notion of the Earth being no more than some 6000 years old was naïve, and just did not hold up in the light of growing geological evidence. Mapping of rock strata, especially in Britain and France, was revealing that the layers of the Earth were cumulatively miles thick and for much of this thickness they contained fossil remains. The idea of all this being deposited by the action of a single or even several great 'Floods' was losing its explanatory power.

The youngest surface deposits, including those forming at the present, were distinguished as the 'Alluvium' by the English geologist William Buckland in 1823. Below them lay the so-called 'Diluvium', which was traditionally considered to have been deposited during the biblical Flood. This, in turn, was seen to lie above yet older strata that had first been recognized as long ago as the 1760s, and characterized as the 'Tertiary'. By the 1820s the Diluvium was being more closely investigated than ever before, and found to contain a variety of recognizable animal bones. However, many of the animals, such as elephant and hyena, seemed to be incongruously out of place in Europe. For a long time the Flood had seemed an eminently reasonable explanation for the existence of such bones.

In 1829 a French scientist, Paul Desnoyers, suggested that Buckland's Diluvium and Alluvium be brought together within a new major system of strata – the Quaternary, which thus acquired an equivalent rank to the older Tertiary system as a chronological division of past time. 'Quaternary' is still used to distinguish the period of geological time that is now known to have started 1.8 million years ago – but the technique of dating certain kinds of rocks did not develop until the beginning of the twentieth century.

Not until the 1860s had enough independent information from England and France turned up for the scientific community in general to accept the need for a new chronology of the Diluvium/Quaternary. By this time, most of prehistory had been carved up into eleven great periods of geological history, from the Precambrian to the Quaternary, and many more subdivisions within this. Fossils were known to have existed as far back as Cambrian times and some scientists were beginning to speculate that the age of the Earth must run into millions of years. In addition, there was increasing evidence that the peculiar characteristics of the deposits of the Quaternary 'Diluvium' were the result not of a universal Flood but of a great Ice Age.

The Palaeolithic has arrived

By the mid-nineteenth century, archaeology and anthropology were emerging as separate scientific disciplines. In England, one of their champions was Sir John Lubbock, later Lord Avebury, a rich and intelligent liberal aristocrat whose family lived near Charles Darwin in Kent. Darwin became something of a father figure to the young Lubbock, who by the age of thirteen had already developed a passion for science and had discovered the first fossil musk-ox remains in England. In the 1860s Lubbock examined Boucher de Perthes's Somme deposits and was impressed by the evidence for the coexistence of extinct animals with humans as evidenced by the stone tools. His 1865 book, *Prehistoric Times*, introduced new terms for what had been called the Stone Age. Lubbock renamed the Old Stone Age with its flaked stone culture as the Palaeolithic, and the younger New Stone Age with its more worked and polished stone culture as the Neolithic.

The Palaeolithic and Neolithic are archaeological divisions of prehistoric time based on the presence of stone tools and other artefacts manufactured by humans. As such, they are a rather different kind of division from those of the geological record of rock strata. Division of most geological strata is based on the occurrence of various fossil organisms, whose changing form we now know to be due to their evolution through time.

Further subdivision of the Palaeolithic was first made by Edouard Lartet. He recognized that sites in the Vézère River valley in western France, around Les Eyzies and the rock shelter of Cro-Magnon, contained different assemblages of tools and fossil remains, including humans. With his palaeontological background, Lartet applied the principles of fossil chronology and suggested that there were recognizable subdivisions within these assemblages which could be named after dominant fossil remains, such as the Cave Bear Epoch and Woolly Mammoth Epoch.

These epochs were soon translated by another French expert, Gabriel de Mortillet, into four and then six stone-tool-based divisions named after specific French sites. De Mortillet, of the Ecole d'Anthropologie in Paris, was a radical champion of evolutionism and believed that the somewhat peculiar Neanderthal skeletal remains did have a place in human prehistory. In his scheme the oldest division, the Chellean, was characterized by massive hand-axes, as was the subsequent Acheulian. This was followed by the Mousterian with a more sophisticated tool technology using stone cores. Then the younger Aurignacian contained bone points as well as long thin blades, followed by the Solutrean with its remarkably fine 'laurel-leafed' points and finally the Magdalenian with bone and antler tools and decorative items.

With minor modifications, this Palaeolithic chronology is still used in Europe today. The Chellean has been subsumed into the Acheulian which is regarded as the Lower Palaeolithic. The Mousterian, associated with the skeletal remains of Neanderthals, forms the Middle Palaeolithic, although the newer division of the Châtelperronian has been introduced between it and the Upper Palaeolithic. The latter includes the Aurignacian, Solutrean and Magdalenian stone and bone technology and was associated with the skeletal remains of those anatomically modern humans known in Europe as Cro-Magnons. There are yet more subdivisions in this complex scheme, as the even more complicated events of the Ice Age have not yet been taken into account. Neither has the dating of any of this history, because the ability to put numbers on fossils (human, animal or plant), artefacts (such as hand-axes), events (such as glacials), processes (such as climatic change) and successive divisions of sedimentary deposits (such as cave or rock shelter layers) had not been developed. In fact, reliable dating methods were not available until well into the twentieth century, but in recent decades they have revolutionized our understanding of prehistory, its evolving life, changing climates and environments, including the evolving peoples and their cultures.

More Neanderthals

By the last decades of the nineteenth century, the search for human remains was gaining ground all over Europe. In 1874 Neanderthal-like jaw fragments and a child's tooth turned up in Pontnewydd cave in North Wales. Again, the find was buried beneath sediment and associated with stone tools and the bones of animals that seemed exotic for this part of the world. They included the remains of rhinoceros, a large leopard-sized cat and bison. This site is still the most northerly known Neanderthal site in Europe, and is now known to date from the early years of their occupation, some 200,000 years ago.

In 1886 two Neanderthal skeletons were found in a cave at Spy in Belgium. These were much more complete than any previously found, and finally convinced more scientists that here was an ancient and distinctive type of human, similar to that found in the Neander valley and Gibraltar. No longer could the old arguments about 'rickety Cossacks' or 'barbarous tribes' of modern humans have any credibility. While these finds clinched the question of the antiquity and distinctiveness of the Neanderthals from other humans, many experts continued to argue about the degree of difference seen in them. There was a general reluctance to admit that a separate species of human could have existed and become extinct.

The problem of 'otherness'

Not far beneath the surface of all the historic problems of recognizing the Neanderthals for what they are lurks another fundamental difficulty. If *Homo neanderthalensis* is, as William King claimed, a separate species of human, then what are the Neanderthals to us? And beyond that question lies our human difficulty with knowing what exactly we are. Most of the major religions of the world portray humans as special kinds of beings and clearly separated from all other animals. Several thousand years of cultural and religious thinking, persuasion and dogma have left their mark.

Since the initial germs of ideas about the evolution of life first surfaced, well before Charles Darwin's day, the position of humans near the top of the ladder has been reviewed. It has been questioned by revolutionary thinkers such as Rousseau, Kant and Lamarck, since the days of the eighteenth-century

Enlightenment and the French Revolution. The process has disturbed the *status quo* and has often been seen as a threat to public stability and order.

The question of who the Neanderthals were got caught up in this intellectual turmoil. And it is still not entirely resolved. The image that was slowly being built up for the Neanderthals was that of a 'barbarous and lower race'. By the end of the nineteenth century, racialist ideas of the superiority of people of European – Caucasian – origin were already widely established. Pseudosciences of characterization by superficial appearance, such as the study of skull shape (phrenology) as a guide to mental faculties, and facial features as a guide to criminality, were also well rooted in western culture.

One of the facial features that was picked on particularly was chin shape. 'The form of the chin seems to be wonderfully correlated with the general character and energy of the race. It is hard to say why, but as a matter of fact a weak chin generally denotes a weak, and a strong chin a strong, race or individual.' This quote comes from a popular book, *Human Origins* by Samuel Laing, published in 1895. How often is the same calumny about chin form and character still trotted out! Needless to say, when it was discovered that Neanderthals had receding chins, this was taken to indicate that they also had fundamental weaknesses of character.

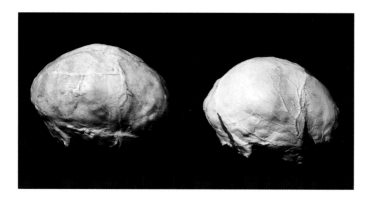

ABOVE Despite having brains just as big as ours, the Neanderthals were seen as witless savages. The larger brain cast *(left)* is that of a Neanderthal from La Chappelle aux Saints, France, while the slightly smaller brain cast *(right)* is Cro-Magnon from Prĕdmostí in Slovakia.

Part of the problem was that by the end of the nineteenth century, the idea of evolution had become much more acceptable. It was one thing to acknowledge that the idea of a hierarchy of command or 'great chain of being', from the lowliest microbes, through worms and other creepy-crawlies to fish, amphibians, reptiles, birds and mammals, had a commonsense appeal. But it was something else to have to acknowledge that within the mammals there had been evolution from monkey-like primates, through higher apes (represented today by such species as chimps) to mankind. As long as there was a reassuring gap between the higher apes and humans, we could still retain our sense of separateness and specialness. But when that gap was actually beginning to be infilled with missing links from the fossil record, then there was the difficulty of where to draw the line between ourselves and these fossil ancestors. What if Darwin and Huxley were right and there was a lineage of ancestral species gradually becoming less human and more ape-like, stretching back into the distant past? What about the 'specialness' of humans – would it disappear?

One solution would be to distance ourselves from the ancestors by characterizing them as very primitive and ape-like, in order to reinforce our own specialness. The existence of the gap allows us to hold on to the idea that somehow a magic wand was waved or a genetic switch was flicked and modern humans were suddenly and fully illuminated with consciousness.

The less comfortable alternative was to consider that there is no great gap, but that the human condition has evolved over a long time and that it is not possible to draw the line between ourselves and our ancestors. If so, what happens to our sense of specialness? Again, the Neanderthals became the focus of the argument. Around the turn of the century, several French finds and one from Croatia did much to influence the immediate outcome and image of the Neanderthals. But before these there was a remarkable find in the Far East.

A global perspective

In 1891 a Dutch military doctor, Eugene Dubois, discovered fossil remains at Trinil in Java. Another very contentious, possibly human ancestor joined the Neanderthals: 'Java Man' (*Pithecanthropus erectus*, generally regarded now as Asian *Homo erectus*). The skull cap shows some Neanderthal-like features, notably a pronounced brow-ridge, but Dubois did not compare his find with those of Neanderthals from Europe. From the start, he had been inspired by the theories of German biologist Ernst Haeckel to search in south-east Asia for the so-called 'missing link' between the apes and ourselves. Haeckel thought that the Papuans and Melanesians were the most primitive of living people and therefore closest to the 'ancestral type'. He had also been struck by the resemblance between human embryos and those of the gibbon apes of south-east Asia and so, as an evolutionist, he argued that the fossil link between apes and the most primitive of living humans would be found in this region. Dubois had set out to prove Haeckel's theory and thought that with his 'Java Man' he had done so. In his mind he had no reason to compare his find with the Neanderthals from Europe. By the turn of the century a German palaeontologist, Gustav Schwalbe, did make the comparison but recognized that 'Java Man' was still much more primitive than the Neanderthals. Even so, human ancestry was beginning to become deeper and more complex.

The Croatian find of Neanderthal remains in 1899 from the rock shelter of Krapina, north of Zagreb, was to prove extremely important for a number of reasons. Several hundred fragments of human bone were recovered, including those of babies, children and adults from what was generally regarded as a Mousterian archaeological context. A Croatian palaeontologist, Dragutin Gorjanovič-Kramberger, who spent years excavating and describing the finds, came to a startling conclusion that did not help the emerging image of the Neanderthals one little bit. He thought that the fragmentary nature of the remains was the result of cannibalism, with the bones being purposefully broken open and in some instances burned by contemporary humans.

Even more important was the 1908 discovery by three priests of the so-called 'Old Man' of La Chapelle-aux-Saints in the Corrèze district of south-west France. But the bones, with their marked Neanderthal features, were not sent to the most obvious experts, the anti-clerical successors of Gabriel de Mortillet at the Ecole d'Anthropologie who, like him, were predisposed to a Neanderthal phase in human ancestry. Instead they were sent to Marcellin Boule in Paris, who was basically opposed to the idea that Neanderthals had any place in human ancestry.

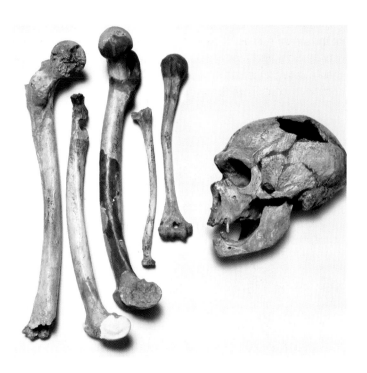

ABOVE These bones from La Chappelle-aux-Saints formed the basis for Marcellin Boule's interpretation of the Neanderthals as brutish bent-kneed savages.

The skeletal remains were found in a rectangular pit beneath a metre or so of Mousterian deposits. From the start, the find was construed as a deliberate burial of a body, and is one of the few reasonably well-documented burials of a Neanderthal. Recently the remains have been dated at around 50,000 years old.

As we shall see, Boule did not disappoint in his characterization of these well-preserved Neanderthal remains. On the one hand, he was one of the first to support King's classification of the Neanderthal as a separate species. But on the other hand, he went to considerable pains to demonize their image. By the time that Boule was researching the Neanderthaler, the Great War of 1914–18 was under way and anti-German feelings were running high in France. Some modern experts see a hidden agenda behind Boule's interpretation of the 'German' Neanderthaler as a savage who had no link to modern humans. We have to remember that by this time the picture of more sophisticated Cro-Magnons who 'originated' in France was well established. Certainly Boule illustrated the facial skull profiles of a chimp and a modern Frenchman on either side of the Neanderthal and concluded that the Neanderthal was clearly a member of one of the 'lowest' races and closer to the chimps than to modern humans.

It took many years to overcome the image that Boule created. The Neanderthals were persistently portrayed as a kind of 'idiot community' of the past, that were and still are the butt of jokes and cartoons from the Flintstones to Gary Larson's 'Far Side' characters. (For a more detailed account of Boule's analysis, see the box on page 64.)

Upheaval in the Levant

The understanding of Neanderthal history was thrown into turmoil by a number of discoveries made in what used to be called the Levant (now the Mediterranean coastal regions of Turkey, Israel, Lebanon and Syria) from the 1930s onwards. The eastern Mediterranean was already known to be of fundamental importance for post-glacial Neolithic developments from around 12,000 (10,000 radiocarbon) years ago, such as the rise of agriculture and pastoralism. But it was not realized that the region had acted as a vital link or crossroads between Africa and Europe for over a million years.

Investigation of the Wadi el-Mughara in Israel (then Palestine), a semi-dry valley which leads down to the Mediterranean coast, revealed a number of caves. The caves overlooked and gave access to the coastal plain and to Mount Carmel. Excavation of the Skhūl and Tabūn caves in the 1930s by an Anglo-American team of archaeologists revealed some well-preserved skeletal remains and stone tools. At Skhūl, the bones of some ten people – men, women and children – were recovered from within a metre of cave-floor sediment, including some that had apparently been purposefully buried. However, at Tabūn bones were less abundant but included the partial skeleton of a woman and the remains of gazelle and fallow deer buried at greater depth within the sediment of that cave. In both cases the skeletal material was accompanied by Middle Palaeolithic (Levallois–Mousterian: see page 132) stone tools. The initial conclusion was that both groups of humans had been contemporaries and probably members of the same regional population.

BELOW Based on Boule's reconstruction, the image of the Neanderthal which became lodged in the public perception through its reproduction in the *Illustrated London News* in 1909.

When the anatomical details of the skeletons from both sites were described in 1939, they showed a remarkable variability. The Skhūl people were quite modern-looking, but the Tabūn woman was very Neanderthal-like apart from being rather lightly built. At the time the conclusion was that these 'Mount Carmelites' were less specialized than the classic European Neanderthals and perhaps more closely related to the Cro-Magnons. Other experts struggled to

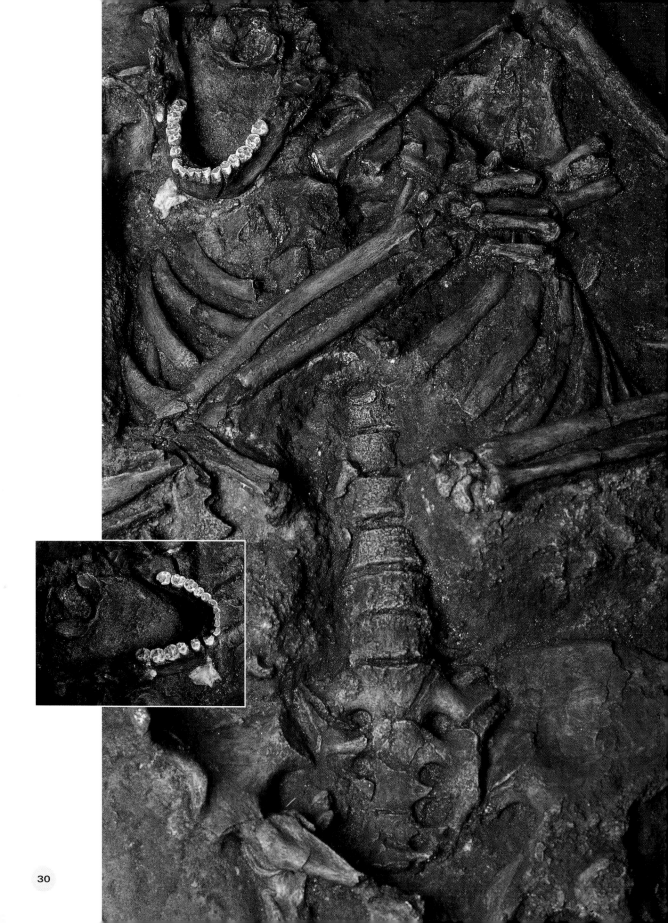

interpret the findings in slightly different ways. Some thought the fossils represented 'missing links' between Neanderthals and modern (Cro-Magnon) humans, even hybrids or perhaps a common ancestral stock for both Neanderthals and Cro-Magnons. The problem was that the dating of the finds was entirely based on the assumption that the stone tools were essentially Middle Palaeolithic (Mousterian) in age.

When Qafzeh cave near Nazareth was first excavated in the 1930s, the remains of seven humans were found and a further fourteen were recovered after World War II. Again, a number of men, women and children had apparently been deliberately buried. These people were similar to the Mount Carmelites in that they seemed to show a modern morphology but, problematically, were associated with Middle Palaeolithic stone tools that were generally thought to be the products of Neanderthals.

Further important cave sites have been excavated in Israel at Amud and Kebara, which is another Mount Carmel cave. Amud contained a Neanderthal skeleton found right at the top of the Middle Palaeolithic, and Kebara has produced one of the best-preserved Neanderthal skeletons known, including the only complete pelvis, although the skull is unfortunately missing.

When the bones of all these people are compared, it becomes clear that the Tabūn, Amud and Kebara finds are predominantly Neanderthal-like, while the Skhūl and Qafzeh people were more modern-looking. Consequently, by the mid-1980s the chronology of the finds was based on this anatomical evidence, with Skhūl and Qafzeh seen as the youngest and perhaps latest Middle Palaeolithic in age. Animal fossils at Tabūn suggested that this Mount Carmel site was older than the neighbouring site of Skhūl. So it seemed possible that the Tabūn people might have lived around 60,000–50,000 years ago and have been ancestral to those of Skhūl (around 45,000–40,000 years ago). But the picture was not at all clear. There was a suggestion from small mammal fossils that the Neanderthal woman at Tabūn was actually younger than the modern people at Qafzeh.

The underlying problem with the interrelationships between these people was dating. The radiocarbon method is very successful for giving chronological dates on a variety of organic materials, especially bone, but could not be used for carbon-bearing compounds much more than 50,000 years old. Luckily, by the late 1980s, new methods of dating archaeological materials were becoming available, such as thermoluminescence dating (TL) and electron spin resonance (ESR). (See the box on pages 32–33.)

When burnt flints from Kebara were dated by the TL method and animal teeth were dated using ESR, they both fell around 60,000 years ago, much as expected. The big shock came when TL dating of the modern human burials at Qafzeh came out at 92,000 years ago. These 'moderns' were not only about three times as old as European Cro-Magnons but some 30,000 years older than the Kebara Neanderthal. Then, to cap it all, when the Skhūl deposits, which also contained modern human remains, were dated by ESR on associated mammal teeth, they too fell between 100,000 and 80,000 years ago. Finally, Tabūn has

OPPOSITE Not until the 1930s were more complete remains of Neanderthals found. The Neanderthal burial of an adult male at Kebara, near Mount Carmel, is one of the best skeletons known and the only one with a well-preserved pelvis. Only the upper part of the skull, the right leg and both feet are missing.

Dating techniques

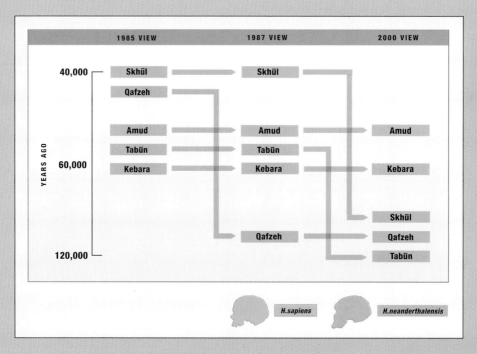

There was no reliable means of dating the geological or prehistoric past available until the beginning of the twentieth century. Previously, scientists such as Darwin and Lyell had attempted various calculations based on estimated thicknesses of rock strata, known rates of erosion of rocks and deposition of sediment. Judging by these crude measures, the Earth was evidently hundreds of millions of years old but it was not possible to produce any exact figures.

Then in 1897, the physicist Lord Kelvin calculated how long it had taken for the Earth to cool from a molten state, which turned out to be between 20 and 40 million years. There was some dismay and disbelief among geologists as this was a lot shorter than expected. In retrospect, Kelvin was way out in his calculations because he had not taken the role of radioactivity into account. The age of the Earth is now known to be 4.6 billion years.

The major breakthrough came with the discovery that certain chemical elements which are common in many minerals, rocks and organic materials have a built-in radioactive isotope 'clock' which measures their age. The principle is simple: radioactive isotopes decay at known and constant rates from so-called 'parent' to 'daughter' isotopes. By measuring the ratio of parent to daughter isotopes remaining in a sample and knowing the rate of decay for the particular isotopes, the date when the 'clock' was originally set going can be worked out. Normally, radioactive clocks are set going when the material is first formed. For example, carbon isotopes can be used to date the formation of bone in an animal's body or wood from a tree and hence give its age relative to the present.

The unfortunate problem with carbon isotopes is that their rate of decay is relatively rapid and they cannot be used to date any carbon-based material older than around 40,000 years ago. But a new radiocarbon method called accelerator mass spectroscopy (AMS) promises to extend this kind of dating back perhaps to 70,000 years before the present. The AMS method counts the radiocarbon atoms directly rather than waiting for them to decay. It has the advantage of allowing very small samples (100–500mg) to be dated and has been used to date carbon-black pigment from cave paintings and drawings.

In recent years, however, another problem has arisen with radiocarbon dating, which is slightly out of kilter with the results obtained by other dating methods such as thermoluminescence (TL) and electron spin resonance (ESR). It turns out that radiocarbon results obtained from 30–40,000-year-old samples are likely to be 3–4000 years too young and many important dates will need to be recalibrated.

Other radio-isotopes belong to a variety of elements such as potassium and uranium, which are mostly found locked up in common rock-forming minerals such as granites and lavas. While these are very useful geologically and can be used to date events in Earth history, they are not particularly useful to archaeologists, except in areas such as the East African Rift Valley where lavas interbedded between hominid-bearing sediments have allowed the dating of our early evolution.

Luckily, uranium is also found in some common carbonate minerals, which form in bone and teeth as well as in caves, where many archaeological finds are made. So dates can be established on a variety of finds, from bones beyond the reach of radiocarbon dating to cave-floor deposits. In the late 1980s, new methods of dating archaeological materials became available such as ESR. The ESR method depends on a buried fossil or artefact being dosed by radiation from surrounding minerals and cosmic rays. The radiation releases electrons which are cumulatively trapped in the crystal structure of the object. The age can be calculated by measuring the rate of radiation input and the dose already received. Crystalline minerals such as tooth enamel are particularly suited for this method which can extend back over 2 million years.

The one major area of difficulty is that it is not yet possible to directly date when stone tools were made, although sometimes a good idea may be obtained by relatively dating the sediments in which they are buried.

been redated and ranges between 200,000 and 90,000 years ago. This means that the Tabūn Neanderthal woman was living around the same time as the early modern people from Qafzeh. The whole chronology had effectively been turned upside-down.

All in all, the confusing evidence here seems to indicate a continuous flux in populations within the region over a long period. Hand-axe makers lived at Tabūn around 200,000 years ago in an earlier interglacial period. They were followed by early Neanderthals, including the Tabūn woman, towards the end of the last interglacial around 110,000 years ago. Early modern humans from the neighbouring site of Skhūl may well have visited Tabūn 90,000 years ago and Neanderthals may have returned when it was colder, 60,000 years ago. Archaeologists are not sure when the Neanderthals gave up living in the region but it may have been some 45,000 years ago. Certainly by 37,000 years ago the moderns were back and this time for good.

Update on the original site

The scenic beauty of the Neander valley and the Feldhofer Grotto was destroyed by the activities of German quarry workers in the mid-nineteenth century. They blasted out the limestone for use in the Industrial Revolution that gripped Germany like much of the rest of north-western Europe.

However, in 1997 two German archaeologists, Ralf Schmitz and Jürgen Thissen, excavated piles of debris near the former site of the grotto. They found the base of the cliff-face below the grotto, buried beneath limestone scree fragments blasted from the original cliff. They also found some of the original cave deposits that had blocked the entrance of the grotto. Searching through the sediment, the archaeologists were surprised to find stone artefacts along with animal and some twenty human-related bone remains. Some of the animal bones have surface cut marks, and the human remains include pieces of a right thigh bone. Since the thigh bone of the original Neanderthaler was complete, it appears that there was more than one skeleton present. But one of the other fragments has now been linked with part of the original skeleton. Carbon isotope analysis of the bone fragments gives a date of about 40,000 years ago.

Discovering the lost relatives

To help clarify the complex history of the discovery of prehistoric remains relevant to the Neanderthals, some of the key events are listed below in chronological order. The full significance of some of the early finds was not realised or appreciated until many years later, as indicated:

- **1698** Edward Tyson (1650–1708), a London physician, scientifically describes chimp anatomy for the first time and shows that they have 48 features in common with humans.
- **1758** Carl Linnaeus (1707–78), a Swedish naturalist, names modern humans as *Homo sapiens*.
- **1800** John Frere (1740–1807), an English antiquarian, publishes the first description and illustration of a worked flint hand-axe but nobody appreciates the importance of the find at the time.
- **1822–3** The English scientist William Buckland (1784–1856) excavates a skeleton buried in Paviland Cave in South Wales. Not until much later is it realised that the remains are some 30–28,000 (26,000 radiocarbon) years old and those of the first Cro-Magnon to be found.
- **1829** Two human skulls are found at Engis, near Liège in Belgium by Philippe-Charles Schmerling (1791–1836). Not until 1926 was it realised that one of the skulls is that of a Neanderthal child.
- **1834** The first fossil ape, *Pliopithecus antiquus*, is found in France and described by Edouard Lartet (1801–71). It is now known to be around 14 million years old.
- **1847** Boucher de Perthes (1788–1868) publishes his description of many worked flints and fossil animal bones found at St Acheul in Picardy. Few experts acknowledge that they represent incontrovertible evidence for the coexistence of ancient humans with extinct animals.
- **1848** A fossil skull is found in Forbes Quarry, Gibraltar but again it is not recognised as of any great interest until 1864 when it is tentatively named as a new human species.
- **1852** Seventeen human skeleton are found in a cave in Aurignac, France. When excavated in 1860 by Edouard Lartet, bones of extinct animals are also found, but few experts accept the significance of the find.
- **1856** Human fossil remains, found in Neanderthal in Germany, are described (in 1857) by Hermann Schaaffhausen (1816–93) but experts disagree about what kind of person they belonged to. Later in 1864 they are formally identified as a new species of human – a Neanderthal.
- **1863** William King (1809–86) identifies the Neanderthal fossils as those of a new kind of human and separate from ourselves – *Homo neanderthalensis*. But few other scientists support the idea.
- **1864** George Busk (1807–86) and Hugh Falconer (1808–65) informally name the Forbes Quarry skull as *Homo calpicus*, a new species of human. Again, nobody pays any attention and not until much later is the skull recognised as that of a well-preserved Neanderthal.
- **1868** The remains of five humans are found at Cro-Magnon, in France. They are excavated by Louis Lartet (1840–99) who finds associated stone tools, jewellery and the bones of extinct animals. Some scholars begin to accept that humans coexisted with extinct animals.
- **1891** Eugene Dubois (1858–1940) finds and describes *Java Man* as *Pithecanthropus* (later called *Homo*) *erectus* but few experts accept his diagnosis as another extinct human relative.
- **1908** A Neanderthal skeleton is found buried at La Chapelle-aux-Saints in France and is sent to Marcellin Boule (1861–1942) in Paris who supports King's original distinction of the Neanderthals as a separate species. Boule portrays Neanderthals as primitive savages compared with Cro-Magnons.
- **1920s** 'Peking Man' (*Homo erectus*) fossils found near Beijing in China.
- **1925** Raymond Dart (1893–1988) describes the first australopithecine from Taung in South Africa and suggests that they capable of upright walking.
- **1925–6** Excavation of the Devil's Tower Neanderthal site at Gibraltar by Dorothy Garrod (1892–1968), who goes on to direct excavations at Mount Carmel.

- **From 1927** The remains of some forty individuals of 'Peking Man' (*Homo erectus*) and many stone artefacts found near Beijing in China.
- **1929–30s** A number of cave sites are found in the Mount Carmel of Palestine (today's Israel) with human remains showing features between those of Neanderthals and Cro-Magnons. They are associated with stone tools and the bones of extinct animals.
- **1940** Franz Weidenreich (1873–1948) claims that the Neanderthals may have given rise to early modern humans.
- **1950s** Thousands of stone tools and, in 1959, an early human relative, *Zinjanthropus* (later referred to *Australopithecus*) *boisei*, discovered by Louis Leakey (1903–72) and his wife Mary (1913–96) at Olduvai in Tanzania and subsequently dated to around 2 million years ago.
- **1964** Fossils of the earliest humans, *Homo habilis*, found by the Leakeys at Olduvai.
- **1971** American archaeologist, Ralph Solecki publishes a controversial account of the Shanidar Neanderthals called *Shanidar – the First Flower People*.
- **1974** Discovery in Ethiopia of the partially complete 3.0 million-year-old skeleton of 'Lucy', an australopithecine, confirms that these ancient human relatives were already walking upright with a modern-like gait.
- **1979** Neanderthal remains at Saint-Césaire in France are found associated with Châtelperronian tools and later dated at 36,000 (34,000 radiocarbon) years old.
- **1980s** New methods of indirect radio-isotope dating archaeological materials, such as electron spin resonance (ESR) and thermoluminescence (TL) are introduced.
- **1980s** A decade of excavation at Boxgrove in the south of England reveals numerous stone tools, animal remains and the shin bone (1993) of a *Homo heidelbergensis* human dated at around 500,000 years old.
- **1987** Differences in modern human DNA suggests modern humans are descended from a cluster of Africans living about 200,000 years ago ('African Eve' hypothesis).
- **1991** Excavation of Moula-Guercy cave in France reveals the butchered remains of several Neanderthals whose bones were also defleshed, perhaps for cannibalism.
- **1992** *Homo erectus* remains from Dmanisi in Georgia are dated at 1.8 million years old (now revised to 1.7 million years ago), by far the oldest human remains in Eurasia.
- **1994** Human remains found at Gran Dolina, Atapuerca, Spain are dated at more than 780,000 years old and are claimed to belong to a new human species, *Homo antecessor*.
- **1997** DNA fragments are recovered from the 'original' Neanderthal skeleton and support the idea that Neanderthals were a separate line of evolution and indeed a separate species from early modern humans such as the Cro–Magnons.
- **1997** Debris from the Feldhofer cave in Germany is found with stone tools, animal bones and more Neanderthal fragments, and dated at around 40,000 (38,000 radiocarbon) years ago.
- **1998** A 27,000 (25,000 radiocarbon)-year-old child's skeleton, found at Lagar Velho, Portugal is claimed to show a hybrid mixture of Neanderthal and modern human features.
- **2000** DNA fragments are recovered from another Neanderthal and reinforce the argument that there was no gene flow between Neanderthals and early modern humans.
- **2000 (June)** Sampling of the human genome completed.

Neanderworld: the Ice Age world of the Neanderthals

chapter two

I T HAS TAKEN OVER 150 YEARS OF SCIENTIFIC EFFORT TO ESTABLISH
the emergence of the Neanderthals as a once-living group of prehistoric
people. It has taken the same period of time and the same amount of effort
by generations of scientists for the complexities of the Ice Age to be realized.
These two stories of discovery and recognition are intertwined, for the
Neanderthals lived through the latter part of the Ice Age – from about 200,000
years ago to 30,000 years ago. Their territory, shown by the accumulated finds
of their remains, stretched from what we know today as Wales to Gibraltar in the
south and the Caspian in the east. This Neanderthal time–space continuum can
aptly be summed up as 'Neanderworld'.

To try and understand the Neanderthals and appreciate their struggle
for survival, it is necessary to have some sense of the realities of their
Neanderworld. Just as the image of those ancient people has at times been
grossly distorted, so the Ice Age has been viewed far too simplistically. The
Pleistocene Ice Age was a prolonged prehistoric episode that exerted an
enormous influence on the landscapes and life of the Earth, reaching back
in time way beyond the Neanderthals. From clues scattered over the
landscapes of Europe, buried beneath the surface and compared with the
living example of glaciation in the Alps, scientists have gradually pieced
together a history of environmental change. Although the most marked
effects were felt in the high latitudes of both hemispheres within the last 2
million years, climate change began much longer ago and had an effect right
down into the tropics.

Over 20 million years ago the beginning of climate cooling and drying
reached as far south as Africa, drastically reducing the forest cover and forcing
some small primates out of the protection of the trees and on to the more open
savannah. From among those primates evolved the upright australopithecines,
our most distant relatives, one of whose lines of descent ended of course with
the Neanderthals.

The chronology of changing environments, and how they influenced the
plants, animals and humans that inhabited them, illustrates the vital
interconnectedness of the physical world. The story is, too, a salutary reminder
that we are more at the mercy of the elements than our modern human hubris
cares to admit. It is a reminder that climates and environments never have been
static and a warning that they never will be. The Neanderthals might have gone,
but the Ice Age has not ended.

Global climates over the last 12,000 years have been unusually
stable, and are certainly getting warmer, but sooner or later the chances are

that the present phase will end. What the past history of the Ice Age tells us is that when the next swing of the pendulum comes it could happen alarmingly quickly. The history of the Neanderthals shows that they managed to survive through numerous 'rapid' swings of climate change but in the end something defeated them. The big question is: What? Was it just one climate change too many, or the arrival of modern Cro-Magnon humans in Europe that finally caused their extinction? While it is possible that competition from the Cro-Magnons applied the *coup de grâce*, the indications at present are that the fortunes of the Neanderthals were intimately linked with climate change.

Europe: an elemental battleground

Europe has been a battleground for the elements for many millions of years, since the formation of the North Atlantic Ocean. The ebb and flow of the elemental conflict between the climates of Asia and the Atlantic still continues. Today, the relatively mild and moist air of the Atlantic Gulf Stream flows over north-west Europe and helps to keep the polar ice at bay, as it has done for the last 10,000 years.

A fundamental cooling of deep ocean water can be traced back at least 30 million years, but its effect on climate seems to have surfaced only around 2 million years ago. Then, climate deterioration speeded up and set into a fluctuating pattern of alternating cold and warm phases, respectively glacials and interglacials. The ice sheets advanced and retreated in a cycle linked to regular variations in the Earth's orbit round the sun: 41,000-year cycles to begin with, and then longer but more intense 100,000-year cycles. At times the temperature in Britain, for instance, dropped from today's summer average of 16°C (60°F) to 10°C (50°F), while winter temperatures dropped drastically to −9°C (16°F). During the very coldest spells, Britain was colder than Siberia is today and winter temperatures averaged around −18°C (0°F). The intervening warm interglacial phases were at least as warm as today and sometimes warmer.

But even the cold glacial phases of the Ice Age were not all relentlessly frigid. Recent reassessment of Ice Age climates shows that the past emphasis on intensely cold climates is misleading. Detailed analysis reveals that for much of the time the climate was much milder. What was significantly different was the way that the climate fluctuated dramatically from relatively cold to warm over very short intervals. During the last glacial phase, between 117,000 and 12,000 years ago, there were at least twenty-four short-lived warm spells, with average temperatures rising over 7°C (12°F) in decades. Consequently, the humans, other animals and plants living through the Ice Age did so in very dynamic and frequently shifting environments.

Today, modern humans can occupy some of the most inhospitable places on Earth and have done so for several thousand years. Our ability to

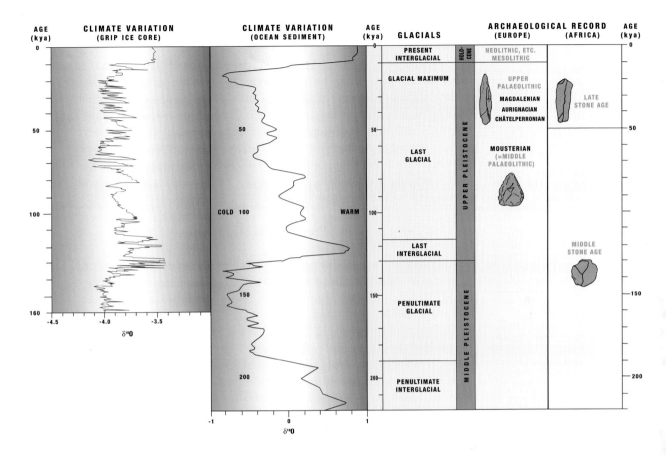

AGE (kya)	CLIMATE VARIATION (GRIP ICE CORE)	CLIMATE VARIATION (OCEAN SEDIMENT)	AGE (kya)	GLACIALS		ARCHAEOLOGICAL RECORD (EUROPE)	(AFRICA)	AGE (kya)
0			0	PRESENT INTERGLACIAL	HOLO-CENE	NEOLITHIC, ETC. MESOLITHIC		0
				GLACIAL MAXIMUM		UPPER PALAEOLITHIC	LATE STONE AGE	
						MAGDALENIAN		
						AURIGNACIAN		
						CHÂTELPERRONIAN		
50		50	50	LAST GLACIAL	UPPER PLEISTOCENE	MOUSTERIAN (=MIDDLE PALAEOLITHIC)		50
100		COLD 100	100	LAST INTERGLACIAL			MIDDLE STONE AGE	
		150	150	PENULTIMATE GLACIAL	MIDDLE PLEISTOCENE			150
160								
	-4.5 -4.0 -3.5 δ¹⁸0	200	200	PENULTIMATE INTERGLACIAL				200

-1   0   1
$\delta^{18}0$

adapt to the polar climates of regions such as Greenland and Siberia has, however, depended upon the advanced technical skills of *Homo sapiens* rather than any major biological adaptation to extremes of temperature. But there are doubts about our future ability to adapt to major changes in plant life, land fertility and use, and changing sea-levels. The Neanderthal people managed to survive extreme conditions for around 200,000 years – there are lessons to be learned from the peoples of the Ice Age.

Our understanding of the Ice Age has been radically transformed over the last decade or so thanks to the discovery of high-quality information about the chronology of events. The old picture showed just four glacial episodes separated by three much longer interglacial phases when the climate was thought to have been much like that of today. Now layers of sediment and the fossils they contain, recovered as drill cores from the ocean floor, turn out to give an indirect but remarkably detailed record of climate change through the Ice Age. When combined with data from ice cores drilled through the ice caps of Greenland and Antarctica and the vast amount of information from many different sources on land, a fascinating and complicated history is emerging.

ABOVE Analysis of ice cores *(left)* and ocean sediments show rapid climate changes during the Ice Age which scientists are trying to link to the archaeological record of stones and bones *(right)*. (The lower part of the ice core is omitted because ice-flow has probably made the data unreliable.)

Identifying the Ice Age

Arguments for and against the existence of a recent Ice Age built up during the early part of the nineteenth century. Luminaries such as William Buckland, Charles Lyell and Charles Darwin in Britain debated the nature of the evidence, from so-called erratic boulders scattered over the landscapes of northern Britain to deposits of shells and sediments stranded high on Welsh and Scottish hills. In continental Europe the same debate was going on, and no more so than in Switzerland where at least they had the benefit of being able to study the process of glaciation at first hand. Foremost among the protagonists for an Ice Age was a Swiss scientist, Louis Agassiz (1807–73). He eventually managed to persuade Lyell and Darwin that much of the evidence originally put down to the effects of the biblical 'Flood' or sea-ice was better interpreted as resulting from the release of glacial meltwaters and changing sea-levels related to a recent Ice Age. Agassiz went on to do an equally persuasive job in North America but then became even better known as an implacable foe of Darwin's theory of evolution.

Dividing the Ice Age

By the latter part of the nineteenth century, an enormous amount of information from many different sources had built up. Studies of landscape features and deposits associated with the Ice Age showed that the history of events was far from simple. There seemed to have been warmer and colder phases during which very different types of life had thrived within the Ice Age. The problem was that the evidence was scattered in patches all over northern Europe and it was very difficult to match a pile of sand and gravel from one place with that from another. Also there was no readily available 'handle' on the chronological dating of the events, apart from the possibility of relative dating provided by fossils – but they were only sometimes present in Ice Age deposits on land.

The realization that the landscapes of the world had been occupied in the not too distant past by a whole range of somewhat familiar-looking but now extinct animals dates back to the early nineteenth century. The French anatomist, Georges Cuvier (1769–1832), had shown in 1799 how the skeletons and teeth of fossil elephants and rhinoceros, recovered from surface deposits in Europe, differed sufficiently in their detailed anatomy from living forms to be identified as separate and extinct species.

As we have seen, the discovery of worked stone tools, associated with such ancient animal remains, also dated back to around the beginning of the nineteenth century but their significance was not recognized at the time. Twenty or so years later, it was generally recognized that changes in the kinds of fossils found in successive layers of sediments could be used to match the sedimentary strata found in different places. By this method, the whole succession of strata back through geological time was being sequenced and subdivided but still without any but a vague idea of how old they were in years.

Experts such as Lyell and Darwin were certainly thinking in terms of hundreds of millions of years for the age of the Earth.

The fossil method of relative dating was also applied, wherever possible, to the more recent surface deposits which were increasingly associated with the Ice Age. The problem was that so many of these deposits did not contain fossils. And then there was the question of human artefacts, the stone tools and other materials that were being found with animal and human remains in these Ice Age deposits. Could the changes in the form of the tools be used in the same way as fossils were used to sequence and subdivide the deposits and events of the Ice Age? The general assumption was that they could, and that the changes would reflect the progress of stone technology as developed by these early humans.

By the beginning of the twentieth century, European geologists thought that they could discern four ice ages, separated by three longer interglacial periods which altogether made up the Pleistocene epoch. Pre-eminent among these scientists were A. Penck and E. Brückner, who named the four glacial phases of the Ice Age after tributaries of the Danube: the Günz, Mindel, Riss and Würm. They estimated that the whole sequence stretched back through some 600,000 years of recent Earth history. Since scientists have been able to chronologically date some levels in the sequence, using the radiometric method, it is known that the Ice Age was more than twice as long as this, with the base dated at around 1.8 million years ago.

Data from the deep sea

One of the problems associated with this classical division is that it was based on the continental sequence in Europe, and there were problems with matching sequences from elsewhere, even from the nearby British Isles. Also, there was a tendency to 'shoe-horn' everything into the classical scheme which became more and more complicated and unwieldy. Fortunately, help came from a completely unexpected source, namely the sediments and creatures of the deep sea.

In the 1950s a massive programme of deep-sea drilling was under way to try and work out what had been going on in the world's oceans, which cover some two-thirds of the Earth's surface. The history of the oceans presented an immense geological problem, which could not be fully resolved until ocean-floor sediment samples were recovered. The sediments record the history of these previously inaccessible environments of deposition.

Ocean-floor muds contain the fossil remains of myriads of tiny shells secreted by single-celled, amoeba-like micro-organisms called foraminiferans. Many of these remarkable little creatures live in the surface waters of the oceans among the plankton. Their shells are made of calcium carbonate, which includes oxygen ions that the organisms extract from the surrounding seawater. The oxygen exists as two different isotopes. When moisture is withdrawn from the oceans during a glacial to form ice sheets, it selectively removes the lighter isotope (O-16). This leaves more of the other, heavier, isotope (O-18) to be taken up by the micro-organisms in forming their shells.

When the ice sheets melt, the reverse happens and foraminiferan shells are secreted with a greater proportion of O-16. So, in a rather roundabout way, the fluctuating ratios of the two oxygen isotopes, locked into the foraminiferan shells, indicates build-ups and melt-downs of ice sheets. By measuring the ratios of the isotopes in successive collections of foraminiferan shells from the different layers of ocean-floor sediment, Cesare Emiliani, an Italian-American geologist, generated a proxy measure of the changing temperature of surface water in the oceans. And, because there is a close link between ocean-water temperature and that of the atmosphere above, the measure can be seen to reflect the climate change which drove the growth and decay of the ice sheets.

Emiliani was able to recognize fourteen stages for the Ice Age, double the number recognized by Penck and Brückner. This is because the ocean-floor deposits preserve a continuous record for the Pleistocene Ice Age, whereas the land record is disjointed and incomplete. Emiliani's method has now been more fully developed by the British scientist Nick Shackleton, who realized that the isotope curves provide a fairly direct measure of the relative quantity of seawater in the world's oceans compared with water locked up in land-based ice caps.

Rock clocks and switching poles

The other crucial innovation was keying in chronological dates to the sediment record. Again, this could not be done directly because the method requires the existence of particular kinds of chemical 'clocks', materials that contain long-lived radio isotopes of certain chemical elements. Radiocarbon isotopes have been used for dating organic materials such as bone, teeth and wood since the late 1940s, but the method is effective only over the last 55,000 years or so. Other elements have to be used to obtain earlier dates and they mainly occur in rocks rather than organic materials. These rock clocks have to be set going by the crystallization of the mineral from a liquid rock (magma) such as a lava. Unfortunately, although lavas form the rocky floor to the oceans they are not found layered between the ocean-floor sediments. But lavas do record the reversals of the Earth's polarity as do ocean-floor sediments.

These reversals happen every few hundred thousand years when for some unknown reason the magnetic dipole within the Earth's liquid core switches north for south and then back again. The last switchover has been pinned down by the radiometric dating of lavas to 736,000 years ago and has been identified in the ocean-sediment record. Scientists use it to mark the boundary between the Lower and Middle Pleistocene. Above it the Middle and Upper Pleistocene contain eight climatic cycles, each of which is made up of a couplet comprised of a glacial and interglacial stage. The boundary of the Middle and Upper Pleistocene is dated at 128,000 years ago.

Once this more complete, detailed and partly timed record had been obtained there was a much better framework for scientists to work with. Other essential background data could now be referred to this much more reliable chronological base, especially the land-based records of environmental change.

Changing pollen

As any hay-fever sufferer knows, plant pollen is remarkable stuff. It is barely visible, produced in vast quantities at certain times of year and can be easily carried by the wind. Amazingly, many individual pollen grains can be identified as belonging to particular species of plant. Luckily for scientists, pollen has to be very tough to survive being carried around by wind or insects. A lot of pollen ends up dumped on the landsurface where it can survive for remarkably long periods of time, even millions of years, although it is no longer viable.

By identifying successive changes in fossil pollen, trapped in ancient sediments, it is possible to get a good idea of how vegetation changed in any particular region. Sediment cores, many metres long, have been obtained from some European sites and these provide detailed records of how the plant cover has changed throughout much of the Ice Age.

Many plants are good environmental indicators, being sensitive to temperature and rainfall. When combined with fossil information from other climate-sensitive organisms, such as beetle remains, remarkably detailed maps of Ice Age environments can be built up. And now these maps can be fitted into the overall chronology of the Ice Age to provide a much better view of the environments in which the plants, animals and humans of the Ice Age lived and died.

ABOVE Neanderthals could not eat the common cottongrass of the tundra, and the small mammals which grazed on this cold-adapted hardy plant would not have provided enough sustenance either.

The ice record

Some parts of the Ice Age record of environmental change seem to show that the climate fluctuated enormously within relatively short periods of time. However, until recently the resolution of the record has not been good enough to realize the exact nature and duration of these changes.

In the 1990s scientists drilled through the Greenland and Antarctic ice caps and recovered the ice cores. Since the ice caps are built up into piles several kilometres thick by the annual accumulation of snow at the surface, the yearly layers form a continuous record that stretches back around 250,000 years. Ice is of course frozen water, with its familiar composition of hydrogen and oxygen (H_2O), so again there is the possibility of analysing oxygen isotopes but this time from the ice cores. In addition, air bubbles trapped in the ice sample the original atmospheric composition at the time a particular ice layer started 'life' as a surface snowfall on the Greenland ice sheet. Analysis of the concentrations of carbon dioxide (CO_2), a so-called

'greenhouse' gas) in these air bubbles provides another, independent, measure of climate change.

As a result of these analyses, more detailed sampling of climate change during the latter part of the Ice Age can be achieved from ice cores than from the sediment cores. The results confirmed the existence of 'sharp' climate oscillations. For instance, between 60,000 and 25,000 years ago there were at least a dozen significant swings of climate that involved changes of as much as 5–8°C (41–46°F). Some of these oscillations seem to have happened remarkably quickly, over periods of a thousand years or so, much faster than anyone had thought possible. That climate change can take place so quickly is particularly worrying for the future of humankind. If we knew how the past changes affected the humans who lived through the last interglacial and subsequent glacial, perhaps we might have a better warning about how such changes might affect us in the not too distant future.

The Ice Age freezer

Many times during the Ice Age, glaciers and ice sheets grew out of the Arctic northern landscapes. From what is known today as Scandinavia and Russia, they built up in the mountains and flowed over the Baltic, taking polar conditions with them on to the northern European plain, Denmark, Germany and the Baltic States. From what is now North America, they extended south to cover most of Canada and encroach into the USA. As they did so, the ice sheets swept everything before them – vegetation was bulldozed, soils were scraped off the bedrock and even the solid rock below was ground down in places. On lower ground, the ice pushed over older glacial debris, moulding it into distinctive mounds, ridges and hollows recognizable today as 'drumlin and flute' topography.

Those animals and humans more used to equable climates had a stark choice: retreat if they could, or perish – eventually. Over the centuries of environmental change, succeeding generations of plants and animals were not able to reproduce and thrive to the same extent as before. Populations would thin out and gradually disappear. Many organisms that now live in more northerly (temperate and wooded) regions of Europe survived glacial phases in refuges far to the south of the ice sheets and permafrost. When the thaw came and the ice melted, those capable of expanding rapidly over long distances quickly established colonies in the newly available northern territories. As a result, relatively few 'founding fathers and mothers' spread their genes over large regions with little genetic variability, a kind of northern genetic puritanism compared with a southern genetic richness. This applies to a wide range of organisms from plants to insects, fish, birds, mammals and mankind.

When the ice returned, life had to retreat as best it could to more southerly refuges but these were already occupied by native species. Many of the refugees from the north suffered extinction and barely survived in the border territories such as Turkey and the Balkans between the north and south. Some life forms became extinct, others managed to survive through interbreeding with the native species of the borderlands and some just survived, perhaps by luck, with reduced populations.

BELOW Siberian frozen corpses and Cro-Magnon art show that mammoths were well adapted to the cold with small ears, short tails, fat deposits and thick coats of hair. The last mammoths survived until 3700 years ago, stranded on Arctic islands.

What we now call the North Sea became icebound and permanent sea-ice extended all the way to Iceland, Greenland and beyond. At an extreme stage, the glaciers from upland Britain covered all but the south of the country. So much water was locked up in the ice that sea-level fell dramatically, maybe by as much as 150 metres (492 feet). As a result, there was no longer an archipelago of islands lying offshore of north-west Europe (known as Ireland and the British Isles today), but a dry and frozen land extension of Europe. The connection formed a thoroughfare for humans and other animals to exploit the natural resources of Britain throughout most of the Ice Age. But none of these prehistoric explorers would have been aware that they would eventually become stranded when the climate improved and sea-levels rose again to create the offshore archipelago that we know today.

ABOVE The landscapes of northern Europe are deeply scarred and moulded by the recent Ice Age. Mountains and rocks were worn down, valleys excavated, dammed with rock debris and filled with meltwater.

The area of the North Sea was a great bay filled by an ice shelf extending all the way to Scandinavia. Most of the ancient mountains of Scandinavia were glazed over by ice sheets more than 2 kilometres (a mile and a quarter) thick. Only a few high peaks stood out above the ice. Winter pack ice filled the Bay of Biscay and glaciers flowed out of the mountains of southern Europe, the Alps and Pyrenees. Even the Massif Central in France had active glaciers flowing down on to the surrounding lowland and casting a deep chill over central France.

But such peaks of glaciation were relatively brief if fairly frequent intervals within the Ice Age. Professor Tjeerd Van Andel of the University of Cambridge reminds us that 'most of the time, conditions were a good deal less severe'. He has criticized archaeologists 'who are fond of setting early human beings in an "ice-bound" Europe of blizzards, tundras and mammoths that fails to reflect the reality of the environment in which modern human beings evolved'.

Beyond the freezer: Ice Age environments

The modern synthesis of information about the Ice Age and its inhabitants – the plants and animals, including humans – is beginning to provide a sequence of snapshots in past time like single frames from a movie that lasts for the best part of 2 million years. Inevitably, the sample of the whole story is still very small but at least it is beginning to be possible to place the fossil evidence of plants and animals within a tighter chronological sequence than ever before. Also, we have to remember that, as with so much scientific information about the Earth and its inhabitants, there are margins of error, which are rarely mentioned outside academic journals.

By selecting one time-slot, an impression can be gained of the variation and sequence of Ice Age environments across Europe. As with today's climate and vegetation zones, the environments changed in a broadly parallel succession from the coldest in the north to warmer ones in the south. As climates changed through time these zonal bands constantly shifted in latitude. During the coldest glacials, as the ice advanced, they shifted southwards. During the intervening warmer interglacials, when the glaciers retreated and even disappeared from mainland Europe, they shifted northwards to give climate zones similar to those of today.

The following description is of an extreme cold-phase sequence, such as occurred 20,000 years ago and 150,000 years ago, for maximum contrast with today's relatively warm environments. The picture is based on the understanding of similar present environments and the organisms that occupy them. This is combined with geological and palaeontological evidence for Ice Age (Pleistocene) environments that lie buried not far below the surface of today's landscapes in the northern hemisphere. The Neanderthals had to face these environments 150,000 years ago and to a somewhat lesser extent many times more through their 200,000-year 'reign'. But by 20,000 years ago the Neanderthals were long gone and it was the Cro-Magnon ancestors of modern ethnic Europeans who had to survive the deep chill. They probably retreated south and waited for conditions to improve.

BELOW Not even the tough Neanderthals could cope in open glacial landscapes; only cold-adapted plants like the purple saxifrage and the Arctic fox can survive in these conditions.

Polar deserts

Beyond the maximum advance of the ice over Scandinavia, northern Britain and the southern shores of the Baltic lay a fringe of barren polar desert stretching from Holland through Germany and across Poland into Russia. The ground was permanently frozen and practically devoid of soils. Fierce winds exaggerated the effect of the bitter cold through the wind-chill factor. Any loose surface sediment was blown away and ended up being dumped as vast desert-like loess deposits hundreds of kilometres away. Today the northern polar desert is confined to the islands of the Arctic Ocean. Even in midsummer, temperatures rise to an average of only 5°C (41°F), and in midwinter drop to a numbing –32°C (–90°F).

Life in this freezer is very harsh but even so some really tough plants – certain mosses, saxifrages and cotton grass – manage to scrape a subsistence living here. Decaying plant material feeds insects, which in turn are eaten by migratory birds such as turnstones and knots in summer. The polar bear, Arctic fox, Arctic hare and lemming can survive all year, especially when the winter snow is deep enough to help insulate them from the coldest weather. The Arctic fox is one of the most remarkable cold-adapted land mammals, able to sleep in open snow

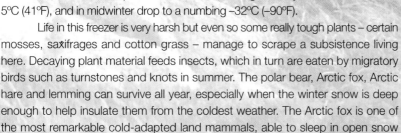

when the surrounding temperature is as low as −80°C (−112°F) without any decrease in its core body temperature. Many of the same plants and animals successfully occupied these inhospitable environments throughout the Ice Age.

The polar deserts extended deep into the glacial terrains along coastlines, where the slight warming effects of the ocean waters and strong winds helped keep narrow corridors of land more or less snow-free. There were similar snow- and ice-free islands of rock where summits of particularly high mountains poked up through the glaciers and ice sheets. Although most of these environments were like hell frozen over, their more sheltered nooks and crannies provided refuges for plants such as sandwort and rare ferns.

Very rarely do modern humans venture into this polar wilderness, except on hunting trips, or scientific expeditions. The extreme climate certainly made it out of bounds even for the cold-adapted Neanderthals or the better equipped Cro-Magnons, who could build temporary shelters and sew skins to make clothing.

Tundra

To the south of the polar desert lay a swathe of windswept tundra and cold steppe, from the south of Britain, across most of France to the Alps and through southern Germany and middle Europe to the Ukraine and beyond to the Caspian Sea. Again the ground is permanently frozen to depths of several hundred metres, although in the few weeks of summer the surface thaws out enough to allow a brief growing season. Some of the permafrost ice also melts, to form standing bodies of water ranging from pools to bogs and lakes. These bodies of water provide crucial 'oases' for plant and animal life, especially migratory animals such as deer and birds. Rivers carrying water from warmer regions unfreeze for several months in the summer and swell dramatically and dangerously in volume with meltwater. Migratory fish move upstream to their spawning grounds. Migratory animals often have to swim across such treacherous waters.

A surprising variety of tough plants are adapted to survive the extreme conditions. Most are very low-growing and dwarf forms, and range from 'trees' such as the Arctic willow and birches, to shrubs such as cloudberry and bilberry, to herbs such as poppies, mountain avens, Arctic white-heather and thrift, and various grasses as well as the even tougher plants of the polar desert.

These plants are adapted to reproduce very quickly during the brief summer season when parts of the tundra become showy flower gardens. The flowering plants have to promote their wares to passing pollinators, mainly insects, as effectively as possible with flashy displays of colour and scent. Their seeds and fruit are dispersed mainly by wind. All provide a basis for an even more diverse range of insects (over 1500 species are known to inhabit today's tundra environment) but relatively few birds (180 or so breeding species) and even fewer mammals (forty-eight living species).

The land-living mammals range from hares and the rabbit-like pikas through rodents to carnivores such as the abundant grey wolf, foxes, occasional bears, ermine and weasels, and the wolverine. Deer of various kinds from moose, caribou (called reindeer in Eurasia), musk-ox and snow sheep are tough and sometimes very abundant. Between 300,000 and 450,000 caribou were recorded from Bathurst Island in the Canadian Arctic archipelago in 1984. Some herds 25,000 to 50,000 strong migrate vast distances (up to 1000 kilometres/620 miles) twice yearly as the season changes. At any one time a large herd may be stretched out over 100,000 square kilometres (38,600 square miles).

During the Ice Age the number of large mammals that ventured into the Arctic tundra was significantly greater, and it is a moot point to what extent the Neanderthals and more importantly the Cro-Magnon hunters were responsible for their extinction. Climate and associated changes in the plant cover certainly played their part. Many of the large Ice Age herbivores, such as mammoths and bison, fed on tundra grasses which have since been replaced by the much less nutritious herbs of today's tundra.

LEFT Giant deer with their spectacular 3m (10ft)-wide antlers ranged from Ireland to China during the Ice Age, and at times were hunted by both Neanderthal and Cro-Magnon people. Like the Neanderthals, the last giant deer sought refuge in the far west, on the Isle of Man and western Scotland, and finally died out about 9000 years ago.

While the cold-adapted animals of the Ice Age could cope with these harsh and treacherous environments, as their surviving descendants do today, it is unlikely that Neanderthals were at home here. They would probably have made hunting trips from more sheltered valley home-bases out on to the tundra, but killing large game in open landscapes is not easy. The Neanderthals might have scavenged carcasses from the tundra, or exploited landscape features such as cliffs and narrow valleys to ambush game.

The mammoth steppe grasslands

Where the landscape drained and when more arid but still cold climates kept soils drier, the shrub and tree cover gradually diminished to leave cold tundra grasslands. The grasslands were a cold equivalent of the grass prairies of North

Analysing palaeodiets

We are what we eat: to some extent the chemistry of our bones, teeth and other body tissues such as hair reflects the chemistry of our food. Recent advances in detailed chemical analysis of fossil skeletal material are giving insights into the diet of the animals and humans of the past. For instance, chemical analysis of hair from the 5200-year-old Copper-Age 'iceman', recently found in the Alps in 1991 and nick-named Ötzi, has shown that plants formed the bulk of his diet around the time of his death. In fact the nitrogen values suggest that he was virtually vegan, subsisting mainly on grains, and this is supported by wear patterns on his teeth. Such chemical analyses are complementary to and independent of the more traditional approaches to understanding what the animals of the past ate, such as their tooth form and jaw articulation.

Well-preserved bones from a variety of animals living at the time of the last glaciation have been found in the Scladina Cave in the Ardennes region of Belgium. Detailed chemical analysis of these 40,000-year-old skeletal remains is showing up the dietary preferences of a number of the Ice Age animals.

Bone and teeth have an organic component 'locked' into their calcium phosphate mineral base. Surprisingly, this organic component, the complex and tough protein collagen, can survive under certain conditions of burial for many thousands of years. The composition of collagen contains chemical signatures (isotopes), especially of the elements carbon and nitrogen, which are derived from the food eaten by the animal. By identifying traces of particular isotopes in bone and collagen, it is possible to gain some idea of the diet of the animal.

The bones found in the Scladina Cave belong to a wide variety of Ice Age animals including plant-eaters such as horse (*Equus caballus*), bovines (*Bison priscus* and *Bos primigenius*), giant deer (*Megaloceros giganteus*), woolly rhinoceros (*Coelodonta antiquitatis*) (*right*) and woolly mammoth (*Mammuthus primigenius*); and omnivores such as brown bear (*Ursus arctos*) and cave bear (*Ursus spelaeus*), as well as the carnivorous cave hyena (*Crocuta crocuta*). The habitat preferences of the plant-eaters include open landscapes, forest and cold climate and suggest that the local environment at the time consisted of grassland and herbaceous steppe with some scattered woodland, in a cool and slightly humid continental climate.

America, which were occupied by bison and Native Americans before the European settlers drove them out. The vast areas of Eurasian cold prairie grasslands are known as the mammoth steppe grasslands because they were home to huge herds of cold-adapted, hairy elephants. There has been considerable argument between experts over the genesis and maintenance of these grasslands, which do not now exist to any extent except in small pockets in Alaska. It is possible that the feeding activities of the mammoth and other grazers helped maintain the grasslands and subdued the establishment of trees and shrubs.

At times, most of Europe south of the Pyrenees and Alps was covered in this kind of open and mostly treeless grassland. In the south of France the average annual temperature was around 1.5°C (35°F), compared with 9.5°C

It turns out that the nitrogen isotope values for cave-bear collagen from Scladina and elsewhere in western Europe are the same as for plant-eaters, and suggest that cave bears were also herbivorous. However, their nitrogen isotope values differ from all other species and may be due to their preference for a forest habitat or some changes in body biochemistry during hibernation. In comparison, the isotope values for the brown bear are intermediate between those of plant- and meat-eaters and show that they were omnivores similar to modern brown bears. It would seem that these two bear species occupied quite different ecological niches, which was why they could share the same territory.

Isotope values for the plant-eaters at Scladina compare closely with those analysed for cave-bear bones found across the English Channel at Kent's Cavern in southern England. But this is only to be expected as, with lowered sea-levels, the two localities were part of the same landmass and were experiencing the same climate at the time. In comparison, the south of France had a milder climate and somewhat different vegetation, and consequently some of the isotope measures from the animals there give different values.

Mammoths have distinctive high-nitrogen and low-carbon isotope measures which have been found in both Siberian and Alaskan specimens. The total isotope pattern in mammoths is different from that of other contemporary herbivores – it is not yet clear why. But the method shows considerable promise for future ecological analysis of both plant and animal remains from specific sites to provide more complete understanding of the original environments.

(49°F) today. Annual precipitation in the form of both snow and rain was low, at around 200mm (8 inches) compared with 830mm (33 inches) today.

One important effect of the aridity was the relatively small amount of snow that fell during the bitterly cold and windy winters. It meant that cold-adapted grazers such as woolly mammoths with their long tusks could easily brush away the snow to get at the dead but still nutritious grass. Summers would have been quite warm because this far south there is a high midday sun and long summers. Moister areas supported the growth of woodland refugia ('reservoirs') from which the landscape was restocked with trees when the climate changed.

The grasslands became the 'larder' for vast herds of grazing mammals. Grasses, as anyone who has had to maintain a lawn knows, do not grow from

the tip of the plant but from the base of the stem close to the ground. Consequently, they can be grazed by animals without their growth and reproduction being seriously set back. By contrast, many other broad-leaf woody plants favoured by plant-eating animals contain much of their nutrients in the growing tips, and if these are completely removed then growth and reproduction may be seriously curtailed. These plants have evolved defences such as pushing their leaf investment high out of reach or lacing leaf growth with unpalatable toxins such as caffeine, nicotine and opium. This chemical strategy is an effective deterrent for most animals, ensuring that the plant is left alone. (In the case of modern humans, of course, those chemicals can incidentally work in the plant's favour as an addictive, ensuring domestic propagation. Coffee, tea, tobacco, marijuana and opium poppies would not be such successful plants were it not for human choice and interference.)

The dominant grazers of these grasslands were bison and horse as well as mammoth; they all seem to have been able to coexist without any difficulty. They were joined by smaller numbers of a wide variety of other grazers such as deer and rhino. The relative proportions of the different megaherbivores change depending on a variety of factors. For instance, in the more upland regions, bison become common. Inevitably this amount of meat protein on the hoof attracted predators, especially the big cats.

But despite the abundant supplies of game, this was a very difficult environment for humans and it is doubtful that either Neanderthals or early Cro-Magnon people were able to exploit it to any significant extent, except at the margins. There was little or no protection or cover, not from the climate, large

predators nor the packs of predatory hyenas and dogs. With the lack of trees there was little or no wood for fire. No doubt Neanderthals probed as deep as they dared into this Ice Age 'game park' in the pursuit of food.

Forest and woodland

Southern Europe, south of the great mountain ranges of the Pyrenees and Alps, was slightly warmer during the Ice Age and covered with woodland and forest. Today, the southern limit of the Arctic more or less coincides with the northern edge of the present European tree-line and an average summer temperature (July) of 10°C (50°F). Where the wind-chill factor is severe, or permafrost persists or the soils are too poor, the development of trees is held back. However, during the Ice Age, the northern boundary of the tree-line with the southern boundary of the mammoth steppe grassland was often unclear as clumps of trees can grow in sheltered or otherwise favoured spots and merge into growth of taller woody shrubs such as willow and birch.

Conifers such as spruce and larch grew in the more exposed areas and on the more barren soils. To the south a variety of pines, along with balsam firs and northern hardwoods such as paper birches, elms and oak, developed. These mixed and deciduous woodlands spread over the lowland and where there was more shelter and better soils.

Much of this kind of vegetation has always been well defended with plant toxins against large browsing animals. However, there are some important exceptions, such as where natural wildfire has reset the succession of plants

Ancient guts

In 1901 the Russian Imperial Academy of Sciences in St Petersburg sent an expedition to Siberia to recover a frozen mammoth, which had been found 100 kilometres (62 miles) inside the Arctic Circle. Led by Austrian scientists Dr Otto Herz and Eugen Pfizenmeyer, the expedition took four months to travel the 9600 kilometres (6000 miles) to the site on the banks of the Beresovka River, a tributary of the Kolyma River which flows into the Arctic Ocean.

The frozen beast *(below)* had originally been spotted by a Siberian deer hunter, who removed the tusks and sold them in Kolyma. By the time the St Petersburg expedition arrived, most of the flesh had gone from the head and the trunk had been eaten by wolves. But the flesh of the rest of the animal, and its long hair, was still frozen solid in the prevailing permafrost.

To retrieve as much of the animal as possible, the body had to be defrosted, cut up and frozen again before it rotted any further. Remarkably, the scientists managed to recover quite a lot of skin, flesh and even some of the stomach contents and bring it all back to St Petersburg, another four-month journey. At times the air temperature fell to –48°C (–54°F). The body parts were reconstructed and mounted and are still on show in the Zoological Museum in St Petersburg.

Later analysis has revealed that the animal was a 35–40-year-old bull mammoth, which had died somewhere between 33,000 and 29,000 years ago, at the end of 'Neandertime'. The mammoth's stomach contained mainly grasses and there was still grass clenched between its massive grinding cheek teeth at the time of death. Clearly it had not died of starvation but rather seems to have fallen back on its haunches and not been able to get up again. Consequently, it may just have frozen to death.

A more detailed analysis of the stomach content of another Siberian specimen, the Shandrin mammoth, found in 1972, revealed 90 per cent grasses and sedges along with some twig tips of willow, larch, birch and alder. With their massive grinding molar teeth, the mammoths, like bison and horse, can use the coarsest end of the grazing spectrum, the poorer quality fibrous plant materials such as coarse grasses, and twig tips of woody herbs and shrubs, which are relatively less defended by plant toxins. Nevertheless, to avoid 'overdosing' on any one plant toxin, these megaherbivores have to eat a variety of plants. In comparison, a 37,000-year-old frozen horse from Selerikan had a stomach content of 90 per cent herbaceous material, mainly grasses and sedge, along with smaller amounts of willow, dwarf birch and moss. Similarly, the stomach of the woolly rhino (*Coelodonta*) from Yakutia, also in Siberia, showed that it had been eating mostly grass.

and allowed the initial growth of more tender and palatable plants; and also where tender and nutrient-rich plants have been able to grow alongside rivers in rich soils that are frequently replenished by floodwaters. Altogether, the many different plants growing throughout this broad zone have formed a diversity of habitats which in turn supported a great variety of animals and humans since the Ice Age.

The large woodland animals were dominated by abundant deer and horse but the variety of habitats also supported a large range of other mammals, the largest of which were bears and big cats (see box, 'Analysing palaeodiets', pages 54–55). The main diversity lay in the medium-sized and smaller mammals, from wolverines, wolves, foxes, boar, beavers and badgers to squirrels, ermine and weasels, and rodents, along with a host of birds.

The very diversity of life in the forests and woodlands provided ideal hunting conditions. The problem for the human hunters was that the environment provided equal opportunity for all hunters – the big cats, bears, wolverines, hyenas and wolves were all competing for potential food. Neither the Neanderthals nor the Cro-Magnon people were individually stronger or faster than the big predators or the pack hunters. Only through co-operation and the manufacture of weapons could the humans compete and survive in the dangerous world of the forests and woodlands of the Ice Age.

LEFT Open grassland terrain provided food for many large migratory mammals such as horse, deer and mammoth, but hunting them on foot armed only with spears was far from easy.

Neanderthal
body-building

chapter three

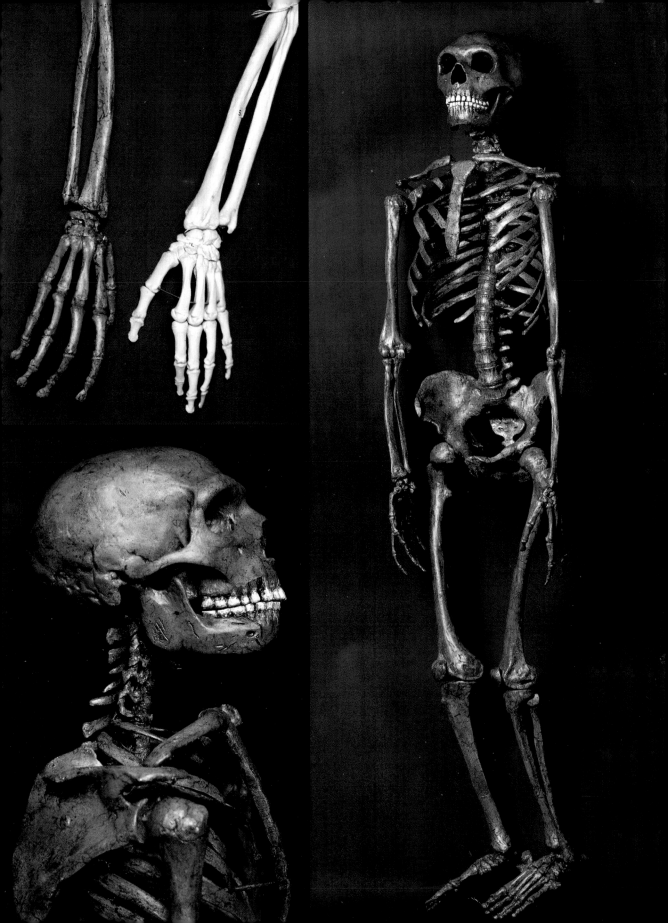

EVEN THE FEW BARE BONES OF THE ORIGINAL 1856 NEANDERTHAL find from Germany revealed features that distinguish Neanderthals from the Cro-Magnon early modern humans and living people. These differences were eventually confirmed and further developed when bony remains from the face and the rest of the Neanderthal skeletal frame were found at La Chapelle-aux-Saints in 1908.

In overall stature, the Neanderthals were not that different from the global average for modern humans, but their bones are significantly more robust and heavier with thick walls. Some of their large limb bones show a clear curvature that was at first mistakenly diagnosed as a sign of malnutrition and rickets. Modern analysis suggests quite the reverse: the bone curvature is a response to a very heavy, muscular body build and considerable strength.

Now after more than 150 years of searching, a much better sample of Neanderthal skeletal remains has been assembled. Altogether, there are fossils belonging to nearly 500 Neanderthal individuals, although only a small percentage are anywhere near complete. Nevertheless, the overall view shows that there was a fairly marked difference in body stature between the sexes, not as much as in earlier human relatives but slightly more than is found today in modern humans.

Unfortunately, no Neanderthal soft body tissue has ever been found, and so the reconstruction of the Neanderthal body build has had to rely on indirect information from the bones. If only a Neanderthal cadaver could be found in a peatbog or the permafrost, like those of mammoths and other Ice Age animals – or the 5200-year-old 'iceman', Ötzi, found in the Alps in 1991 (see box on pages 54–55) – a lot of our ignorance about Neanderthal build, appearance and clothes would be dispelled. While the chances of finding one are probably zero, there are nevertheless a number of interesting and important conclusions about the appearance of the Neanderthals that can be drawn from the fossil evidence.

Neanderthal stature

Calculating the height of a Neanderthal from the bones of the skeleton is not quite as easy as it might at first seem. The human spine is curved, and overall posture can make a significant difference to the calculations. When the Neanderthals were first 'reconstructed' by a French expert, Marcellin Boule, in the early decades of the twentieth century (see the box on page 64), they were assumed to have been ape-like. Consequently they were given bent legs and a

Old bones

The Neanderthal skeleton known as the 'Old Man' of La Chapelle-aux-Saints *(right)* was discovered in 1908 by three French priests in the Corrèze district of France. The bones were sent to the Museum of Natural History in Paris, where they were subjected to exhaustive study by Marcellin Boule.

Boule's very detailed work set new standards of exactitude for the future description of fossil skeletons. Importantly, he compared the Neanderthal skull with those of a chimp and a modern Frenchman, his illustration of the side profiles of the three skulls highlighting the differences.

At the one extreme, there is the chimp's face that slopes back from a prominent muzzle with no bony support for the nose that is, as a result, flat. Above the eye sockets, a double-arched, bony brow-ridge is joined in mid-face above the nose. Above the brow the skull slopes back without much forehead. At the other extreme is the modern face, almost vertical and flat but with a clearly developed bony nose bridge and high forehead before the skull roof slopes back. In between lies the Neanderthal with a face showing less slope than the chimp but more than the modern. The reconstructed nose is distinctly prominent and large, as are the brow-ridges. The forehead is low and sloping, more like the chimp's than that of the modern skull.

As a result of his investigations, Boule concluded that Neanderthals are sufficiently separate from modern humans to be seen as a species in their own right – *Homo neanderthalensis*. In doing so, he agreed with the earlier diagnosis by William King in the nineteenth century.

Boule was certainly very thorough in his forensic examination of his 'patient'. Because the skull was remarkably intact and complete, he was able to make a cast of the inside of the skull. The resulting 'endocast' replicated the surface of the Neanderthal's brain in some detail. Boule interpreted its relatively simple appearance and 'development of different parts of the grey matter' as indicating that Neanderthals had 'rudimentary intellectual faculties'. Surprisingly, even the remarkably large size of the brain (just over 1600ml, compared with a modern average of 1200–1500ml) was not regarded by him as any particular sign of intelligence.

When Boule reconstructed the skeleton, he saw his 'vertebral column and limb bones as having numerous simian characters and, in particular, a less perfect bipedal or upright carriage than in modern Man'. In other words, Neanderthals were relegated to being somewhat ape-like beings of low intelligence. Boule had put up a barrier that emphasized differences and distanced the Neanderthals from us. As Chris Stringer and Clive Gamble point out, Boule's 'yardstick was the Caucasian ideal which confronted him every morning in his shaving mirror'.

There was an inherent racialism in the approach and attitudes of many of the early investigators of human ancestry who were carrying all kinds of conceptual baggage with them, some quite consciously so. Skull and brain shape and size were linked to intelligence and behaviour in a very crude way, inherited from pseudosciences such as phrenology and character typing based on facial features. Such racialist characterization is strongly repudiated by modern experts.

hunched posture, with the head carried forward; thus their height was minimized. Now, it is assumed that their posture was much more like that of modern humans. Also, most of the Neanderthal height statistics have been based on various formulae devised for making calculations from partial skeletons. These formulae have been worked out from the relative proportions of individual bones in the modern human skeleton in relation to overall height.

At about 169cm (5ft 6in), the average adult Neanderthal man might seem somewhat 'vertically challenged' by modern western height standards, which have climbed to 175cm (5ft 9in) or more since the 1950s. A Neanderthal woman would also seem slightly on the short side at 160cm (5ft 3in), compared with the 165cm (5ft 5in) average for women, again achieved since the 1950s. But both Neanderthal measures are well within the normal range of modern westerners and very close to the average of other modern groups found in parts of Spain and southern Italy. In the early nineteenth century, even western people had average heights somewhat less than that of the Neanderthals. There has been a 1 per cent or so increase in height each decade since then.

However, as with any population of living beings, Neanderthals varied in height. So far, from a very limited sample of skeletons – most of which are also incomplete – the tallest Neanderthal known came from the Amud site in Israel and was 179cm (5ft 10½in). The shortest are two adult females, both 155cm (5ft 1in), and they come from sites in France and Iraq. By comparison, modern adult humans show an enormous range in height from well over 195cm (6ft 5in) down to 145cm (4ft 9in) or less. But not all populations show such a range and there are important demographic differences in average heights. For instance, in subtropical New Guinea today, men are less than 160cm (5ft 3in) and women 150cm (4ft 11in), while one of the shortest groups of modern humans, the Bushmen of the southern Kalahari, range between 150cm (4ft 11in) and 145cm (4ft 9in).

Tallness in men always seems to have been seen as a desirable feature – even today, with society's emphasis on wealth, success, good looks and intelligence. We might joke about the increased chances of the tallest candidate always winning the American presidential race, but there is a recognized phenomenon at work here. Modern diet, especially in the early years of babies' growth and development, has led to a steady increase in average height for both men and women, at least in the developed world, where malnutrition is rare. But even here, there are other well-documented selection processes at work and, perhaps not surprisingly, these have to do with sex.

Recent studies reveal that young women show a distinct and often quite unconscious preference for taller men. With all the complicating factors of modern birth control and breeding habits, such preferences do not necessarily affect the subsequent size of our offspring in a direct or immediate way, but sexual selection for height may well have been going on for well over 3 million years in our ancient relatives, perhaps ever since they started walking upright. The first height benchmark was established by 'Lucy', the first partially complete skeleton of an ancient human relative to be found. Discovered in Afar, Ethiopia, in 1974 by the American palaeontologist Don Johanson, the skeleton has been dated at 3.5 million years old, and preserved enough bones to show that it belonged to an upright walking australopithecine. (She was called Lucy after a favourite Beatles song of the time, 'Lucy in the Sky with Diamonds'.) She is estimated to have stood a mere 110–120cm (3ft 6in–4ft) – below the lowest end of the modern height spectrum. Other individuals of the same species, *Australopithecus afarensis*, seem to have varied considerably in height, between 100 and 150cm (3ft 3in and 4ft 11in).

The rate of increasing height over time was probably very uneven, as many different factors, such as diet and climate, play important roles. While Neanderthal women may well have selected their males for height, there seems to have been another male characteristic that they were more enamoured with and that had a distinct selective advantage: namely brawn.

Neanderthal muscle

More significant than height from the biological and evolutionary point of view is body mass: weight and size. Body mass determines many aspects of food requirements, behaviour and way of life. Detailed measures from living animals shows that body mass is clearly related to what happens during growth and development, such as the length of time a baby spends in the womb, metabolic rate and life expectancy.

Over the last 100,000 years or so, as humans spread from the equator to the poles, our bodies have adapted to the range of climate extremes. Equatorial people have maintained less body mass than their more polar contemporaries. In general, native people in the tropics have relatively longer limbs, thinner bodies and proportionally more skin (that is, a greater surface area) than people adapted to colder climes – though nowadays cultural development is increasingly interfering with this basic pattern.

The body mass of fossil members of our genus *Homo* can be estimated from skeletal remains using models developed from living primates, including humans. These calculations can be tricky, to say the least – Neanderthal bones are definitely more robust, with thicker walls and larger muscle attachment areas, than modern specimens – but they do give a reasonable basis for analysis.

From such analysis, some remarkable differences emerge. To begin with, average body mass increased through time from about 50kg (8st) around 4 million years ago to 60kg (9st 7lb) between 1.8 million and 600,000 years ago. Then there was a further increase to a peak of 66kg (10st 6lb) between 600,000 and 150,000 years ago, in mid-Pleistocene times, before falling back to the modern global average (for men) of 58kg (9st 2lb). Consequently, the Pleistocene humans were some 8kg (17lb) heavier or 10 per cent larger than the living human average. Nestling within the Pleistocene sample are the Neanderthals, who were significantly more robust. A sample of seventeen

Neanderthals produced an average body mass of at least 76kg (12st) – about 30 per cent more massive than the average modern human, although only 24 per cent more than modern humans who live in high latitudes. We would probably be at something of a disadvantage in any arm-wrestling competition with a Neanderthal, male or female!

However, there was a considerable difference in body mass between Neanderthal males and females, just as there is in modern humans. As mentioned above, the global average weight for a man is 58.2kg (9st 2lb), while for women it is 46kg (7st 4lb). The sex differences would probably have been at least as great for the Neanderthals, if not slightly more than those of modern humans, but the bone samples of Neanderthal women are not abundant enough yet to really ascertain.

Most modern males in the west with Neanderthal-type stature and build – who are no more than 169cm (5ft 6in) high and weigh 76kg (12st) – would be regarded as overweight and probably quite flabby. The exceptions will be those men whose extra weight is muscle rather than fat: body builders, weightlifters, wrestlers or other athletes. In fact, it may be more appropriate to model Neanderthal musculature and body mass on modern professional athletes, especially those who participate in power sports and can weigh as much as

90kg (14st 3lb). No doubt the Neanderthals lived very physical lives to the limits of their strength and endurance. Many of their bones preserve forensic evidence of this: healed fractures are common and occasionally evidence of mortal wounds. Famously, the Neanderthals from Shanidar in Iraq show a whole catalogue of injuries to their arms, legs, feet, ribs and heads (see page 119). The Neanderthals could well have been similar in build to those modern models – if so, they would have typically carried some 25kg (55lb) more muscle power than the average modern human. Awesome indeed, if true.

Interesting evolutionary implications arise from this kind of modelling and estimation of body mass. Is there a connection between brawn and behaviour in these ancient people? There must have been selection pressures that promoted the increase in brawn. Certainly part of the answer lies in the move north to higher and colder latitudes which favour high body mass relative to limb length and surface area. However, the large size of some of the ancient people from tropical Africa (one of whom, from Namibia, is estimated to have weighed 93kg (14st 9lb)) suggests that there were other factors at work.

The most plausible explanation for the large body size of Neanderthals is their way of life, along with the imperative of sexual selection. There is good evidence from a number of independent sources to show that they were confrontational game hunters who relied on their muscle power to kill powerful animals such as horse, wild cattle and even mammoths, with hand-held or thrown heavy spears. Also, there would have been competition among males for access to females. This is found in the higher apes today, and the same basic trait is likely to have been found in the common ancestors we share with the higher apes and the Neanderthals. One result is a distinct difference in size and weight between the sexes, so-called sexual dimorphism. Chimps show a 13 per cent difference in body weight between the sexes and it is also marked in ancient australopithecine hominids (between 4 and 2 million years old). Within the rugged and often stressful lifestyle of the Neanderthals, a greater premium may well have been placed on strength rather than height.

It's all in the head

As mentioned earlier, a curious feature of the early characterization of the Neanderthals was the way that their remarkable brain size was largely ignored while more 'primitive' features of the skull were emphasized. Although soft brains do not fossilize, brain tissue fills the cranial space of the skull quite tightly. By taking a mould of the cranial space or simply filling it with uniform-size glass beads, the brain volume can be measured fairly accurately. One of the first measurable Neanderthal skulls, the 'Old Man' of La Chapelle-aux-Saints, had a cranial space and consequently brain that was over 1600ml in volume (see the box on page 64). Since this Neanderthal brain is significantly larger than that of the average modern human (which is 1200–1500ml), it was peculiarly perverse to characterize these ancient people as 'stupid primitives'.

Just as body size increased as humans evolved, so did brain size. Ancient human relatives, the southern apes (australopithecines, living between 4 and 1.2 million years ago), had brain capacities between 300 and 560ml. The lightweight, so-called 'gracile' australopithecines had smaller brain sizes, similar to those of chimps, while the heavyweight 'robust' australopithecines had bigger brains like those of gorillas. The first humans, who lived more than 2 million years ago, showed a marked increase in brain size to between 650 and 800ml, which is also seen in the newly found 1.7-million-year-old human skulls from Dmanisi in Georgia. So it would seem that it was not increase in brain capacity that facilitated the first move of humans out of Africa. But within the considerable diversity of these ancient humans, the long-lived lineage of *Homo erectus*, who subsequently moved into Europe and Asia from Africa, there is an enormous variation in brain size between 650 and 1250ml. However, many of these measures, especially the older ones, are not yet well founded because they are based on very small samples and skulls reconstructed from incomplete and/or distorted bony fragments.

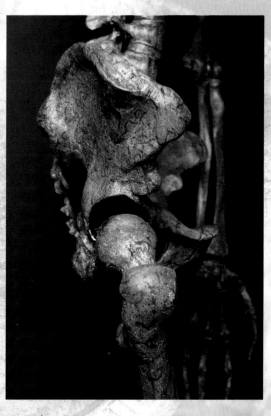

Also, such crude measures of brain capacity have been notoriously abused in the past. Brain size is only meaningful when related to body mass – which is why male and female Neanderthals, with their different body sizes, also had different brain sizes (averaging 1500ml and 1300ml respectively). Similar differences are found between the sexes of most primates today, including modern humans. The sexist slander that women are less intelligent because they have slightly smaller brains has long been buried.

Because it is necessary to relate brain capacity to body size to obtain meaningful measures, the problem of the fragmentary and incomplete nature of the fossil record becomes increasingly worrisome. By comparing the body mass of various living primates with the sizes of their bones that are most commonly fossilized, various formulae have been derived. For instance, the width of the hemispherical head of the thigh bone (femoral head), which articulates with the pelvis, has a good correlation with body mass because the hip joint bears much of the load of the body. And since the femoral head is a fairly massive bony 'knuckle' it is more often preserved as a fossil than smaller bones or those that are often destroyed by scavengers or natural processes such as weathering and erosion.

ABOVE Since the articulation of the leg bone and hip bears much of the body's weight, the size of the ball and socket joint is related to body weight and can be used to estimate that weight from fossil material.

When calculations of body mass are compared with brain capacity, another measure is obtained: the 'encephalization quotient'. And when the ancient record is revisited, using this measure, the increase in relative brain size turns out to have been 'stepped'. The early humans, living between 1.8 million and some 600,000 years ago, did not show any significant increase in relative brain size, which was 30 per cent less than that of modern humans. But by about 120,000 years ago, in Neanderthal times, there had been a significant increase.

The Neanderthals turn out to be only slightly less 'encephalized' than the Cro-Magnons, whose relative brain size continued to increase until around 35,000 years ago. Importantly, the Neanderthals were much closer in relative brain capacity to modern humans than they were to more ancient humans. Following this evolutionary highpoint of encephalization, there has actually been a decrease to the modern global average. Some experts believe that in fact the relationship in size between brain and body has been maintained by the decrease in body size of recent humans. This downward trend has been particularly emphasized in European and other high-latitude populations and has been reversed only in recent decades. By comparison, the stature and relative brain size of tropical populations has shown much less change over the last 35,000 years.

So, if the Neanderthals had such relatively well-developed brain capacity, why did they not show greater evolutionary potential, especially when compared with the Cro-Magnons? Increasing body stature coupled with decreasing relative body mass and increased encephalization in the Cro-Magnons suggests that there was another change in selection pressure at work. The interesting question is: what benefit was there in having a relatively smaller body size and relatively larger brain? So far, the changes cannot be linked to specific technical innovations, such as improved weaponry for hunting. However, the trend towards less muscular bodies of Cro-Magnons means that they did not have to rely on sheer muscle power to the same extent as the Neanderthals. They must have been behaving in some significantly different way, which allowed them still to thrive, but without such an active lifestyle.

In the past, attention has been focused on possible reasons why the relative brain size increased initially in modern humans. Perhaps the problem might be more easily resolved by looking at the possible reasons for selecting smaller body size. One obvious explanation may be that there was a change in social behaviour and structure based on increasing group activity. Co-operative food-gathering might have put a greater premium on better communication skills. Increased activity and restructuring of the brain would have stimulated its growth and development. Larger brains are more energy-hungry. If the advantage of having a larger, more active brain outweighed the advantage of a more massive body, then there would be a selection pressure for energy supply to be diverted to the development of the brain rather than body building.

The earlier inattention of palaeontologists to the size of the Neanderthal brain may have had something to do with their focus on the very striking characteristics of the Neanderthal face.

The Neanderthal face

Confronted by a Neanderthal skull, one is particularly struck by the huge size of the face. Reconstruction of the prominent nose is based on the large nasal opening and the angle at which the bones, right at the top of the nose, project. It is thought that their noses functioned as 'air conditioners', moistening and warming the incoming cold and dry air, which could otherwise damage the lungs or cool the brain too much. An acute

sense of smell would also have been useful to these people. The Neanderthal combination of considerable nose length and width is certainly unusual.

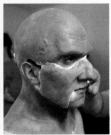

ABOVE The Neanderthal skull is sufficiently different from ours to require a substantial 'nose-job' and the addition of 'beetle-brows' to make the conversion.

While modern cold-adapted people such as the Inuit do also have long noses, they tend to be narrow. A wide nose in modern people is more of a tropical characteristic. It has even been suggested that the Neanderthal nose was a 'radiator' that could be used to help promote cooling of the blood during high levels of activity. Darwin noted that the Indians of Tierra del Fuego often bled from the nose following strenuous activity like prolonged running.

Neanderthal front teeth are basically large and prominent, but they are also often heavily worn down or faceted with particular wear patterns that are even found in children as young as seven years old. The faceting on the front teeth is at a distinct outward-facing angle to the bite surface; consequently, it cannot be a peculiar occlusion related to some unknown eating habit. Similar wear patterns are known from modern human people, such as the Inuit, whose teeth are used in the preparation of animal hides. They are also found on the front peg-like teeth of certain large long-necked plant-eating dinosaurs! Here, they are thought to have been produced by the animals using their teeth as 'rakes' to strip foliage from branches high in the canopy.

Detailed examination of the Neanderthal patterns has revealed microscopic scratch marks on worn tooth facets and tiny cut damage to the surface of the front teeth. This wear evidence suggests not only that they used their teeth as a vice to hold one end of an animal skin or plant fibre, but also that they were right-handed; the left hand was used to hold the other end of the skin. The damage to the front teeth is angled such that it was probably caused by a stone tool, such as a scraper or blade, held in the right hand. While scraping or cutting the skin, the tool accidentally hit and marked the front teeth every now and again.

Another unusual feature of Neanderthal dentistry is the large pulp cavity in some back molars, extending down into the roots, which are not so divided as in most modern humans. Interestingly, the condition can be common in some modern populations such as the Inuits. The characteristic may be an adaptation for heavy wear, since such teeth can continue to operate as effective chewing surfaces even when the crown is worn through.

The prominence of the Neanderthal mid-face pulled the jaws forward with the result that a distinct gap was opened up behind the wisdom teeth in the lower jaw. This so-called retromolar space is a useful distinguishing feature of Neanderthal jaw fragments, along with tooth structure, wear pattern and the lack of a well-developed chin, especially among the later Neanderthals. The front chin area of the lower jaw is structurally weak in many mammals. This is because the area where the two jawbones join is relatively small and yet the jaw is subject to considerable stress. So, according to one theory, the area of the join has to be reinforced and in the Neanderthals there is an extra bony strut or buttress that lies within the jaw. A similar structure is found in the higher apes and more ancient human relatives. In no way can the Neanderthal lower jaw profile be construed as signifying a 'weak character'. Cro-Magnons and modern humans have the lower jaw buttressed on the outside where it forms the chin.

Neanderthals are perhaps most distinguished by their prominent brow-ridges, but this characteristic is also found in more ancient human relatives and in the living higher apes. However, the Neanderthal bony brow-ridge was not a solid bony structure like that found in older *Homo erectus* people, nor was it well developed around the side of the forehead as in *H. erectus* and *H. heidelbergensis*. In Neanderthals, the brow-ridge is lightened internally by air spaces; it is present generally in both sexes and appears in children as young as eight. There has been much speculation about the function of the ridge. The most popular argument has been that it acted as a structural cross-member that reinforced the top of the face and allowed powerful biting and chewing forces to be transmitted over the whole front surface of the skull. It was thought the size of the ridge was a good indicator of the relative size of the jaw muscles.

Although the argument seems eminently reasonable, mechanical experimentation and analysis with monkey skulls does not support this explanation. Other speculation that, when animated with muscles and covered with eyebrow hair, the brows were used to signal emotion, especially threats, is not much more convincing. But who knows? We still use the phrase 'brow-beating' to signify intimidation.

Neanderthal skin

Questions over Neanderthal hairiness and skin colour will never be satisfactorily resolved. It was originally assumed that the people must have been very hairy, to fit in with the 'primitive' ape-like image. So far there has been no fossil evidence for their relative hairiness, since skin and hair are very difficult to fossilize – but not impossible. Fifty-million-year-old mammalian hair and soft tissue have been preserved in the Messel lake deposits near Frankfurt in Germany, and even older hair-like structures have been found recently on some Chinese dinosaurs. Perhaps in the future some Neanderthal remains will be found with preserved traces of skin and hair.

Most mammals and primates retain their body hair, either as a shield against heat and ultra-violet light from the sun's rays or as an insulating layer to help retain body heat. In the tropics hair tends to be short whereas in polar regions hair is longer and otherwise modified to increase its insulating properties. Those large mammals that have mostly lost their body hair, such as elephants, rhinos and whales, have thick tough skins with substantial layers of subcutaneous fat. The fat has replaced hair as shield or insulation.

Against this biological background, we humans are fairly exceptional in the underdevelopment of our body hair, no matter where we habitually live. Humans still retain several million body-hair follicles, like other mammals, but human hair is generally very light and short except on the head and where associated with secondary sexual characteristics – principally pubic and underarm. So the interesting question is: when did our ancient human relatives 'lose' their hair – before the Neanderthals evolved or not? The possible advantages and disadvantages of body hair can be considered in relation to sexual selection and by comparison with cold-adapted modern humans such as the Inuit, Sami, Siberians and Fuegian Indians. Interestingly, none of these people have increased development of body or facial hair – quite the reverse. But then most of them do have very sophisticated clothing to deal with extreme cold, something the Neanderthals probably did not have.

Hair is a good insulator but can cause problems. For highly active people, excessive body hair is detrimental because it does not allow the skin to lose heat easily through sweating and can lead to overheating. The most useful place for hair in a cold environment is on the head but not necessarily on the face. In very cold conditions, facial hair around the mouth and nose traps moisture and freezes. Male polar explorers like to be photographed with ice on their eyebrows, moustaches and beards because it emphasizes their toughness, but Inuit men have very little facial hair.

The Fuegian Indians of Tierra del Fuego might provide a better model for Neanderthal appearance in that they lived fairly basic lives in harsh but not extreme polar conditions. The Fuegians were observed by explorers and traded with since Magellan in 1520. The reports of these early explorers often remark on the ability of the Fuegians to withstand cold, windy and wet conditions with only the most basic clothing of a fur cape and skin 'apron'. Their body hair is very underdeveloped, even lacking secondary sexual hair, but they do have thick black and straight head hair. Fuegian body proportions also show typical cold adaptations with relatively short limb extremities, that is, their forearms and lower legs are proportionally shorter than the thighs and upper arms of other people.

There are some problems with this model in that the Fuegians are modern humans and thus quite different from the Neanderthals in many ways. It depends on whether the Fuegians' ancestors were equally 'smooth-skinned' and whether genetically they could have evolved hairier bodies as a cold adaptation or not. Nevertheless, they provide an alternative model for Neanderthal appearance, which was originally thought to have been very hirsute, like the apes.

The arguments for skin colour can also be looked at from basic physiological considerations. With the long adaptation of Neanderthals to European conditions and then even cooler climates of Ice Age northern Europe, there was plenty of time for the benefits of paler skin coloration to have been selected over the generations. Certainly, their ancient human and australopithecine ancestors from Africa would have been dark-skinned. A change in skin colour might seem dramatic and has been overladen with all manner of cultural and racial baggage by modern humans, but biologically all that happens is that the pigment-forming cells (melanocytes) in the skin are less active in pale-skinned peoples'; the number of melanocytes does not change.

ABOVE Charles Darwin remarked upon how the native Indians of Tierra del Fuego managed to live in harsh glacial environments with little clothing or body hair.

The advantage – indeed importance – of paler skin for people living in high latitudes is that sunlight can more easily penetrate the skin and better activate the synthesis of vitamin D. The downside is that without the protection of pigmentation, pale-skinned people have a greater propensity to skin cancer.

For Neanderthals, perhaps the best compromise would have been to have had some skin pigment protection and consequently a Mediterranean type of coloration; low levels of body hair but plenty of head hair. Whether they were actually like this, of course, remains a matter of speculation.

Neanderthal clothing

When it comes to trying to work out whether Neanderthals wore clothing or not, and what it was like if they did, the evidence is also indirect but even slimmer than the anatomical evidence.

ABOVE There is no direct archaeological evidence that the Neanderthals wore animal skins because such organic materials do not normally fossilise. However, indirect evidence such as tooth wear suggest that animals skins were prepared, perhaps for clothing.

As we all know, being able to put on or shed clothing at will confers enormous advantage in coping with changes in temperature on a daily basis. The adoption and use of clothing is one of the distinctions that separate modern humans from the higher apes. The question is: when did our ancient relatives first adopt the practice? As long as they lived in tropical climates there was not much benefit to be gained. But as soon as the ancients moved north into more temperate and then colder climates some thermo-regulation through the use of clothing would have been advantageous.

Certainly, the Neanderthals were among the first humans to have been confronted with seriously cooler climates, not just as a result of moving north but also because of rapid climate deterioration during the Ice Age. We know that they could manufacture and use a range of stone tools, including scrapers and basic blades, for butchering game. Cut marks on the animal bones show that these were effective tools and consequently skinning game would not have been a problem. Indeed, it was probably a normal first step in the butchering process, so animal skins would have been available.

However, processing skin to make it into a lasting and supple material, suitable even for the most basic kind of clothing, requires considerable work and knowledge. More importantly it implies conscious intent and planning. While there is no direct evidence for Neanderthals being clothed, some remarkable indirect evidence has been uncovered in recent years. As mentioned earlier, wear patterns and cut marks on Neanderthal front teeth indicate that they were using their teeth as vices to hold something so that one hand, normally their right hand, was free for another activity.

Comparison with similar tooth wear in modern human cultures provides a good model for Neanderthal processing of animal skins and other organic materials. Preservation of animal pelts requires the removal of all fatty tissue from below the skin layer. Inuit people make pelts supple by working them with their front teeth and their teeth suffer considerable wear as a result. Neanderthals may well have used this simple but effective means of preparing animal hides. Since no sewing implements have been found associated with Neanderthal remains, it is thought that any skin 'clothing' they had can only have been tied or joined in a fairly primitive way with animal sinews or plant fibres.

LEFT Fat has to be scraped away from a skin to stop it from rotting.

Our knowledge of what the Neanderthals looked like when their bones are fleshed out has grown enormously, but many aspects are still largely unknown. Inevitably there are considerable differences of opinion between the experts – but not nearly as much as when we consider the social aspects of the lives of these extinct people.

Neanderworld society

THERE IS PLENTY OF ARCHAEOLOGICAL EVIDENCE TO SHOW THAT Neanderthals lived in groups, but how were these groups organized? Social organization develops in all animals that live in communities, whether they are ants, apes or humans, and is clearly necessary for the survival of a group as a viable entity. The size and structure of a group depend on a number of factors, such as the roles of individuals within the group, their inter-relationships, and how the group as a whole relates to the outside world and other groups of similar beings. Fundamental to group survival is the ability of its members to obtain food, protect themselves from predators and reproduce.

Most primates, higher apes and their more human-like relatives, including the Neanderthals, are or were neither particularly strong, well armed or fast moving in comparison to the common game animals they lived among and hunted. A single wolf can easily outrun and probably kill an unarmed adult human, let alone a child, and a horse or large deer can easily break a human limb with a single kick. Consequently, primates have tended to form social groups of various sizes and kinds. The big question here is not so much when they formed groups but what kind of groups they formed, and how Neanderthal society differed from that of more modern humans. Was Neanderthal society essentially just a more simple and primitive form of modern human society, or did it differ in some fundamental way? Perhaps Neanderthal society had a closer resemblance to ape society?

An outstanding problem here is that primate and higher ape society is enormously variable, ranging from the solitary, monogamous families of Asian gibbons to the male-dominated harems of mountain gorillas. Consequently, it is very difficult to generalize or extract what might have been the most 'primitive' model that the earliest humans and their australopithecine relatives inherited from the past. By comparison, there are a number of organizational and behavioural patterns that tend to recur in modern human communities and can be considered to be fairly basic to the modern human condition.

These patterns include the establishment of pair bonds between male and female adults that are fairly permanent throughout life. Such basic family units tend to connect regularly with a few other families that are genetically related over significant periods of time to form clan-type groupings. Within the families, food is commonly shared between the sexes and their dependent children. When it comes to reproduction, the clan groups commonly practise exogamy, in which females move away from the immediate parental group and are 'imported' into other clans.

PREVIOUS SPREAD, INSET One of the most contentious aspects of the Neanderthals is their way of life.

OPPOSITE As hunter-gatherers in the harsh realities of their Ice Age world, the Neanderthals had to have some basic form of social organisation and cooperation in order to survive.

The clans regularly establish 'home-bases' in particular locations that provide the focus for a variety of activities such as food preparation, eating, socializing and sleeping. In addition, families tend to retain long-term relationships with blood-relatives, even over considerable distances and intervals of time. This is one of the most distinct differences between modern human and living non-human primate communities. Trying to extract common factors that relate to the division of labour and the distribution of social and economic roles between the sexes is almost impossible from the wide variation found in modern human societies. So again the question is: which pattern of social organization was Neanderthal society closer to, that of the apes or modern humans?

Evidence and interpretation

In general, the archaeological evidence from the relatively small size of cave sites, with the limited scattering of their stone tools and remains of butchered prey, can be interpreted as patterns of organization and behaviour which show that Neanderthals were hunter-gatherers who lived in small social groups. Sometimes the signs of activity are so constrained as to suggest that only one

or two individuals might have been present. Exactly how these groups were structured depends on how the evidence is interpreted. Analysis of one particular site in France, Combe Grenal, by the American expert Lewis Binford has provided a highly speculative interpretation claiming that Neanderthal society was radically different from home-based models that lie more on the human side of the ape/human divide. In Binford's view, there was a fundamental social separation between Neanderthal males and females, with foraging troops of males living apart from the females and their children for most of the time. The males visited the females only occasionally, maybe for a few days a month and then for the specific purpose of mating. Other experts, such as Paul Pettitt of Oxford University, disagree with Binford's interpretation of Combe Grenal but have not had a chance to examine his detailed evidence (see the box on page 86).

In contrast to Binford's model, the home-base interpretation is founded on archaeological signs of repeated patterns that have been well documented by recent socio-ecological studies of primate organization. There are two main factors particularly relevant to the social organization of Neanderthal society: an increasing reliance on animal food and the increasing delay in child maturation.

Although there are physical differences between Neanderthal men and women, the women were also powerfully built. The bones of Neanderthal women show just as much damage as those of males, suggesting that at times they were also active hunters of wild game. There are interesting questions of whether they hunted with the males or separately or whether they only hunted game of a certain size. They certainly would have had difficulty taking part in particularly active or risky hunts if they were heavily pregnant or engaged in child rearing. They could however gather food such as plants, small and easily caught animals such as tortoises, snakes or shellfish by the coast, and perhaps have hunted small mammals and birds. Their children seem to have developed somewhat faster and perhaps matured earlier than modern children. This may have allowed them to fend better for themselves at an earlier age than children can today. However, compared with all earlier primates and ancient human relatives, the Neanderthals had large brains and heads, similar to those of modern humans. And, as in modern humans, such large heads develop in the foetus. They create considerable problems for the birth process and large-headed offspring inflict a heavy cost in terms of nutritional and care investment by the mother. Consequently, the mothers would have been much less mobile and less able to engage in far-reaching searches for food while engaged in bringing up their young. The most 'cost-effective' resolution would be for small groups of females and children to be directly supplied with food by males.

ABOVE To maintain their food supply the Neanderthals needed all able-bodied members of the group to participate in the hunt. The women and older children would certainly have caught small game like wild boar and rabbits.

Thus the underlying biological demands of the evolving child development pattern would have reinforced social patterns of increasing group integration and mutually co-operative food sharing, to ensure the survival of dependent children. These arguments have been extended to consider increasing male involvement in the group so as to ensure their safety from animal predators and perhaps other human groups. Thus the males would have been further drawn into parental investment and the establishment of more lasting pair bonds. These models envisage convergence of evolutionary biological, ecological and social pressures towards the formation of nuclear family groups. Such close-knit groups would have shared food that was prepared at selected home-base sites, where child rearing also took place.

As relatively long-lived and intelligent beings, living in small groups, the Neanderthals may have formed reasonably well-developed understanding of one another and have been able to predict the actions and responses of other members of the group. Blood ties among siblings would have reinforced such ties but may have been tempered with competition and rivalry. Nevertheless, for survival, the dominant members of the group would have had to ensure that they 'pulled together'.

Increasing reliance on large-animal food was partly a consequence of environmental change and partly the increasing demands of larger groups of dependants. Within the changing climates and environments of Ice Age Europe,

ABOVE In times of need the Neanderthals resorted to scavenging other predators, kills – even a few bones could still yield some nutritious bone-marrow.

the only locations that could provide an abundant supply of smaller-animal food were areas such as rocky coasts where shellfish and the eggs of seabirds were easily obtainable. To regularly supply family groups of several adults and dependent children with a subsistence level of food would have required deliberate hunting of medium- to large-sized game, or prolonged searching for the remains of large animals killed by other predators. In turn, such hunting would have required the co-operation of males to locate the game, pursue and then kill selected beasts.

Such scenarios all require considerable co-operation and integration of males and females in localized groups, which is at variance with the much more gender-exclusive Binford model.

Evidence from France

The archaeological evidence to support the idea of small groups of Neanderthals using regular home-bases as sites of habitation and centres of social organization comes particularly from south-western France. The many sites in this region were far removed from any direct glacial disturbance and some provide good records of occupation between 110,000 and 45,000 years ago.

Archaeologists have looked for evidence of changes in occupation patterns throughout this lengthy period. Overall, there is little change in the spatial selection of sites for occupation apart from a late shift in location of some sites, which may have been related to climate deterioration and the exploitation of migratory reindeer.

The artefact evidence from the French sites indicates a considerable diversity of activity. A range of tool types was produced on site, using unworked flint imported from elsewhere. Also, a considerable variety of game was being hunted and processed, with skinning, butchering and the extraction of bone-marrow and brains all taking place within any one site. In addition, several of the sites contain multiple human burials. As far as can be seen, there was no significant or readily measurable difference in the diversity and intensity of activities undertaken at these sites throughout the whole period.

Nevertheless, trying to assess the length of time that any one group occupied a site is incredibly difficult, if not impossible. For there to be any record at all, there needed to have been continued import of materials to the site, the debris being discarded on-site and then to accumulate as a new floor level on top of pre-existing levels. Remarkably, this does often seem to have occurred, but still there is the problem of measuring the duration of occupation. There are a few instances of site improvement, where occupants appear to have levelled the dwelling surface, laid cobble 'pavements', constructed hearths, disposed of refuse and possibly erected some type of shelter.

According to Paul Pettitt, all this evidence emphasizes the simply organized and structured activity of the Neanderthals, associated with repeated episodes of quite intensive occupation, and supports the 'home-base' idea rather than the more basic Binford model. There does not seem to be any clearly defined change in these patterns throughout the 110,000- to 45,000-year interval, apart from a generally simpler organization and shorter-term occupation by smaller groups in the earlier period.

The restricted size of the groups can be seen as a strategy for survival in a harsh environment that put less stress on the natural resources. Larger groups or an increase in the number of groups within a territory could lead to overhunting and famine. However, just as the game fluctuated in numbers so might the predators, including the Neanderthals – but on a longer timescale because of the relative slowness of their reproduction compared with the greater fecundity of game animals such as horse and deer. We do not know if the Neanderthals also suffered from periods of 'boom and bust' – feast and famine – but it is quite likely, considering the often rapidly fluctuating climatic conditions and environments of the Ice Age.

Certainly by 40,000 years ago and the onset of Upper Palaeolithic times, there is evidence of larger and more structured groups occupying sites for longer periods of time. These Upper Palaeolithic levels are associated with the appearance of personal ornaments as artefacts. These are thought to reflect the advent of more clearly defined social roles, complex language and symbolic expression, typical of modern humans.

The Binford interpretation of Combe Grenal

Combe Grenal is a very important French rock shelter that preserves a record of use over a period of some 75,000 years, from 115,000 to 40,000 years ago. The distribution of the artefacts at each level through time was plotted by the excavators, and has provided the basis for interpretation of changing occupation patterns and environments. These changes range from the last interglacial into the last glacial and cover about 70 per cent of Neandertime.

According to an analysis by the American expert Lewis Binford, the spatial distribution of hearths, stone tools and animal remains carries significant sociological implications. He sees a well-defined central hearth area with scattered ashes and abundant animal bone debris (mainly horse and bovid) showing evidence of burning, splintering and fragmentation

along with denticulated stone tools and flaking debris. Binford sees this as the central nest of the site where there was intensive processing of selected parts of animal carcasses. Long bones were splintered for marrow extraction and skulls fragmented for access to tongues and brains. Then there is a more peripheral zone of more marginal activity associated with some more concentrated hearths and different tools such as scrapers and points, which were used for primary or preliminary butchery of carcasses.

The bone remains in this outer area are mainly the detached knuckle ends of long bones and sometimes broken jawbones.

Binford also detects a difference between the raw stone materials found in the nest and those of the more peripheral areas of the site. The raw material of the nest area is more locally derived (from within a kilometre or two) and of poorer quality than that of the periphery which may have been more carefully selected and transported over greater distances (up to several kilometres). Binford interprets all this as indicating a sexual division of labour where females operated in the core nest, extracting high-protein marrow, tongues and brains from selected bits of carcasses. The periphery was more specifically an area of heavy-duty butchery of carcasses by males.

The nest female group consisted of between five and ten closely integrated adults and their children. Binford claims that they were only occasionally visited by the foraging males, who effectively exchanged the game they had killed for sex.

Paul Pettitt has also examined the Combe Grenal site and disagrees fundamentally with Binford's interpretation. According to Pettitt, the only spatial separation to be found in sites like this is a basic division into two kinds of areas: firstly, where butchering of carcasses took place and rubbish (mainly bone debris) was dumped; and secondly, living spaces where there were hearths and fires, which doubled as sleeping quarters. But neither of these spaces was permanently fixed in any way – it was all pretty simple habit-based activity that could change its location almost on a day-to-day basis.

Social hierarchy

All human and primate societies have some sort of 'pecking order' or social hierarchy, generally based on dominant males, especially where there is strong sexual dimorphism. The physical differences between Neanderthal males and females were slightly greater than those found in modern humans and consequently it is likely that their groups were more male-dominated.

Each Neanderthal group is also likely to have been self-contained, with closely related males dominating the group dynamics. The problem with such social dynamics is that they are largely based on physical strength and aggression. Underlying tensions of competition from other potential dominant males would have been held in check by the 'alpha' male as long as possible. The dominant position is primarily acquired by virtue of size, strength, intelligence and experience. The sheer physicality of the Neanderthals suggests that sexual selection and subsequent breeding tended to emphasize these patterns of dominance.

In such societies, actions may well have spoken louder than words. Even so, the greatly heightened consciousness of Neanderthals over more primitive primates, such as chimps, suggests that they may have had the human ability to observe developing behaviour in others, predict and then pre-empt future threatening action. Even chimps have been observed to have some basic predictive ability.

BELOW Detailed analysis of associated stone tools and animal bones from Neanderthal sites can tell a great deal about how these people lived.

Then there is the question of how different Neanderthal groups interacted. Their 'home-base' sites are geographically separate one from another and they appear to have used only fairly local raw material sources for making tools. Analysis of rock sources for tools found at individual Neanderthal sites suggests that their territories were not very extensive, probably less than 70 square kilometres (27 square miles).

The vast majority of the rock sources for the flints found at Neanderthal sites in south-western France lie within 4 kilometres (2.5 miles) of the home-base. These sources could therefore have been used on a daily basis, if need be, with only a few hours' travel. Indeed, quite a number of home-base sites are situated right next to good rock sources. However, some sites contain a surprising variety of stone tools from as many as a dozen different sources.

Intriguingly, several sites, especially those in south-western France, contain some stone tools (rarely more than 5 per cent) that have been sourced from much further away, up to 30 kilometres (18 miles) and occasionally (1–2 per cent) as much as 100 kilometres (60-odd miles). And these rare materials are often sourced from several different and equally distant rock outcrops. Most of these rarer materials have particular qualities that more locally derived material does not. The fact that Neanderthal groups recognized that a few sources provided superior material and somehow were able to obtain it, is in itself interesting. Obtaining rock material from so far away suggests deliberate selection, but, according to Paul Pettitt, does not necessarily mean that organization and planning were involved.

How these more distant sites were actually accessed is a problem and raises questions about the relationships between Neanderthal groups. Was the rock material obtained through trade with neighbouring groups, through rare longer journeys by small bands or by seasonal visits as part of longer-range annual movement by the whole group? And, if so, were such sources used by several different groups at different times or the same time? Were the Neanderthal groups involved in much more complex patterns of interaction and exchange of raw materials than previously thought? Experts such as Paul Pettitt think that there were only very limited relationships between Neanderthal groups. Access to the more distant sites was simply achieved by the normal mobility of the groups. They agree that there had to be some exchange, but it would have been limited to social interactions such as the swapping of unattached members of the groups in marriage. Such exchanges would have been essential for the continued reproductive viability of otherwise isolated small bands.

All these sociological interpretations, based on the distribution of stone materials, are as yet highly speculative.

Neanderthal food

A primary necessity for the survival of all animals is food. We all need to secure at least an adequate food supply and preferably one that takes into account any fluctuations in the source of that food. The food supply, whether animal or plant, and its availability determines the number of individuals or groups that can be supported within any given area.

From the biological point of view, the modern human gut has quite a slow transit time (twenty-four to thirty hours) for the throughput of food, probably inherited from our plant-eating ancestors. By comparison, meat-eating non-human animals typically process their food within seven to twenty-six hours. Our human digestive system, like that of the earlier primates, is basically adapted to slowly digesting plant food. We have also inherited another mammalian herbivore trait, an inability to make vitamin C, which is in plentiful supply in the plant food.

But our digestive systems also show signs of being modified by a long history of meat eating. Like many carnivores, we produce low levels of certain enzymes and completely lack those that make the amino acid taurine, which is plentiful in meat. By comparison, plant eaters have high levels of these enzymes, especially those that convert beta carotene in vitamin A and change certain fatty acids from plants into the fatty acids that animals need.

Even the physical structure of our gut has been modified since our ancestors moved away from plant-based diets. Humans in good physical shape do not have 'pot bellies' typical of so many habitual plant eaters such as the chimps and gorillas. We have a shorter colon and longer small intestine, more like that of a carnivore. So, from the evolutionary point of view, the expectations are that early humans would have had mixed diets of plant and animal food. But the archaeological evidence for Neanderthal diet suggests that it was much more meat-based than might otherwise be expected. This dietary interpretation is reinforced by recent isotope analysis of Neanderthal bones, which closely compare with those of wolves – known to be predominantly meat eaters. The reason for Neanderthal reliance on meat was the relative abundance of game and relative scarcity of easily digestible plant food in northern Europe during the latter part of the Ice Age, and especially during winter.

When the food source is itself 'animated' and mobile, its pattern of movement also influences the predators. They have to be mobile too and capable of some degree of planning to execute effective kills; otherwise they would be dependent on the more risky strategy of scavenging the kills of other predators. Where the prey animals are medium- to large-sized game, then co-operation by the predators also helps increase the success of the hunt.

BELOW Plant foods would have been used to supplement the staple diet of game meat. Knowledge about them, and gathering the plants, may have been a female role.

Assessing the evidence

One of the great problems encountered in trying to understand prehistoric subsistence patterns is the difficulty in assessing the role of plants in ancient diets. Little or no fossil record is left of the extent to which wild plants have figured as food sources. By comparison, many animal residues, mostly bones and teeth, are resilient and can be recruited relatively easily to the sediment record at settlement sites and then persist indefinitely as fossils. But there are also considerable problems with the interpretation of these prey food remains.

The bones of small animals are often selectively removed during the natural processes of recruitment into sediment and subsequent fossilization. Other bones may be introduced to settlement sites by animal predators, such as wolves, hyenas and lions that habitually used caves and rock shelters as dens. Fortunately, many of these animal predators and scavengers leave characteristic chew marks on the bones that they have introduced. When stone tools are used to dismember and butcher carcasses by humans, they tend to leave distinctive cut marks and fractures on the bones. Careful assessment by taphonomists (scientists who study burial processes) is needed to distinguish between animal and human feeding activity.

ABOVE Cooking meat releases more of its food value, makes it quicker to digest and kills any harmful parasites or microbes.

A major difficulty is encountered in trying to unravel the history of food use at any one site. The food debris may accumulate over considerable periods of time and consequently the record of multiple occupancy may all be compressed into a single layer. Even so, careful mapping of individual occupation levels at a number of sites has revealed particular distributions of animal remains, stone tools and hearths.

A significant number of bones found at Neanderthal sites are charred, suggesting that at least some of the meat was cooked. However, there are also plenty of unburnt bones and it is highly likely that much of the meat was eaten raw. The advantage of cooking meat is that it aids digestion and so is nutritionally less wasteful. The large protein and starch molecules in the flesh are broken down by heat, allowing them to be more rapidly absorbed by the body. Cooking meat also makes it safer to eat by killing dangerous parasites and microbes that could otherwise have been transferred live into the Neanderthal body.

When meat is eaten raw, much of the nutritional value passes through the body unused and is wasted. Therefore more meat needs to be consumed to provide basic energy requirements and more time has to be spent obtaining it. In addition, protein provides only a limited amount of energy, about the same per unit weight as carbohydrate and only about half as much as fat. Nevertheless, all the indications are that the Neanderthals did consume raw meat and would therefore have had to spend more time hunting than necessary, had they had more sophisticated food preparation techniques. They boosted their energy intake by eating fat obtained from brains and, especially, bone marrow.

During freezing winter conditions, fire may also have been used for 'defrosting' frozen animal cadavers, which other predators could not touch. Many of the frozen Ice Age cadavers, such as the mammoths recovered from the Siberian permafrost, show partial consumption by animal scavengers. However, it is also clear that even wolves, with their powerful jaws, could not make much of an impression on solidly frozen cadavers. But Neanderthals armed with stone tools could have recovered some body parts and defrosted them for their own consumption.

As shown by energy studies of game-hunting communities, hunting is actually a fairly inefficient way of obtaining food. A lot of time and energy has to be expended on hunting game, recovering the carcass and preparing it for consumption. However, compared with today, game was very abundant during the Ice Age and consequently Neanderthal hunting may well have been more efficient. Studies of living hunter-gatherers show that the role of plant foods in their diets has been greatly underestimated; this may apply to the distant past as well.

Human body chemistry requires certain nutrients that cannot be obtained from a meat diet alone. Over a lifetime, the human digestive system needs an appropriate intake of plant proteins and plant-derived nitrogen. It is highly likely that the Neanderthals did supplement their meat diets with plant food such as fungi, roots, nuts and fruits, especially berries which are rich in ascorbic acid. If there was any division of labour within Neanderthal groups, then it is probable that the women played a significant role as gatherers of a variety of plant foods.

ABOVE Many Neanderthal sites preserve the broken shards of animal long bones which have been cracked open for their nutritious marrow.

The problems and benefits of high-protein diets

There is epidemiological evidence that eating too much meat is bad for modern humans. By comparison, vegetarians are healthier and much less likely to die of coronary heart disease and heart attacks. The main reason for this is the relative fattiness of farmed meat and the use of fats in its cooking. However, the picture is more complicated and it is difficult to make direct comparisons with the past.

By itself, a diet of lean game meat does not provide enough energy for an active predator with a human digestive system. The extra energy requirements have to be derived from other sources such as fat from bone marrow and brains. While lean meat is rich in iron, a necessary trace element in the human diet, too much iron can cause severe liver damage (cirrhosis). Modern hunting communities such as the Inuit, who traditionally lived off large quantities of meat that was often raw, have suffered in this way in the past.

Historically, by early middle age many Inuit suffered from enlarged livers and cirrhosis. Consequently, their life expectancy was about fifty years, largely as a result of their diet and the rigours of their way of life. Severe tooth wear from chewing raw blubber and processing animal skins also meant that by middle age many of them could barely chew food at all.

Consumption of high meat protein diets can also lead to certain vitamin deficiencies or excesses. Plants are necessary to provide thiamin and ascorbic acid. Lack of thiamin results in beriberi, a neural and cardiovascular condition that leads to loss of ankle movement and peripheral paralysis. Ascorbic acid (vitamin C) is required to counteract scurvy, which results in poor wound healing, swollen joints and subcutaneous bleeding. An excess of vitamin A from eating too much liver can lead to 'fluid on the brain' and be fatal. Again the condition has been found in the Inuit. All these symptoms would have been seriously incapacitating if not fatal for a Neanderthal.

Eating people

One of the most emotive and debatable topics concerning Neanderthal behaviour is cannibalism. The practice has been attributed to them for over a hundred years but never really confirmed until recently. It has been argued that with dwindling numbers and an increasing scarcity of food, some Neanderthal groups may have turned to cannibalism as a feeding strategy.

The evidence comes from sites in Croatia (Krapina and Vindija) and French caves (L'Hortus and Moula-Gercy). The largest selection of skeletal evidence came from Krapina, which was excavated by the Croatian palaeontologist Dragutin Gorjanović-Kramberger at the beginning of the twentieth century. He had found evidence of burning of some human bones and attributed this to cannibalism. More recently, this interpretation has been criticized. Cut marks found on the Krapina bones have been variously interpreted as resulting from the kind of defleshing of a cadaver which the Neanderthals normally employed when butchering a kill for food. But other experts regard it as evidence of 'postmortem processing of corpses with stone tools, probably in preparation for burial of cleaned bones'. There does not seem to be any evidence of the Krapina bones being processed for marrow extraction.

The most detailed and sophisticated analysis comes from recent work on the Moula-Gercy cave in south-eastern France by a Franco-American team of scientists (see the box on page 95). Seventy-eight pieces of bone, belonging to at least six humans, have been found scattered among some 400 fragments of other animals. The debris covered over 20 square metres (215 square feet) of a 100,000-year-old Mousterian cave-floor deposit buried beneath younger layers of sediment.

Three pieces of a large human thigh bone each had marks showing that the muscles had been cut away. In addition, impact marks on the fragments showed that the defleshed bone had then been set on a stone anvil and smashed open with a stone tool to reveal the nutritious marrow. Cut marks on a clavicle revealed how an arm had been disarticulated and cut away at the shoulder. There are clear cut marks across the bones of the feet, elbows and ankles, which indicate that the tough Achilles tendons have been slashed to release the muscles from the bone.

There is evidence that long flat chewing muscles have been cut and stripped from skulls and the lower jaw removed. Braincases of both deer and humans have been cracked open, presumably for the removal of the brains. Other marks on the jaw of an adolescent show where the tongue had been cut out. Since there are few signs of burning, it would seem that if this meat was being consumed, it was eaten raw.

This is fairly clear evidence of butchery of the carcasses. The only debatable point regards the purpose, and some experts argue that removal of the flesh in this way does not necessarily mean that the meat was being eaten. The cadavers could have been defleshed for ritual purposes. Or, if there was cannibalism, it too could have been ritualistic.

Certainly, there are various aspects of the Moula-Gercy material which point to cannibalism. There is very little evidence of interference with the remains from scavengers such as hyena chew marks. And, most importantly, the human remains have been dumped among the bones of other butchered animals. There is no sign that the human material was treated differently from the other prey animals. This is pretty convincing circumstantial evidence for cannibalistic butchering of Neanderthals by Neanderthals, and strengthens other older and less secure evidence from Krapina and Vindija in Croatia.

Our modern revulsion with cannibalism is largely a cultural taboo. Nevertheless, despite our deep-seated western revulsion, there are well-documented historical instances of cannibalism in modern human societies from the Aztecs of Mesoamerica to the Fore of eastern New Guinea. For the Aztecs, cannibalism may have been primarily ritualistic but could also have been for nutritional reasons – their largely maize-based diet lacked meat-based protein. In more recent times even western accultured people have been pushed into cannibalism at moments of crisis, such as shipwreck. Famously, in 1820, the surviving crew of an American whaler, the *Essex*, which had been sunk by a sperm whale, resorted to cannibalism to survive at sea until they were finally picked up. And more recently there was the well-reported case of a plane crash in the Andes, the survivors of which resorted to eating their dead fellows to stay alive. If we can do it *in extremis*, then Neanderthals living on the cusp of survival may have done so as well.

Interestingly, a lethal side-effect of cannibalism – especially where it includes the eating of brains – is a disease known as kuru. It was quite prevalent in the Fore people until their practice of cannibalism ceased. Also known as the trembling disease, it is a progressive degeneration of nerve cells in the central nervous system and particularly affects that part of the brain controlling movement. Kuru mainly attacks women and children and can prove fatal within a year of onset. It has been linked to a virus but there are also suggestions that it is linked to Creutzfeldt-Jakob's disease (CJD), which is now known to be caused by a prion, an abnormal kind of protein.

It seems that eating human brains on a regular basis is not such a good idea – there are very good biological and health reasons for not doing so. Whether the Neanderthals suffered from any ill-effects as a result of their cannibalism is not yet known.

Social grooming

Interpersonal grooming may well have been the 'glue' that held Neanderthal society together, especially if they had only limited language ability. Furthermore, according to Paul Pettitt, the body was very important for Neanderthals; he considers that they used body language as an important element of communication and expression of feelings. There is no direct evidence for this, but most primates are very body-orientated and use grooming to establish and

Cannibal cave

The Moula-Guercy cave site in Ardèche is on a hillside about 100 metres (320 feet) above the west bank of the Rhone River; it preserves a rare glimpse of the transition from the Middle to Upper Pleistocene around 130,000 years ago. The excavation was opened in 1991 and has since revealed the remains of twelve humans, some of which are thought to have been butchered for cannibalistic practices.

The thick succession of cave-floor deposits begins with the lowest level, laid down during a cold phase at the end of the Middle Pleistocene. Above this the sediments record the temporary occupation of the cave by Neanderthals during Mousterian (Middle Palaeolithic) times, dated at somewhere between 120–100,000 years ago. Climates had improved considerably and the region was covered with temperate forest at the time. The record continues through to some 72,000 years ago and is dated by some volcanic ash.

The Middle Palaeolithic level contains Mousterian stone tools, such as scrapers and debris from Levallois-prepared core stone working. There is evidence of three hearths, a stone wall, seventy-eight human and 392 identified animal bone fragments, with many more that have not been identified. All were scattered over some 10 square metres (100-odd square feet) and represent a scene of considerable human activity. Analysis of the remains shows that at least six humans and five red deer had been butchered along with ibex.

The human remains are all Neanderthal and include at least one large and one smaller adult, two 'teenagers' (fifteen to sixteen years old) and two younger children (six to seven years old). The bigger Neanderthal is one of the largest known. Cut marks on the bones are typical of defleshing and dismemberment associated with butchery for consumption. Some of the human bone fragments which can be joined together to form single bones were scattered over 9 square metres (about 100 square feet) of cave floor. All human and animal fragments were mixed together. Some polish on the bones suggests that the floor level was occupied for some time after the butchery.

The archaeologists who have excavated the site and studied the remains conclude that they definitely represent cannibalism, but cannot say whether it was motivated by the stress of diminishing resources or other social factors.

maintain social relations, as do some modern humans. Interpersonal bonds are cemented on the basis of 'You scratch my back and I'll scratch yours'. It not only works as a demonstration of loyalty and interest but also gives pleasure. In addition, grooming has a practical purpose in helping to maintain hygiene, and as a strategy for securing favours such as sex and food.

Studies of chimps show that a considerable amount of time is spent grooming one another, and grooming may be actively solicited. It has an important function within the social pecking order, maintaining networks of social exchange. Apparently, such intimate and reassuring touch during grooming stimulates the production of natural opiates in the brain, leading to a sense of well-being and relaxation. Many primates use grooming activity to lower tension, not just in individuals but in the group as a whole.

Extensive and common grooming is mainly developed where there is copious body hair in which lice and ticks can hide. The parasites are normally eaten by the one doing the grooming, along with any salt crystals that have been deposited on the hair from sweat glands. The latter has an important conservation function, where salt is otherwise unobtainable. If Neanderthals lacked extensive body hair, grooming would have been restricted to head, armpit or pubic hair. Depending on the effectiveness of their hunting and small group size, Neanderthals, like other primates, may have spent 20–30 per cent of their time grooming one another. The body was probably crucial in Neanderthal society, and much of their social discourse may have communicated through gesture. As Paul Pettitt says, 'It is undeniable that Neanderthals were creative social actors but it was the mime of their bodies accompanied by a simple dialogue, in a theatre low on props and devoid of scenery, which created and constrained their social systems.' Out of this comes the question: how do we know they possessed true spoken language?

ABOVE 'Scratch my back and I'll scratch yours'. Mutual grooming helped social bonding within Neanderthal groups as well as maintaining personal hygiene through the removal of common ticks and lice.

Language

A crude definition of the human condition portrays us as 'chattering apes', since many monkeys and higher apes possess rudimentary forms of language, even though their vocal equipment is not nearly as sophisticated for modulated sound production as ours. Furthermore, language in its widest sense includes a large range of body movement, especially facial and limb gesture, sound, sign and symbol. Fundamentally, language is communication and this can be transmitted in many different ways, although humans put a premium on vocalization. Nevertheless, much human communication is still non-verbal. There is little doubt that even the most ancient of human groups was capable of some basic form of verbal language. The possession and evolution of language is perhaps the most important 'tool' that has allowed humans to dominate so much of the Earth.

The question here is what evolutionary 'station' the Neanderthals had reached on the route between ape-like vocalization and that of modern humans. But this begs the question of how language evolved: was it a fairly gradual, step-by-step process with gradual increases in complexity and structure or were there some abrupt 'steps' linked to some significant and relatively sudden evolutionary biological novelties?

These 'steps' might have been related to some genetic change or 'rewiring' of the brain – neurological reorganization. Was there some critical threshold between primitive and more advanced syntactical language and, if so, which side of the divide did the Neanderthals lie? And anyway, how is it possible to recover any information about the language of the Neanderthals?

One line of evidence has been through study of language development in young children, based on the notion that such human ontology might reflect ancient developmental stages. The so-called protolanguage of very young children has virtually no grammar or syntax and tends to be comprised of strings of words that generally refer to the 'here and now' only.

LEFT Human hunters like the Neanderthals depended on communication by speech and gesture for cooperative hunting. Just how sophisticated their speech was is not known.

There is a significant and qualitative gulf between this and adult language in modern humans. Adult language is highly structured and can cope with the past, future, speculation, thought, cause and so on. Consequently, there is a considerable difference between the two language states in modern humans and some experts argue that the jump from one to the other may well reflect a similarly 'punctuated' evolution in human language skill and use. And some experts think that the Neanderthals were definitely in the early-child stage of language development, and this explains some of the radical transformations in behavioural patterns observed between the Middle and Upper Palaeolithic.

The evidence for Neanderthal language

Some Neanderthal skulls have been sufficiently well preserved to allow casts to be made of the inside surface of the brain case. These brain endocasts preserve enough detail to show features of the brain's topography, including the size and sites of some of the major blood vessels.

The patterns of folds on the surface of the modern human brain have now been extensively mapped over several hundred years. More recently it has been possible to match some of the features of this brain map to particular human attributes, such as language. Two specific areas of the brain map are related to language: Wernicke's and Broca's areas. The first is specialized for language comprehension and the latter deals with speech articulation.

Language ability initially develops in both brain hemispheres but generally shifts to the left hemisphere by the time a child is five years old, when the abandoned area in the right hemisphere is given over to other mental activities such as those that govern gesture. Recent brain scanning techniques have shown that other areas are involved as well. Different parts of the brain respond when someone is shown a word, asked how many syllables it contains and asked to consider what it means. Broca's and Wernicke's areas have been tentatively identified on Neanderthal brain endocasts.

Anatomical study of the basal region of the Neanderthal brain case and jawbone has suggested to some experts that Neanderthals did not possess a fully developed vocal tract. In Neanderthals the skull base is flat and the voice box or larynx may have been positioned high up in the throat, similar to the condition seen in modern human babies. The arrangement of the vocal tract in babies constrains the movement of the tongue and consequently the range of sound that they can produce. Similar limitations probably restricted the vocal range and language of the Neanderthals.

As modern babies grow, the larynx gradually descends to its adult position and allows the full development of the voice, but in the Neanderthals the juvenile-like position was permanently fixed. Consequently, they were perhaps physically incapable of producing the full range of vowel sounds or rapid changes of sound that characterize modern human speech patterns. Their large noses may even have given their vocalizations a distinctly nasal sound.

However, another critical feature associated with language is the small hyoid bone, which lies in the throat and is linked to the structure of the vocal tract. In the early 1980s, a single hyoid bone from a Neanderthal was found at the Kebara site in Israel. And its form is practically identical to that of a modern human.

The archaeological evidence

One of the defining hallmarks of fully developed language is its link to elaborate symbolic expression. The lack of hard evidence for such expression by Neanderthals is perhaps one of the most telling arguments against their possession of advanced language. Few convincing decorative or artistic artefacts have been found associated with Neanderthal remains. Nor is there any really convincing evidence for ceremonial burial by Neanderthals. And then their stone tools generally show much less diversity in form than those of the Cro-Magnons.

The British archaeologist Paul Mellars has argued that the Neanderthals lacked what he calls well-defined 'mental templates' for the construction of

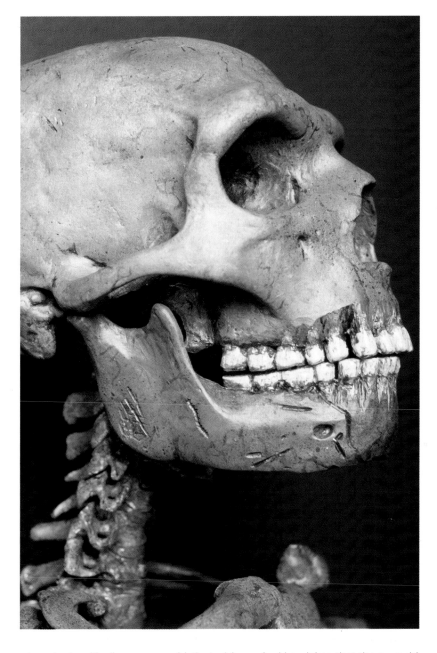

stone tools with diverse or sophisticated form. And he claims that there would have been links between such limited tool- and language-making capabilities. Mellars suggests that there was a marked increase in the number of categories of tools produced by Cro-Magnons in the Upper Palaeolithic and that this may mark an important transition in language as well.

There is similar evidence for significant change in patterns of social planning and organization of activities over this same period. There was a marked change in the way raw materials were procured, food was stored and the movement of game predicted, and it all involved more complex logistics and probably a sense of time. As such, these more advanced and organized activities would seem to predicate the use of more structured and grammatical language by the Cro-Magnons, whereas the evidence from Neanderthal archaeology points to a much more basic language ability.

ABOVE Blood brothers – perhaps blood ties amongst Neanderthal males helped foster cooperative hunting.

Other advantages of developed language include the ability to share information with others, both individually and between groups. This would lead to increased social cohesion, an improved capability for storing information in the long term and ability to deal with the unpredictable. The latter facility would have been especially advantageous in the face of sudden climate deterioration. The evidence is that the Neanderthals were not able to make such changes, whereas the Cro-Magnons did, and they were the ones who survived.

Nevertheless, the Neanderthals must have had a substantially more effective communication than chimps or earlier human relatives, but apparently had not crossed the linguistic watershed into a more advanced form of language. Some experts, such as Paul Pettitt, think that Neanderthal language would have been very limited in vocabulary (maybe with as few as forty words) and grammar, without tenses to describe or remember the past or speculate about the future. Pettitt thinks that they could have interpreted what was in front of them – for instance, changes in the colour of leaves and other natural signs of autumn would have been known to foreshadow the coming cold – but whether they could further link this to a predicted change in the behaviour of the animals is more doubtful. Neanderthals lived much more in the present and dealt with time and life step by step. As Pettitt puts it, 'For the Neanderthals, every day was like the first day of their lives.'

As the sole human occupants of Europe for so much time and operating in small independent bands within fairly constrained territories, they did not have much need for a complex language to engage with the world at large. The basic language of the Neanderthals may have been linked to differences in the organization of their brains compared with modern humans, but we do not know.

However, the Neanderthal world was suddenly turned upside-down with the arrival of the Cro-Magnons. There is compelling evidence from Upper Palaeolithic artefacts that the incomers did have complex language. Whether either side ever got to communicate with each other in words, we shall never know, but making contact would have been a much greater problem for the Neanderthals. In his novel *The Inheritors*, the novelist William Golding was probably not far off the mark in his portrayal of the limitations of Neanderthal communication skills and their bruising encounter with the Cro-Magnons. Golding's Neanderthals have few words and are often uncomprehending of what is going on around them. They can imagine scenes but not always put them into words.

As Golding also realized, his portrayal of the Neanderthals and Cro-Magnons could not be complete without imagining what sex and death meant to these peoples. The scientific investigation of such past behaviour and social practice is fraught with difficulty. As we shall see, just as Golding based his interpretation on his understanding of modern sexual instincts and basic attitudes towards the death of a close relative, so does the sociologist of the past.

Cave to grave: birth and death in Neanderworld

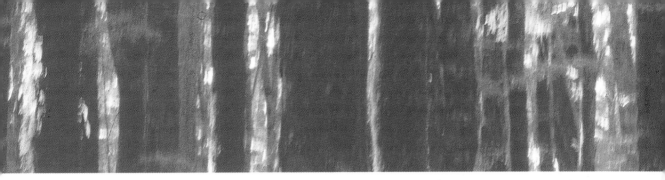

T HE INITIAL SUCCESS OF THE NEANDERTHALS IN SPREADING throughout such a vast terrain of Europe and the Middle East suggests that they had no problem reproducing themselves. But our understanding of their sexual practices and relationships is almost entirely speculative, although some educated guesses can be made. Sex in primate societies is used not just for reproduction but also for pleasure, for the maintenance of relationships and as an expression of dominance.

Modern humans and the bonobo chimps are unusual, even among the primates, in being sexually active all year round with females capable of becoming pregnant at any time of the year. The interesting question is whether, in terms of sexual behaviour and reproduction, the Neanderthals lay on the ape or modern human side.

Back to basics

All primates are slow in maturing and tend to live a long time. After a lengthy gestation (six to nine months), most primates produce one large-sized, large-brained (roughly half the volume of the mother's brain) and dependent offspring per pregnancy. Infants are breastfed for considerable periods of time (up to four years in chimps, gorillas and even some humans) during which time the female's reproductive cycle is suppressed to a variable extent.

The costs of breastfeeding in terms of energy and nutrition are very high, adding between 20 and 50 per cent to demands made by everyday life on the mother's system. If she breastfeeds her infant frequently, she generally does not become pregnant again until the infant has been weaned (although, as many modern humans have found, breastfeeding is not a guaranteed contraceptive). Because children mature slowly, reproduction does not start until quite late in life compared with many other mammals, and there are relatively few offspring produced by each female during her fertile years. With such a reproductive strategy, primates have to take great care of their offspring to ensure survival. These basic controlling factors have developed over some 60 million years since the primates first evolved at the beginning of Eocene times.

As social animals, most primates live in permanent groups comprising at least one adult male and one adult female, along with the female's children, which may also be the offspring of the male partner. Some primates are monogamous like the gibbons but most are polygamous and have more than one male in the group. Characteristically, there is relatively little difference in body size (sexual dimorphism) between male and female in monogamous groupings but, in polygamous groups, dimorphism is more pronounced.

Two basic kinds of social and reproductive groups are recognized among the primates – female-bonded and male-bonded. Most primates are female-bonded, with related females forming the core of the group and males moving away when they become sexually mature. The females form stable hierarchies based initially on dominance through success in aggressive encounters which gives priority of access to food and so on. Higher apes form male-bonded groups but these male hierarchies are less stable than the female equivalents and may rely on changing alliances or coalitions.

Ape models

Chimps are most closely related to modern humans, and share over 98 per cent of their genetic makeup with us. Inevitably they have been taken as the closest available living model for the prehuman condition in terms of biology and behaviour – although it should be remembered that it was over 5 million years

RIGHT The basic sexuality and reproduction of the Neanderthals was the same as in modern humans. Sexual activity was continuous and as female oestrus was not evident to males, paternity was not secure.

ago that humans and chimps shared a common ancestor. Nevertheless, chimps have not developed nearly as much as humans over this time and there is good reason to believe that they are biologically and socially very conservative.

Sexual dimorphism is pronounced in the orang-utan and gorilla, with adult males weighing twice as much as the females. Chimps show much less dimorphism, with a 25 per cent difference between males and females which is not that different from the situation in modern humans, where the difference is about 20 per cent. And there are related differences in brain size. Chimps live in extended communities that can contain as many as 100 individuals sharing a home range, but live and feed in small groups without any permanent large-group associations.

Chimp 'family' groups tend to be made up of related males, and females that are the outsiders in terms of blood relationships. Females are more solitary and live with their young in small territories that overlap with those of other related females from the larger community. Adult females are passively tolerant of one another and meet at preferred feeding sites. The males are more social but with mixed co-operative and competitive tendencies. They range more widely, co-operating to defend the community territory, occasionally hunting together, and competing to find sexually receptive females.

Female chimps become sexually mature when they are about ten years old and have their first babies at thirteen to fifteen. Their sexually receptive (oestrus) phase lasts just some nine or ten days and can occur irregularly. The males are sexually interested in them only at this time, so have to be constantly on the alert for when the females are in oestrus. Mating is promiscuous but dominant males often manage to achieve the majority of copulations with a receptive female. Pregnancy lasts about eight months and, because of lengthy breastfeeding, chimp mothers may not reproduce again for another five years.

Chimp males have important roles as protectors of females and their offspring. Male hierarchies are well established but power struggles between growing adolescents and weakening older males are common. The formation of co-operative gangs and social manipulation is an important and time-consuming aspect of their lives. In these terms, chimps are not so very distant from modern humans. But can the chimp model be used to get some idea of Neanderthal sexuality?

Human models

Human reproductive biology is very similar to that of the primates, with similar sexual cycles, long pregnancy and the birth of single (usually), large and helpless offspring who have to be fed and nurtured by their mothers for lengthy periods of time. Normally, females marry out of human family groupings. However, there are some important differences. Oestrus is largely concealed and so males do not know when the female is ovulating. Sexual activity is not confined to oestrus but may be more or less continuous. Human babies are more immature and helpless at birth than those of other primates.

Very few people, if any, surviving today still live in the way our hunter-gatherer ancestors did. Some generalizations can be drawn from the remaining hunter-gatherers such as the !Kung of southern Africa. Basically, such human groups tend to be centred around the nuclear family, usually consisting of a mother or mothers, one father and their offspring. The pair bondings can be very variable, ranging from single male–female (monogamy), to single males with more than one female (polygyny) and, rarely, a single female with more than one male (polyandry). Families are based on ceremonial couplings with either the male or female moving away from their family (exogamy). Marriage involves complex economic and reproductive rights.

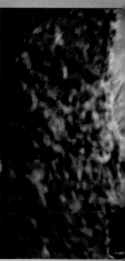

THIS SPREAD Neanderthal social groups were probably male dominated and comprised of related males with females being 'imported' from other Neanderthal bands. The important benefit of this arrangement would have been the prevention of inbreeding and the enlargement of the gene pool. The big question is, were the females coerced or kidnapped? Since there is no archaeological evidence for cooperation between bands, it is thought that young females were probably kidnapped, but we do not actually know.

Families are often clustered in communities and marriages are contracted mostly between families within the community, which is thus held together by blood-ties. Links between families are usually maintained by males, who may co-operate to initiate aggression against other communities over resources or territory.

Neanderthal sex

Neanderthals show slightly greater sexual dimorphism than modern humans; proportionally, Neanderthal body size differences between the sexes are closer to those found in the chimps, especially the bonobo chimps. Among primates, such sexual dimorphism usually implies that there is a sexual imbalance in adult partnerships; generally, dominant males mate with a number of females. But also, the norm among primates in general is that family groups are female-bonded. However, most of the higher apes, who are more closely related to humans, live in male-bonded groups.

So, which model is more appropriate to the Neanderthals? It is thought unlikely that females dominated Neanderthal groups. As we have seen, there is skeletal evidence that females participated in dangerous, challenging activities that left them damaged; presumably such pursuits would include hunting for food. Whether they would take part in all hunting activities or just some is not known. The demands of Neanderthal carnivory and the necessity of hunting large or at least medium game animals, with the associated physical dangers, suggest that provisioning was nevertheless male-dominated. Certainly pregnant females and those with young children would have been largely dependent on the males for protection and sustenance. However, the importance of plant foods to the Neanderthals and the possible female role in gathering them is as yet unknown. Experts still disagree on the interpretation of some of the archaeological evidence here.

Ovulation was probably hidden in Neanderthal females as in modern humans, and consequently the balance of sexual power and dominance may have been shifted more towards the basic human model.

ABOVE AND BELOW
Neanderthal women were powerfully built. Any newly introduced female would have been confronted by the dominant female who would have had to exert her authority over the incomer.

OPPOSITE 'Alpha' males may have tried to monopolise sexual access to the females, but no doubt there was considerable rivalry.

But it is very difficult to assess which model the Neanderthals adopted. The basic, more chimp-like model envisages males forming hunting and foraging bands which spent considerable periods of time away from home-base nest sites where the females and young lived. On their periodic return to base, the males exchanged food for sex, which was largely controlled by the dominant male. Only in this way could the dominant male be sure of fathering any offspring.

However, the considerable strength of female Neanderthals and the complex demands of childbirth and child rearing in environments that were often stressful might suggest that sexual relationships were much more complex. At times environmental factors, such as harsh winters and nutritional stress, may have resulted in seasonal breeding patterns. Babies may have been conceived in summer and born in the following spring. With more food available for the mother through the summer months, the baby would also have benefited before the lean winter months set in.

Prolonged and frequent breastfeeding by Neanderthal women could have meant that there were lengthy periods over which they could not become pregnant but that does not mean that they were not receptive to sexual advances. Sexually, they are more likely to have been continuously active, following the modern human and bonobo pattern rather than the general primate pattern. If so, this could have had a considerable influence on the way Neanderthal relationships were conducted.

The development of mental and social skills in early humans had many benefits in terms of organization and co-operation and the ability to use past experience to predict future behaviour in others. There is also, though, an escalating 'arms-race' element to the growth of such skills and all the potential for antisocial or anarchic behaviour by individuals. One well-known manifestation of such 'selfish' behaviour involves sex. Sexual infidelity – 'cheating' – is not confined to modern human society but is found in most otherwise monogamous pairings throughout the animal kingdom, practised by both sexes. Within the confines of the Neanderthal

group space, it is likely that sex was performed publicly, except perhaps where it was illicit 'cheating'. We do not know to what extent social cohesion within the Neanderthal bands was achieved by consensus or by coercion, but the likelihood is that there was at times all the potential for violent confrontation between males over access to the females.

Pair or poly-bonds?

The development of sexual relationships in humans is related to the promotion of a bond between male and female which is advantageous when their reproductive strategy relies on low numbers of offspring born at relatively long intervals. The greater the parental investment in the offspring, the greater the chances of survival. However, in stressful environments, infant mortality can be high and it makes sense for females to make alliances with dominant males who are better able to look after them and their offspring. These kinds of conditions would have applied to the Neanderthals.

The question of whether Neanderthals practised monogamy or polygyny is highly speculative. Some experts think that most of the Neanderthal men had just one partner but the most powerful 'alpha' men may have had several. If there is only one female, the dominant male may have sole sexual 'rights' to her. Alternatively, Neanderthal females may have allowed selected males sexual access in return for food when they were feeding very young offspring and unable to obtain much of their own food.

Neanderthal fecundity

In the small, tightly bonded world of the Neanderthals, birth was probably an infrequent event. The Neanderthal females had reproductive lives of less than thirty years, compared to thirty-five or so years for women today. The onset of puberty was not so different in terms of physical changes from that of modern children. In the Neanderthal adolescent, around the age of ten, those changes included developing such distinctive physical characteristics as the exaggerated brow-ridges. The Neanderthal women probably had not even reached the menopause before they died at the age of forty or so.

Their fertile period was still long enough to produce quite a few children, theoretically. But given the demands of their way of life, it is unlikely that they had many children at all or at least many that survived. The average Neanderthal woman may only have had about five pregnancies. How many of these came to term successfully and survived the trauma of birth is unknown, but it was almost certainly less than five. There is fossil evidence for significant infant mortality between the ages of four and seven and so the number surviving into reproductive adulthood may have averaged three or less, just about enough to keep the population going.

Female physiology

The fossil record is rather limited in what it can tell us about the reproductive anatomy of extinct human relatives such as the Neanderthals. However, the discovery of the first relatively complete and well-preserved Neanderthal pelvis from Kebara in Israel shows some interesting differences from the Cro-Magnon and modern pelvis. The curved (iliac) 'blades', which rise at the back and sides of the pelvis, are longer and broader in the Neanderthal. As a consequence, the hip joints are more sideways oriented. The front of the fossil pelvis (technically known as the superior pubic ramus) is comprised of two curved bones that extend forward from the hip joints and meet to form the pubic bone. These curved bones enclose the birth canal and are longer and thinner and extend somewhat further forward in Neanderthals. Somewhat paradoxically, it seems that at least part of the Neanderthal pelvis is more lightly built than that of modern humans.

These differences have led to some interesting speculation about their function in the Neanderthal pelvis. The increased pubic length may have increased the volume of the Neanderthal birth canal by up to 20 per cent and may have allowed the women to give birth to bigger and more mature babies.

Comparison with the cold-adapted Inuit people of the Arctic provides another possibility. They too have large heads relative to their body stature and

ABOVE The Kebara pelvis has been analysed to see if there were any significant differences between Neanderthal and modern human reproduction. As it belongs to a male it is difficult to draw much of a conclusion.

their pelvic structure shows some similarities to the Neanderthal condition, such as a longer pubic ramus. However, the Inuit show no difference in length of gestation or foetal growth rate from other humans.

In any case, all this speculation is founded on very slim and problematic evidence in the form of one Neanderthal pelvis. Furthermore, it turns out that the long Neanderthal pubic ramus of the Kebara skeleton belongs to that of a large male. There is as yet no complete female Neanderthal pelvis and so building ideas about gestation and birthing from male pelvis data is somewhat premature.

Yoel Rak of the University of Tel Aviv has examined the Kebara pelvis in considerable detail and reckons that there is a quite another reason for the differences. The longer pubic bone widens the pelvis at the front and rotates the iliac blades outwards – which is why the Neanderthal hip socket also faces outwards more than that of modern humans. There is no difference in volume of the birth canal and the lengthening of the pubic bone starts well before puberty. Such differences are probably primitive characteristics inherited by the Neanderthals from their more ape-like ancestors. However, the angle of hip articulation did not stop the Neanderthals from walking fully upright like modern humans, the only difference perhaps a slight roll to the gait.

Birth and beyond

There is some evidence to suggest that Neanderthal babies were born with large heads relative to their body size, even proportionally greater than found in modern humans. There may be a connection with the slightly different shape of the Neanderthal pelvis and birth canal, but this is still very much a matter of argument.

The birth process for Neanderthal women was almost certainly just as difficult and dangerous as for those modern women who do not have the benefit of modern medicine and technology. Neanderthal babies still had to rotate during the birth process so as to emerge head first. The implication is that the women would also have needed assistance. As in hunter-gatherer groups today, that role would have been filled by an older and more experienced woman in the group. The need for such assistance has further implications for social bonding between the women and is often linked to male exclusion.

As yet there is hardly any available evidence that allows us to assess infant and maternal mortality associated with birth among Neanderthals. Given the relatively large size of the babies at birth, it is highly likely that there was a high mortality rate associated with birth.

For those infants who did survive the hazards of the birth process, life did not get any easier. A baby born in winter would have been confronted with extra problems – hypothermia would have limited infant life expectancy. Some experts think that the Neanderthals may have been able to adopt seasonal breeding to avoid such problems, but such a strategy would have involved some method of timing conception. Many cold-adapted animals have such reproduction patterns but they are biologically based rather than dependent on conscious decision making. Since there are no cold-adapted higher apes living today (they all live in equatorial regions), there are no appropriately close equivalents whose biology can be compared with that of the Neanderthals regarding this issue.

It is thought unlikely that Neanderthals had any biologically driven reproductive patterning which related to the seasons. Certainly modern humans do not show any but, on the other hand, the Neanderthals had much longer to evolve one. Neither is it likely that they would have been capable of planned seasonal reproduction. Nevertheless population control could well have been critical for the Neanderthals, especially during colder glacial climate intervals. There is some evidence to suggest that they may have practised the crudest form of population control – infanticide.

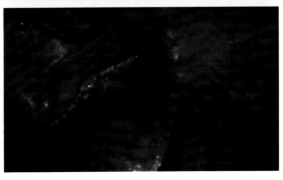

Infanticide

Neanderthal caves are often littered with tiny pathetic fragments of babies' skeletons, suggesting that infant mortality was common. It has been estimated that over 40 per cent of Neanderthal remains are those of infants and children. But, as always, the interpretation of such remains can be fraught with difficulty.

Infanticide is still a method of population control in some hunter-gatherer tribes today, especially in harsh environments where food is in short supply. Rates of infanticide as high as 50 per cent have been found. Extrapolation of these kind of data to the Neanderthals has suggested that in some circumstances, they may have practised infanticide to a similar extent, but we do not know for certain.

To our modern sensibilities, such a crude strategy for population control seems brutal and repellent, but it may have been necessary within the harsh realities of marginal existence for some Neanderthals, when climates deteriorated and game was scarce. During a particularly bad winter, feeding an extra dependent mouth could put its mother's health at risk. The loss of an adult female would be much more serious to a Neanderthal clan than the loss of an infant.

ABOVE Birthing was just as traumatic for Neanderthals as for modern women, but much more risky. Their babies also had big heads and had to be born head first.

Growing Neanderthals

A major concern about Neanderthals is their evolutionary position relative to more ancient and more modern humans. For a long time the assumption has been that the Neanderthals probably lie somewhere between the two groups of humans. It has been thought that many attributes of early humans such as *Homo erectus* were significantly closer to those found in great apes than in modern humans. But were the Neanderthals closer to the apes or modern humans? On the evidence of their brain size they should be thought to be nearer to modern humans, who have a familiar and distinctive growth pattern. Living babies, toddlers and young children grow quite slowly in terms of height. Then comes the famous adolescent growth spurt that peaks earlier in girls (14.5 years) than in boys (16 years). The standard measures of growth and development rates, which have been used for many years now, are derived from thigh bone (femur) length and stage of tooth eruption and calcification.

Recently, samples of gorillas, *Homo erectus*, Neanderthals, early modern (Cro-Magnon) humans and modern humans have been compared to test whether the Neanderthals really do have an intermediate position between ancient and modern humans. Gorilla growth rates can be clearly differentiated from those of modern humans, being considerably higher and over a shorter time period, and ceasing at about eleven years old. Although only a single sample of *Homo erectus* is suitable, it does fit into the gorilla pattern. Early modern (Cro-Magnon) humans fit within living human patterns.

Surprisingly, the Neanderthal pattern fits neither ancient nor modern pattern. The Neanderthals either show a slower and more even (linear) juvenile growth pattern relative to modern humans, or advanced tooth development. It is interesting, though, that the Neanderthal pattern is closer to that of modern humans than it is to the ancient pattern. Put another way, Neanderthal children may have grown in stature at a slower but more steady rate without the typical growth spurt of living adolescents; or their teeth developed more quickly than those of modern children. At present it is not possible to tell which option is more likely because there is no independent measure of the actual chronological age of the individual Neanderthals.

One of the main problems in working out the details of Neanderthal development is the lack of well-preserved and complete juvenile skeletons. One well-preserved skull of a four-year-old Neanderthal child was found at the Devil's Tower site in Gibraltar. Enough of the skull is preserved to calculate its brain size, which measures an astonishing 1400ml, close to the average for an adult modern human and bigger than that of a modern child of the same age. And jaw fragments contain molar teeth which are advanced in development for a

ABOVE The skull of a 4-year-old Neanderthal child from Gibraltar *(left)* contrasts with that of a modern girl of about 8 years old *(right)*.

child of this age. Here the evidence suggests that Neanderthal children grew up rather faster than the average child today.

From the evolutionary point of view, the conclusion that – however interpreted – Neanderthal development was somewhat different is particularly interesting. It suggests that the Neanderthals might have been separated from both the *Homo erectus* and early modern (Cro-Magnon) human lines for a considerable period of time.

A case study

In 1993 a small Neanderthal skeleton was unearthed in the Dederiyeh Cave, Syria by a Japanese–Syrian team led by Osamu Kondo. Unusually, much of the body skeleton is preserved but, unfortunately, just fragmentary remains of the skull. Even so, the skeleton is important as it provides an opportunity to test ideas about Neanderthal growth and development. The stature of Neanderthals is normally calculated from limb bone length.

Although most of the skeleton has been preserved from Dederiyeh, there are considerable problems associated with trying to reassemble it accurately. The child was clearly very young because the articulating surfaces of the individual vertebrae are incomplete and this makes it difficult to work out the curvature of its spine. And, in any case, can we be sure that the posture of Neanderthal children would have been the same as that of modern children?

A recent analysis by the team of anthropologists of the skeleton assumes that it was. Also, they had to take into account the cartilage discs between the vertebrae which are not preserved and so their thickness has to be estimated. Then the thickness of various soft tissues, such as the scalp and soles of the feet, have to be added. Again, measures from living children have to be used as models.

ABOVE Japanese scientists have reconstructed this fragmentary skeleton of a Neanderthal child from Syria. If the child was only two years old then, with a height of 82cm (2ft 8in), it was very similar in development to modern American children, but the Neanderthal may have been older.

LEFT With so many powerful and dangerous predators around, the young were particularly vulnerable and the old may have helped justify their existence by caring for them.

The measured and calculated height of the child totals about 82cm (2ft 8in). If the child's height had been calculated using the normal procedure of using leg bone length, the total would have been estimated at 82cm for a boy and 81cm for a girl, which shows a very good correspondence. As a result this method of using leg bone length as an estimate of stature seems pretty good. There are only two other young Neanderthal skeletons that allow such measures of stature, both from France: one is 82cm and the other 83cm high.

To put any meaning to these measures, it is necessary to know the chronological age of the children. The standard procedure is to use tooth development, which in modern humans is a very good guide for estimating age. Using modern tooth development measures as a guide, the Dederiyeh child was just under two years old (its lateral milk incisor, canine and second molar had not fully erupted) while the French Neanderthals were between three and five at death.

Taking both height and age estimates and comparing them with modern American children, the Neanderthals were below the normal American range if they were five years old or close to the norm if they were just three years old. However, the Neanderthal children definitely differ from modern Americans in the relative proportion of their limb bones. The proportional length of Neanderthal thigh to shin bones is much closer to the Finnish norm than the American one. Global measures show that there is gradation in these proportions from the tropics to the poles. Cold-adapted people like the Finns, living near the poles, have relatively shorter shin to thigh and forearm to upper-arm bones than people living in hot climates.

Finally, there is another problem relating to the rates of Neanderthal tooth development. We cannot be sure that they compare exactly with those of modern humans and if they do not, then their age estimates will be incorrect to some extent. If and when more remains of young Neanderthals are recovered, it will be interesting to see whether a better idea of Neanderthal development will emerge. Clearly the early development of their cold-adapted body proportions shows that it was entrenched in their genetic makeup.

Care in the community

The fossil bones of the Neanderthals often bear eloquent witness to their rugged way of life. Healed fractures and lesions are common, even in the remains of young children. Most were not life-threatening injuries but many were

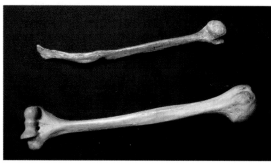

ABOVE The catalogue of injury and disease recorded by the bones of Neanderthals from Shanidar in Iraq reflects a population living on the edge. A rib bone *(top)* with a partially mended stab wound suggests that not all their injuries were sustained during hunting wild game. A withered arm bone *(bottom)* compared with a healthy one suggests that nevertheless the injured must have been cared for to some extent.

sufficiently incapacitating to have temporarily prevented them from being active members of the group. A broken limb would have seriously impaired an individual's ability to obtain food and could have had fatal consequences. The fact that some Neanderthals did survive such serious injuries suggests that they must have been receiving sufficient care from the group to keep them alive.

Some of the most dramatic fossil examples of injury come from another site in Iraq – Shanidar, which has produced a whole series of important Neanderthal remains. Nine Neanderthal skeletons ranging in age from very young infants to 'old' men were excavated between 1953 and 1960 by a team of archaeologists from the American University of Columbia, led by Ralph Solecki. A male rib was found with a dramatically deep cut mark. Acting as palaeodetectives, the scientists carried out forensic analysis of the lesion on his eighth rib and showed that the victim was stabbed in the ribcage by a very sharp and heavy weapon. From the angle of the cut, it seems that the wound was inflicted by a right-handed assailant in a face-to-face attack.

ABOVE Close-encounter combat with wild animals was probably the source of most injury for the Neanderthals but some scars may have come from more personal conflict.

The weapon almost certainly punctured his lung and dealt a mortal blow. But detailed examination suggests that the victim probably survived for a few weeks before finally succumbing to this and maybe other soft tissue injuries for which we have no evidence. Whether he was cared for or not by the group is not clear, but his survival for that length of time suggests that he may well have received some sustenance. And there does seem to be evidence of even longer-term care. Another skeleton in the Shanidar cave, an adult, had a diseased and withered right arm that he had had since childhood. Solecki concluded that this individual could not have survived as long as he did unless he had been cared for by the other members of the group.

No matter what support there was available from other Neanderthals, most (80 per cent) were destined to die before they reached the age of thirty-five to forty.

The question of whether Neanderthals looked after injured or decrepit members of the group is intriguing. Some experts have speculated that, as a survival strategy, the Neanderthals would only have provisioned those individuals who still had some value to the group, either practically or emotionally. An older individual might have some particular skills or knowledge which could still benefit the group, or they might retain some authority which bolstered the social cohesion of the group. Any Neanderthal unable to obtain food would have been a 'passenger' and a drain on the resources of the group. Survival may well have depended on playing a useful role. Perhaps the elderly gathered plant food and firewood, tended children and fires and thus had a role to play.

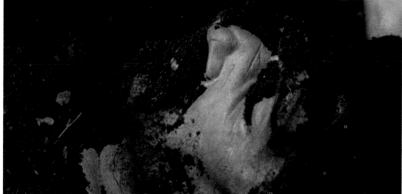

Nevertheless, life for the elderly and young must have been precarious. The fossil record shows that there was considerable infant mortality, especially after the age of four. Some 40 per cent of all Neanderthal remains are those of children between four and eleven which suggests that, on the whole, they were left to fend for themselves. Common enamel defects on children's teeth shows that they frequently suffered from dietary deficiencies that may well have been seasonal.

Once weaned and without the antibodies from their mother's milk, infants would have been increasingly prone to infection. They would also have been vulnerable to predation. Just as the Neanderthals picked out young or weak individual animals as easier prey, so would predators, such as wolves, hyenas and possibly the big cats, have picked out young and frail Neanderthals as easy meat.

Death and ritual

Another of the intriguing but frustrating aspects of studying Neanderthals is the question of how they responded to death. Again, we cannot actually know what they felt about the death of a friend, relative or foe. Did they experience feelings of loss and grief or have any sense of an afterlife? The lack of convincing emblematic or symbolic artefacts at Neanderthal sites suggests that their lives lacked ritual or religion, but there is evidence of some care for their dead through burial. And another important question is whether Neanderthal burial was accompanied by any form of ceremony.

Today, the death of individuals and the celebration of their life can be marked in many different ways depending upon the belief system of the culture to which the dead belong. Nevertheless, some ceremony is generally regarded as essential for relatives and friends. People will go to great lengths to try and recover the remains of their loved ones and ensure a 'proper burial'. Disappearance of a loved one, presumed dead, for whatever reason, is particularly hard for the victim's family to accept: they need the body.

The great leap forward

It would seem that the basic act of burial of a body is the simplest and perhaps most ancient way of recognizing death. Burial is a social act of recognition of an individual. For a member of a social group not to be buried by the group is to deny that individual's existence. Non-burial is a social sanction because the 'victim' truly has become a non-person. So the introduction of the act of burial has very great social and developmental significance. It marks the transition to intentional group activity that recognizes individuality. The one who dies lives on in the minds of the others as an 'I'. For such a realization to take place, there must be conscious thought and it must be articulated for the group action to occur. So the act of burial is a very important marker for the transition from feeling to thought, which was perhaps one of the greatest leaps forward for humanity.

Evolution of burial and religion

For social animals, such as most of the living primates, which live in tightly knit groups, group obeisance is instinctual as it is generally paramount for survival. In the primitive group situation there is a suppression of any latent individualism. In more advanced groups where individualism has already evolved, there is pressure to regress to the instinctual behaviour of the group. Deviance is punished by the physical aggression of the dominant individual. The transgressor can make a physical challenge for leadership and risk serious injury, back down or leave the group. For most social animals, ostracism – whether voluntary or enforced – is a severe punishment. Not only does it challenge their instinctual need for community, but also the exile will not have the support of the group in hunting for food. The transformation of these threats on to the unconscious psychological level was probably an important step in the early evolution of our ancient human relatives.

The next step may have been consciousness of selfhood and the formalization of group and individual identity through burial. Up until this point the individual in the group was mostly a unit with very limited autonomous determination. This development and expression of selfhood has been equated with the formation of the most basic form of religion. It is thought that the individual, being conscious of selfhood, makes a distinction between the 'I' and the 'I-of-the-group', in other words, myself in the group. The group is the world for that individual and takes on an inflated importance. As a result, the outside world and strangers are devalued almost to the point of obliteration. Because the group activity is closely controlled by its need to survive, any unusual event may be a threat to its survival. The unusual, whether real or imaginary, is beyond the world of the group and imbued with imaginary and perhaps supernatural powers which in turn invoke fear. It could be a mountain which occasionally rumbles, smokes or erupts because it is a volcano, an astronomical phenomenon, an unusual animal or a strange human.

The fashioning of a local world and the population of that world with supernatural beings may well have been an essential step in the emergence of consciousness and primitive religion. An important manifestation of that religion was burial with ceremony.

Archaeological evidence

Enough fully articulated skeletons of Neanderthals have been found to indicate that active burial did occur. In the natural state, unburied bodies are potential food for a variety of predators and scavengers from lions, hyenas and birds of prey to a host of microbes. The bigger scavengers tend to tear off whatever parts of a carcass they can manage and remove them to where they can feast in a less competitive environment away from their fellows. Consequently, scavenged carcasses are dismembered and dispersed but, fortunately for archaeologists, the action of scavengers usually leaves tell-tale signs on the bones.

Of the relatively complete Neanderthal skeletons that have been found, some are positioned on their sides in a foetal position, sometimes with the hands cushioning the head. Such attitudes certainly suggest careful positioning of the bodies. Most of these bodies are found inside caves, which may have been favoured sites for burial because the bodies would have been less available to some scavengers (but not all).

Many of the scavengers, such as some lions and hyenas, themselves used caves as dens. These animal cave dwellers actually brought back their pickings to the safety of their caves to consume them – some fragmentary Neanderthal remains found in caves, such as Monte Circeo in Italy, may have been hoarded by big cats or hyenas, which are strong enough to drag back quite sizeable chunks of prey.

Also, conditions outside cave environments do not normally promote the long-term persistence of skeletal remains. Even active burial does not guarantee that bones will survive in the ground long enough to become potential fossils, just waiting to be found by some scientist. Much depends on soil conditions, the amount of water in the ground and its chemistry. The infrequency of Neanderthal skeletal remains outside caves and rock shelters does not mean that they did not occur; it could well be that either they were not preserved or they have not been found.

The most important evidence comes from three sites in south-west France where there seems to have been deliberate burial within a Middle Palaeolithic (Mousterian) context. Although La Chapelle-aux-Saints was originally excavated in the early years of the twentieth century, careful records were made of the geological context of the find (see the box on page 64). The plans and sections show that there was a rectangular burial pit, right at the base of the Mousterian deposits, and that it is extremely unlikely that the burial was the result of any non-human natural process. The same conditions apply to at least one of the six skeletons found at La Ferrassie in 1934, which was photographed in its flexed position before being fully excavated.

Altogether, there were seven individual Neanderthals buried at La Ferrassie and ten at Shanidar in Iraq, including a number of children who had small and relatively delicate bones. It is highly unlikely that so many bodies would have survived intact unless they had been deliberately protected from scavengers by burial. The thorny question of whether or not the Neanderthals used any ceremonial or ritual in connection with burial is still largely unresolved.

Stone tools and animal remains accompanying the burials at La Ferrassie and Le Moustier were probably introduced during the original act of digging the burial pits down through older occupation layers which are full of scattered tools and bones. At Teshik Tash in Uzbekistan, there is a record of the horn cores of Siberian mountain goats with their points driven into the ground around the partial skeleton of a Neanderthal child. Whether this was a deliberate act to try and protect the corpse from scavengers or was part of some ceremony is unclear. The skeleton of another young child, the one in Dederiyeh Cave referred to earlier, was found buried 1.5 metres (5 feet) deep in layers of cave deposits. As the sediment was carefully excavated layer by layer, the body was found lying on its back with arms extended and legs flexed. There was a slab of limestone lying by the crushed skull and a small piece of triangular flint lying close to where the child's heart would have been. The team of Japanese and Syrian archaeologists who excavated the site say that the limestone slab is rare in these deposits and conclude that all these features are indicative of an intentional burial.

Conjecture can sometimes be further complicated by human intervention. In 1939 an isolated skull was discovered in the Grotta Gauttari, near Monte Circeo in central Italy. Alberto Blanc, the archaeologist who worked on the find, published a drawing that showed the skull placed upside-down in a circle of stones. Blanc concluded that it had been placed there as part of a ritual.

But it turned out that the find had originally had been made by a workman who had stumbled on it by accident and in the dark had picked up the skull from among many bones scattered around on the cave floor. No one knows exactly where the skull was originally positioned and further work has shown that the cave was a hyena den. The bones could well have been brought back to the cave by these scavenging animals.

Buried with flowers?

Better known is the highly contentious find at the Iraqi cave site of Shanidar, mentioned earlier in the context of wounded or handicapped individuals. In the sediment surrounding one of the burials here, there is a scattering of pollen grains, interpreted as the remains of a ceremonial garland of spring flowers placed on the corpse. Ralph Solecki published an account of the excavation in 1971, *Shanidar – the First Flower People*, which was enormously popular. Suddenly the image of the Neanderthals was changed and they became seen as caring people who looked after the 'lame' and buried their dead with ceremony. While it makes for a good story, the evidence has been critically reappraised and it is thought that the pollen was probably introduced by burrowing rodents or groundwater percolating through the sediment.

Only two Middle Palaeolithic burials contain convincing grave goods or offerings, both in Israel. Djebel Qafzeh incorporates a large pair of fallow deer antlers, apparently clasped in the hands of a child's corpse; while at Skhūl there was the complete lower jawbone of a boar, again placed in the hands of the dead, this time an adult. Most importantly, these two most convincing burial goods turn out to be associated with anatomically modern humans rather than Neanderthals. Both burials are dated at around 90,000–100,000 years old.

Bin-ends or burials?

The big question concerns the extent to which the Neanderthal burials reflect symbolic behaviour. Is the act of burial itself evidence of symbolic behaviour, or could it have been mostly functional? The number of bodies buried at sites such as Shanidar would seem to argue against a purely functional interpretation because there would be much less labour-intensive ways of disposing of corpses. For instance, at Atapuerca, near Burgos in northern Spain, the remains of some thirty-two humans have been found jumbled together at the bottom of a 15-metre (50-foot) deep shaft within the cave. This 300,000-year-old deposit could be interpreted as one of the simplest ways of disposing of the dead and one that was primarily functional – body bin-ends.

However, the Spanish archaeologist Juan Luis Arsuaga, who has excavated the find, has claimed that the bodies of the dead were purposely dumped into the pit and that therefore this represents intent and concern for the dead, possibly a belief in the afterlife, even if the method of disposal was pretty crude. The problem is that if this really is the case then the remains should consist of complete skeletons, but they do not. Teeth of thirty-two different individuals have been found but the limb bones of only twenty. Continuing work on the remains may well redress the balance.

However, again many of the bones are covered with scavenger, mainly fox, chew marks and the odd puncture mark of a larger carnivore such as a big cat. This suggests that the remains were accumulated by scavengers. Another Spanish archaeologist, Yolanda Fernandez-Jalvo, thinks that the bodies may have been intentionally left at one of the entrances to the cave and were later disturbed and redistributed by scavengers.

Another curious facet to the story is that the bodies are mostly those of adolescents who are thought to have been fairly closely related in time and perhaps genetically. Many of them were in pretty poor medical shape – there is evidence of general bone disease, deafness, jaw disease and a severe dental problem and malnourishment. It is even possible that they all died in some epidemic but the picture is not yet clear.

These Atapuerca people were perhaps among the ancestors of the Neanderthals and if they were truly disposing of their dead with intent, then the origin of 'burial' in its simplest form may be very ancient.

Burial goods?

Stone tools and animal bones have been found closely associated with Neanderthal skeletons and some of these have been interpreted as 'grave goods'. The suggestion is that they were put there on purpose as part, perhaps, of some kind of ritual 'send-off'. But this is another highly contentious area. Other experts see the association as largely accidental because such items tend to litter the floors of Neanderthal caves anyway. And we do not know how much disturbance of the sites has occurred after the event. At a cruder, more practical level, such burials may well have been no more than a means of disposing of a body in a cave which continued to be occupied by the Neanderthals.

There is as yet no evidence of any increase in the number of Neanderthal 'burials' over the last millennia of their existence. The sample size is still far too small. Their numbers may well have been decreasing over a long period and it would be hard to distinguish any increase in mortality rates.

Birth, sex and death may have been fundamental to Neanderthals, as to any other being. But another fact of life was that without food, their journey from cave to grave would have been very short. The basic need to survive, to eat, in the Ice Age environments of Neanderworld, presented huge challenges to our ancient relatives. Eating plants alone was not a sustainable option – an adequate diet demanded animal protein. Those animals not easily captured would have to be hunted. Hunting required weapons for the kill, and tools for making the weapons and carving up the carcasses. To survive, the Neanderthals needed technology.

The arms race: technology and hunting

chapter six

ONE VITAL SKILL THAT THE NEANDERTHALS BROUGHT WITH THEM into Europe was their tool and weapon-making technology. Our view of this technology is heavily biased towards stone tools because, generally speaking, these are the only ones that are preserved in the archaeological record. It can be difficult to decide whether a lack of organic artefacts was because they were not made or because they were not preserved. Tools and weapons made of organic materials such as wood and even bone, horn and ivory are not so easily preserved. However, some sites have now been discovered where special conditions of preservation have allowed these less durable materials to survive.

The stone tools are the most important evidence we have of the Neanderthals' existence and activities, apart from their fossil bones. Being able to make stone tools for a variety of purposes – though driven by the need to obtain food – was critical in helping the Neanderthals survive in the ever-changing environments of western Europe and Eurasia. Surprisingly, perhaps, the rock record seems to show that for a long time the Neanderthals demonstrated little innovation in their tool technology.

Understanding stone tools

The craft of making tools from stone is not as simple as it might seem to the uninitiated. Only certain rock types will take an edge or point that is sharp enough to cut or penetrate tough animal hide, especially when it is covered in fur. And most tools whose design extends beyond a simple single flake broken from a stone nodule require an element of conceptualization and design that took a very long time to evolve.

The method of making stone tools is now fairly well understood, thanks to careful collection of stone fragments and the reconstruction of the original stone nodules or blocks from which they were struck. The work is like putting together a three-dimensional jigsaw from many stone flakes and fragments found at certain sites, where there has been active tool-making. Often the final tool at the core of the reconstituted block is missing because it was taken from the site to be used elsewhere, but the very process of putting the pieces back together reveals the process of making the tool in reverse.

In addition, recent experimental research has replicated the techniques required to produce flakes and edges of various sizes and shapes in the range of common rock types used for tool-making. Quite a good understanding of stone tool manufacture has been achieved by combining this knowledge of both the sequence and process of fragmentation.

The big problems with stone tools are the difficulties of sequencing and dating their development and relating them to particular groups of ancient people. It used to be thought that there was a linear progression in the development of stone tool technology, and it was just a matter of sorting out the dates of the different developmental stages. The hope was that since durable stone tools are often found without any other fossil remains or artefacts, they could be used as a kind of proxy chronometer for the Palaeolithic and its further subdivision.

The Lower, Middle and Upper Palaeolithic were originally characterized by the occurrence of particular types of stone tools. The Lower Palaeolithic's trademark tools are the hand-axe and chopper. The Middle Palaeolithic has a variety of tool types, most of which involved modification of the edges of flakes struck from a core; the flakes have been classified according to their supposed use. The Upper Palaeolithic tools are more standard in form and generally more sophisticated, and include the manufacture of long, thin blades.

This chronological development was thought to show an increasing efficiency in use of stone and was related to advancing cultural differences in the succession of peoples who manufactured them. In 1868, the discovery at Cro-Magnon in France of the skeletal remains of anatomically modern humans with blade-type stone tools led to the conclusion that this advanced stone tool technology was characteristic of the Upper Palaeolithic and Cro-Magnon modern people. The subsequent discovery, in the early part of the twentieth century, of Neanderthal remains with Middle Palaeolithic stone tools led to the further connection of this tool-type with the Neanderthals. However, recent research has undermined some aspects of such a simplistic chronology.

An evolving technology

The making of the most basic and crude stone tools appears to have started by 2.5 million years ago in Africa. Stone tool manufacture has been particularly associated with evolving humans ever since. One of the most distinctive stone tools to emerge during their long development was the hand-axe, which first appeared in Africa around 1.5 million years ago. Hand-axes are developed from a lump of stone in a step-by-step process. The basic hand-axe design can vary enormously but many have a flat pear, almond, drop or oval shape. The idea of the shape, the conceptual design, has to be in the stone knapper's mind before work begins.

Firstly, a suitable piece of rock was selected. It had to break in the right kind of way and retain its cutting edge. This is not as simple as it might seem since there are relatively few rock types that are suitable for making stone tools. Secondly, a hard stone hammer (a pebble of suitable hardness and weight) was used to strike off flakes and form a rough outline. In the process, most of the outer surface 'skin' of the nodule or stone block was removed to reveal the fresher inner stone. Then a softer hammer with a smaller head, such as a deer antler, was used to give better control on the shaping process. The flakes broken from the core stone were used for other purposes such as blades. The final shaping of the axe removed smaller flakes to form the axe's cutting edge and again required the use of the 'soft' hammer and a stone anvil. Many axes but not all were worked on both sides, or 'faces', and are known to archaeologists as bifaces.

This type of axe typifies the Acheulian stone industry, named after the French town of Acheul, where they were first found in the nineteenth century. But the Acheulian hand-axe originated in Africa and was spread throughout much of the Old World by the dispersal of ancient humans around 1 million years ago. This ancient type of large hand-axe was largely superseded by smaller and more knife-like hand-axes by the time the Neanderthals appeared on the scene, by about 300,000 years ago.

An ancient tool-kit

In the geological context of most of Europe, especially the lowland areas, much of the available rock is too soft for making effective stone tools. However, flint is one particular – and in many ways unusual – rock type that occurs as nodules and occasional bands within these otherwise relatively soft rock strata. It could be argued that it was the presence of flint as much as anything else that made the Palaeolithic occupation of Europe possible. Neanderthals clearly knew how and where to find the right kind of rock material in each region that they occupied. Like their African forebears, they had to know their rocks.

The Middle Palaeolithic tool-kit typically consists of a variety of stone tools, mostly flakes that have had their edges modified by secondary working. They have been variously characterized as scrapers, points, denticulates, tanged tools and so on. The French archaeologist François Bordes spent a lifetime trying to categorize these tools and make sense of their patterns of occurrence in south-west France. He thought that he could recognize over sixty different tool types, which fell into just five kinds of assemblage, each with a particular proportion of tool types.

Bordes suggested that these five assemblages reflected different traditions or cultures of tool-making belonging to five separate 'tribes' of Neanderthals who had little contact with one another. However, more recent work has suggested that expediency, and availability of particular materials, was the dominating factor. When raw material is to hand, tools are less well finished or worked because they can easily be replaced. Further away from material sources, it was easier to modify and rework existing tools rather than fetch new ones. Consequently, the apparently more worked, variable or sophisticated tools are not separated according to social group or time but convenience.

Analysis of stone tool assemblages and degree of modification from some Italian sites suggests that purpose may be even more important than distance from source. Where there was active hunting, relatively unworked raw materials were stockpiled on site. When game became available, the hunters would have had no time to start manufacturing their stone tools from scratch. But where they lived mainly by scavenging and foraging, especially at coastal sites where there was a fairly regular and predictable supply of small food, more time was spent reworking stone tools that could be used for a variety of purposes.

The original hope of using stone tools for the basic chronological subdivision of the Palaeolithic, in the way that palaeontologists use fossils to subdivide successions of rock strata, has not been fulfilled. However, the more complex picture of how stone tools were prepared, and perhaps used, is providing a richer view of the Neanderthals and how they lived.

Developing technology

From an early phase of their existence around 350,000 years ago, there is evidence that the Neanderthals had developed the so-called Levallois technique of tool-making. Named after the French site (now in the suburbs of Paris) from which these advanced tools were first found and described, the Levallois technique shows a significant technological advance. Here there is an intermediate stage which has to be conceptualized to a much greater extent and prepared before the final Levallois flake can be struck.

Previous stone technology simply involved flakes being struck off a stone core. With the advanced Levallois technique, a core stone had to be prepared and roughly shaped before it was possible to strike off a suitably formed piece, which could then be worked on and modified in a number of ways to produce the tool. Typical Levallois tools were relatively large but thin flakes, and a triangular point, which may well have been hafted on to a long wooden stick to make a much more effective spear than was previously available. Wear patterns have been found just on the front surfaces of some stone points, suggesting that the rest of the point was protected by a covering of some sort, which has not been preserved. The most likely explanation is that the point was hafted on to a spear with a binding of animal sinew or plant fibre, but there is no direct evidence of how it was done.

As earlier, some wooden shafts were just cut and scraped to a point and sometimes hardened at the tip by fire. One of the great advantages of the Levallois technique was that at least six times as many flakes could be prepared from the same amount of stone as a single Acheulian hand-axe. They would have made a significant contribution to the effectiveness of hunting, especially when used as a very hard and sharp point to a heavy wooden spear.

The edges of stone tools, formed by knapping flints, can be exceptionally sharp. The problem is that such edges are fragile and easily break so that they constantly need to be reworked to maintain their sharpness. Stone knapping techniques allowed the Neanderthals to produce a variety of tools for different purposes such as skinning carcasses, cutting meat and tough sinews and scraping hides.

Tool-kits from the Dordogne

A good idea of Neanderthal working methods can be obtained from the large numbers of stone tools scattered over the limestone plateaux of the Dordogne region of south-west France. There is evidence of some 300 temporary, open-air Neanderthal camps as compared with only about twenty-five cave or rock shelters in the same region. The vast majority of the open-air sites have been identified as Neanderthal as they contain Mousterian-type tools, especially triangular hand-axes. It is difficult to assess such sites: how many people occupied them, what they were doing, how long they stayed and whether they repeatedly visited the same sites from year to year.

Because of their very openness in the landscape, these sites have often been disturbed over the intervening millennia by subsequent human activities. Typically, such locations do not accumulate layers of sediment in the same way that more protected cave sites do. Consequently, artefacts do not tend to get buried and preserved beneath younger sediment but accumulate on one surface over a considerable period of time.

The richer and more extensive open-air sites seem to be concentrated on high altitude plateaux that separate the deep river valleys of the Dordogne. Even here, there is the problem of knowing whether they reflect a few long periods of occupation by relatively large groups or are simply the compounded results of repeated visits by smaller groups. One thing is sure: when layers of stone tools are found they show that the sites were occupied at many different times throughout the Palaeolithic from the Acheulian through to the Aurignacian or upper Perigordian. The abundance of the tools and repeated evidence of occupation suggest that there was something highly favourable about the sites that attracted a succession of peoples to them.

Surveys have shown that the overall distribution pattern of sites over the landscape breaks down into distinct, separate clusters, each with a small number of sites. For instance, several sites have been found concentrated on the Meyrals plateau in the Sarlat region and other clusters have been found on the Plateau Cabrol and Plateau Baillard in Lot-et-Garonne. At the

BELOW A Neanderthal (Mousterian) flint tool kit consisting of a hammer stone *(clockwise from top right)*, pointed cleaver, point, small hand-axe, disc and side scraper, all from Le Moustier in the Dordogne, south-west France.

large La Croix-Guémard site in Deux-Sèvres, which is close to a rich source of flints, mapping of stone tool finds has revealed very distinct clusters, especially of Mousterian, Upper Palaeolithic and post-Palaeolithic tools, while older Acheulian and younger Neolithic tools are more scattered.

This kind of detailed survey reinforces the view that there were indeed frequent visits to the same locations by relatively small bands of people. By comparing the types of tools at different sites, French archaeologists have been able to get some glimpses of what the sites were used for.

Categorizing campsites

Quarry sites were those used for the extraction and initial working of local flint sources, usually of high quality. There is evidence that the flint workers went to considerable lengths to check the quality of the flintstone nodules before working on them to any great extent. At Lascabannes in Lot-et-Garonne, the outer surface 'skin' of some nodules has been scratched to assess the nature of the flint; flakes have been removed from others to check the quality of the interior of nodules and some have had all the outer white layer removed to reduce the weight for greater ease of transport from the site.

Workshop sites were devoted partly to extraction of flints and partly to working nodules into fully prepared flakes. At Lagrave in Lot, close by a source of high-quality flint, production was focused on hand-axe manufacture. Those axes found at the site tend to be abandoned as unfinished or broken.

The best home sites are those that combine evidence for the widest variety of activities, and have been estimated to account for some 20 per cent of the open-air sites in south-west France. They too are generally sited on good quality flint sources and include the basic tasks of quarrying and preparing flakes, but they also include significant numbers of retouched tools. With the variety of stone tool work going on, of all the open sites, they most resemble the cave and rock shelters of the region. Consequently, these may be the sites that were the most domestic or residential of the open-air sites. They tend to occur on the higher plateaux and usually command extensive vistas over the surrounding terrains and 'game reserves'. They were probably the sites which were most consistently occupied.

Less notable sites were those that were little more than temporary stopovers, but probably include the majority of open-air sites. The evidence for distinguishing these sites is similar to that of the other kinds but it is thought that they were used for some short-term or specialized working of the local flint sources. They tend to be fairly widely scattered over both plateau and river-valley locations. Further close research at these sites may reveal evidence for distinct activities by individuals or single-occupation episodes.

An example of the potential for this kind of investigation is seen at the Carrière Thomasson site, which gives a rare glimpse of at least part of a specialized tool-kit. A small cluster of tools was found, including four side scrapers, two naturally backed stone knife blades, a single notched flake, two flint cores and a group of twenty-six flakes. They were all found near the bones of a single mammoth that had either been hunted and killed, or scavenged. The tools were part of a butchery kit, some of which might have been made on site for this particular purpose from prepared cores, which the group had been carrying with them.

Interesting patterns have emerged from comparison of the raw material sources for the tools found at the different campsites. Stone tools found at open-air sites tend to be much more locally derived than the tools found at caves or rock shelters. Between 82 and 98 per cent of campsite tools have come from within a 4–5-kilometre (2.5–3-mile) range, compared with 66–89 per cent of those found at cave and rock shelter sites. These patterns reinforce the idea that most open-air sites were essentially short-term sites for certain specialized hunting or scavenging activities. Their use was much more ephemeral than that of caves and rock shelters. However, a few of the larger open-air sites show patterns of tool sourcing much more like those of caves and rock shelters, with a significant proportion of the tools being derived from distances of up to 80 kilometres (50 miles) away. These were the 'five-star' sites more frequently used by larger groups, often with the privilege of commanding good vistas over the landscape.

Interpreting their use

The common occurrence of the open-air sites on higher ground suggests that it was not unusual for small bands of Neanderthals to stay away from the main group for a night or two. At these campsites, they probably made fires, cooked meat and slept over. We cannot be very sure about what exactly went on because very little apart from the tools are preserved at most open-air sites. Hearths and organic materials, such as bone, are mostly preserved in cave and rock-shelter sites. Exceptions are open sites such as Dolní Věstonice in Moravia, where there is indisputable evidence for the use of fire in a hearth, over a burial and the firing of clay but, at 27,000 years old, this was the work of Cro-Magnons not Neanderthals.

For Neanderthals, there would have been more game to hunt on the higher plateaux of south-western France and consequently a greater likelihood of contact from time to time between groups competing for the same game. Territorial boundaries may have been less well defined in these open landscapes and perhaps more disputed.

Travelling at night would have been very hazardous, and it is much more likely that they would have set up camp with a fire to deter the other predators of the time, the big cats, wolves and hyena. The abundance of simple hearths shows that firemaking was an essential skill for the Neanderthals and one of the keys to their initial success as a species.

Making fire

ABOVE Making fire was crucial for survival in Neanderworld, it provided heat for warmth, cooking and protection from predators such as wolves and big cats.

As with most prehistoric hunter-gatherer tribes, fire is likely to have been made by rubbing a pointed wooden stick against a wooden base. To modern humans inexperienced in survival skills, it might seem surprising, if not almost magical, that such an apparently crude and simple technique can generate enough friction to make fire, but it does. The friction heats the wood sufficiently that dry tinder placed on the wooden base begins to glow with red heat. Controlled and sustained blowing provides oxygen to the glowing ember, increasing its temperature sufficiently for it to eventually burst into flames.

It is likely that the Neanderthals employed the same basic technique. The more advanced and efficient variant of using drill friction was probably beyond their ability but may well have been employed by the Cro-Magnons. With this method, a long pointed stick is loosely anchored at one end by the teeth and the other end rests in a hollow on a wood block. A string or sinew is wound around the stick and held at each end. By moving the hands and arms to and fro, the stick is rotated like a drill, much faster than can be achieved by hand alone, and so the frictional heat builds up more quickly. The Oxford archaeologist Paul Pettitt thinks that the wear patterns on Neanderthal front teeth may have been produced while gripping sticks during fire making.

To be able to make fire wherever they went, they had to carry the basic tools and dry tinder with them. Dry lichen, fungi, tree bark and pine cones all made useful tinder.

Hunting

The hunt required preparation: the weapons had to be in order, and tools for rough butchering of the kill had to be carried with them. Polished wear patterns, found on some tools, suggest that they may have been carried around in some sort of bag or pouch in which they rubbed together. Any such bag would probably have been made of animal hide and may have carried some provisions as well as stone tools. There is speculation that a typical Neanderthal hunters' 'picnic' consisted of the long bones of animals that contained marrow. Bone marrow is an extremely rich source of protein and fat and could have provided one of the quickest energy boosters available to them. They could also determine the health of the animal they had killed or scavenged from the colour of the marrow. Healthy animals in good condition have pink marrow, which is high in fat, while red marrow indicates poor health.

The composition of the hunting party in terms of people is not known. It may well have depended on the distance being travelled, the conditions at the time and the game being hunted. More local hunts with the least dangerous prey probably included all the able-bodied members of the group – only small children and the infirm elderly would have been excluded.

Hunting techniques

Having a home territory would have had some advantages for the Neanderthals. They would have known the detailed lie of the land, where best to watch the movement of game, where to set ambushes, where best to drive game over a cliff and so on. Some valley side caves and rock shelters provided natural viewpoints for watching game. But generally they would have sought out higher vantage points with vistas over the surrounding countryside. From there they would have watched out for signs of game – dust clouds or circling birds of prey. Neanderthal hunting was probably opportunistic and not particularly planned, which was fine as long as the game was in plentiful supply. Anything more sophisticated such as building up a detailed knowledge from season to season would have required communication by language. As we have seen, it is not clear how well developed Neanderthal language was. It certainly would have helped in predicting the movement of game, especially herds of migratory animals such as reindeer, horse and mammoth.

The distribution of bones in some sites shows that Neanderthals had fairly definite hunting territories extending over some 20–30 kilometres (12–18 miles), which would have been adequate when game was plentiful but had severe limitations when game was scarce.

Neanderthals hunted specific types of game at particular times of year. A site in western France preserves the bones of reindeer that they hunted in winter, and red deer hunted in summer. Occasionally, in the absence of these most

THIS SPREAD Killing wild game armed only with spears takes considerable skill. Animals are alert to the slightest sense of danger and so, for close-quarter killing, have to be taken by surprise. The Neanderthals' main advantage as hunters was their intelligence. They had the ability to cooperate, communicate and plan the hunt to some extent. But it was a risky business. Limb and upper torso damage in Neanderthal skeletons provides evidence of what could happen. Even deer can break a human limb with a single kick.

common prey animals, they were forced into hunting more dangerous game such as wild cattle (auroch), bison and even perhaps elephant or mammoth.

As predators, humans are physically ill-equipped for the hunt. Even the powerful Neanderthals were not individually very well suited for taking on an animal the size of a fully grown wild horse. They could not outrun a horse or deer, nor were they strong enough to kill such game single-handed and unarmed. The main weapons in the human and Neanderthal armoury are cunning, co-operation, communication and technological clout.

The cunning was their ability to predict the movement of game, and set ambushes in which surprise was a major factor in their favour to overcome the animals' natural turn of speed. Co-operation was their ability to work together to target a group of prey animals and drive them into the prepared ambush. Alternatively, the hunters would sometimes target individuals, either more solitary animals or those separated from a herd.

Communication allowed them to develop hunting strategies, enact them and, importantly, respond to the rapidly changing circumstances arising from hunting wild, unpredictable and often dangerous animals. Nevertheless, accidents did, as we know from skeletal evidence, happen.

Clout was provided by the Neanderthal hunting tool-kit of heavy thrusting spears, tipped with sharp stone points. Dealing mortal blows to an animal like a wild horse required considerable upper body strength to handle the heavy weaponry. There is anatomical evidence that the Neanderthals did have well-developed upper arm muscles to stabilize their arms during strong forward thrust movements. Similarly, the evolution of powerful and dextrous hands capable of performing a great variety of tasks was an essential ingredient in the overall evolution of humans. Neanderthal hands had very strong fingers with relatively large finger bones and less difference in length of the fingers than in modern humans. The large bones increased the strength of their hands without affecting their dexterity. Their fingertips were especially well developed and probably gave them a very powerful grip.

The kill still involved getting very close to the prey, which, unless rendered helpless by the first thrust of the weapon, could yet retaliate with dangerous kicks or headbutts. Such close-contact hunting techniques involved considerable personal risk, as shown by Neanderthal skeletons with wounds and fractures of the upper body and limbs. At one Neanderthal site in Croatia, the majority of the skeletons (85 per cent) show some damage to the upper body with fractured collar bones, ribs, lower arms and skull damage.

RIGHT Flint flakes have razor-sharp edges which are quite adequate for fashioning wooden spears.

There is evidence that Neanderthals were capable of orchestrating mass drives and slaughter of herd animals by stampeding them towards cliff edges, trapping them in narrow valleys and using other traps exploiting the natural landscape. The La Quina site in the Dordogne region of France preserves an accumulation of bones of aurochs, horses and reindeer beneath a steep cliff, some 100 metres (over 300 feet) high. These animal-bone graveyards resulted from the development of the relatively low-risk hunting strategy of the cliff drive. Mauran on Haute-Garonne was a natural hollow, perhaps containing a lake, where bison were trapped and butchered. Their broken bones form a deposit 30–40 centimetres (12–15 inches), extending over at least 1000 square metres (nearly 1200 square yards).

The problem with such techniques is that they may have been too successful in killing more animals than could be consumed at any one time. This would reduce the reproductive capacity of the herd, leading to fewer animals the following season. Even modern humans do not seem to have fully learned the lesson of maintaining the sustainability of prey animals by controlling hunting activity. From whales to bison and cod, we have practically wiped out some important food sources through persistent overkill. Conversely, hunting game as a vital, practical activity has practically disappeared in today's world; now it is more of an emotive issue, or perhaps a symbolic one. Some people see the deliberate killing of wild or semi-wild animals as not only acceptable and

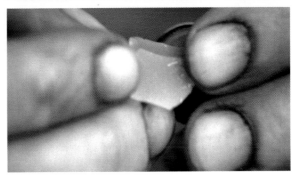

honourable but as a means of maintaining a connection between wildness and humanness, nature and culture. There is little doubt that hunting is a very ancient human predatory habit that was originally forged out of necessity.

Off-setting this emphasis on meat is the good fossil evidence that our primate ancestors were largely plant and fruit eaters. In between these two modes of subsistence lies another, more intermediary, scavenging habit. So the interesting questions are: When exactly did we change from being herbivores into predators? And where do the Neanderthals lie on this pathway?

ABOVE With a fairly basic kit of scrapers, blades and hammers, the Neanderthals prepared the necessary tools of their 'trade' as game hunters.

Until the 1980s it was generally accepted that the Neanderthals had been active hunters of game, even killing some animals as large as mammoths. But then there was a critical reappraisal of the archaeological basis for these claims. Analysis of animal bones found associated with Neanderthal remains suggested instead that these people were more likely to have been scavengers.

ABOVE Neanderthal children had to help gather food as soon as they were physically able.

Perhaps they opportunistically exploited the kills of other animal predators. But there was also evidence of a significant change in behaviour around 55,000 years ago when late Neanderthals in Italy forsook scavenging for hunting. Since then, close examination of more and more sites in Europe has pushed back the origin for the start of hunting by Neanderthals. Now some experts claim that hunting dates back right through 'Neandertime' in Europe and perhaps back over 500,000 years and that prime-age animals were often selected rather than young or weak ones.

Reading the bones

One of the most remarkable sites providing high quality information about Neanderthal hunting behaviour is Salzgitter Lebenstedt in northern Germany, not far from Hanover. Radiocarbon-dated at between 58,000 and 54,000 years old, this site is particularly interesting because it lies close to the northernmost margin of Neanderworld. More strictly, it contains the northernmost Neanderthal remains in continental Europe but it is not far from the Baltic coast, which certainly formed a natural barrier to Neanderworld.

During late glacial times, the site lay at the junction of a steep and narrow valley where it opened out into a wide glacial valley with a large river. A large amount of well-preserved artefacts and animal remains were found buried in waterlogged sediments. Some 840 worked flints have been discovered, including hand-axes, scrapers and Levallois flakes. In addition, over 3000 animal-bone fragments have been found along with the remains of two Neanderthals and thirty bone tools. These bone tools are particularly exciting as they are some of the first unequivocal bone tools to be found associated with Neanderthal remains. They have been whittled from mammoth bone and closely resemble the bone daggers used by today's Sami people to finish off wounded reindeer.

The vast majority of the animal bones are those of reindeer, followed by mammoth, horse, bison, a few woolly rhino and rare wolf remains. Many of the reindeer bones have human-inflicted cut and impact marks while some of the other remains have animal chew marks. Well-preserved plant remains include dwarf birch and cold-adapted willows, characteristic of a shrub tundra environment. Radiocarbon dating and pollen analysis date the remains at around 58,000 to 54,000 years ago, in the last glacial when temperatures were falling.

The fracture patterns on the reindeer bones are typical of bone marrow extraction, but with a pronounced selection of adult bones that contain significantly larger amounts of marrow. The bones come from some eighty-six animals, mostly adult males. The condition of the antlers suggests that the animals died around September.

It was difficult to resolve the length of time over which the remains accumulated, but it is thought that the site was probably used repeatedly over a considerable period of time for autumn hunting of migratory reindeer. Reindeer move in vast herds along well-defined routes and it appears that the Neanderthals' seasonal hunting pattern crossed that of the reindeer at Salzgitter. Presumably, the Neanderthals were taking advantage of the lie of the land to ambush the herds. The hunt itself appears to have been unselective regarding animal size, but subsequently they selected the bones of adults for marrow extraction. This was systematic game processing that was apparently routine for these northern Neanderthals.

ABOVE Skinning game that have tough hides requires sharp blades, and the butchering of carcasses needs heavier choppers – the Neanderthals either had to find suitable stone locally or carry the tools with them when they went hunting.

Altogether, there are now a number of sites in France, Germany and Russia with similarly good evidence for Neanderthal hunting of fully grown members of the Ice Age megafauna, especially bovids. Crude stone tools from these sites support this interpretation. These are all open-air sites, dating from the first half of the last glaciation, and the animal remains are restricted to just a few species. Again there is the suggestion of repeated visits to favoured sites, with hunting focusing on a few animals at a time of one kind. Supporting evidence from Kebara cave in Israel suggests that Middle Palaeolithic Neanderthals were perfectly capable of hunting both large and small game by 60,000 years ago.

Indeed, recent finds take evidence of hunting activities even further back in time. There are signs, from 120,000 years ago, of young woodland rhinos being hunted in the interglacial forests of central Europe. And a yew spear was found at Lehringen in Germany, lying beneath the bones of a straight-tusked elephant, which probably dates from around the same time.

Beyond this time there is still very visible evidence of human interference, in the form of cut and impact marks, on the animal remains. The 200,000-year-old site of Biache-Saint-Vaast in France preserves evidence of a hunting focus on bovids, especially aurochs, which make up some 70 per cent of the bone remains. Here again there is an association with flint Levallois points which some experts believe were used, like the Syrian example, as projectile points for hunting.

Recently, a spectacular series of wooden spears, between 300,000 and 400,000 years old, have been found among the remains of twenty horses at Schöningen in Germany. And in 500,000-year-old deposits at Boxgrove on the south coast of England, a horse shoulder blade is perforated by a circular hole, made by a hunting spear. This same site contains the remains of rhinos, horses and hippos that have been butchered. These two sites suggest that active hunting may have evolved in ancient European humans even before the Neanderthals moved in.

Full circle

Reassessment of Neanderthal hunting proficiency now seems to have gone full circle. There is good evidence of selective killing of particular kinds of large game rather than opportunistic scavenging, which inevitably gathered a greater diversity of animals. Scavenging typically results in incomplete remains of animals being butchered and accumulating at sites. No doubt both strategies were employed by the Neanderthals, depending on availability. The big argument has been about whether they were capable of active confrontational killing of game. The answer seems now to be a definite 'yes', and they may well have been able to employ this mode of hunting right from the start of their occupation of Europe and Eurasia. The remaining question asks how important hunting was relative to scavenging; it is hoped that the use of stable isotope analysis will resolve the issue (see box on pages 54–55).

There is an important caveat to this view. There is, as yet, no evidence about how the kill-sites fit into the wider issue of Neanderthal subsistence. These were temporary sites and do not provide evidence for home-bases or dwelling structures, with sharing of food. What they do indicate is constant Neanderthal mobility within the environment, at times ranging over 100 kilometres (60-odd miles) in the more open northerly landscapes. Movement

was determined primarily by the availability of food. Experts such as Paul Pettitt interpret this as indicating the fundamental opportunism of the Neanderthals, with a decided lack of forward planning or prediction. It was a strategy that worked well while there was plenty of game about. However, the recurrent use of certain sites by Neanderthals does indicate that knowledge of the sites was being transmitted over many generations. Apparently these people had solved the problem of living in a highly seasonal environment and overwintering in a landscape where most food was highly mobile.

In having no evidence of home-bases, these outdoor Neanderthal sites differ significantly from the early Cro-Magnon people who did develop home-bases and build shelters, however temporary. A recent critical review of home-

ABOVE A dead or dying mammoth mired in a boghole would have been easy prey and provided a good supply of food, skin and other materials for the Neanderthals. Sharpened mammoth ribs have been found at a Neanderthal site in Germany.

OPPOSITE Small
mammals were an
important part of the diet;
they were easier to kill
than larger prey, and fast
breeders like rabbits
and birds were
soon replenished.

base evidence claims that only a few possible dwelling structures pre-date the
last glacial maximum but none of these is particularly convincing and none is
more than 30,000 years old – in other words, they were not Neanderthal structures.

Small game looms large

We tend to hear mostly about the big game hunted by our prehistoric relatives
and almost nothing about the smaller animals that formed an important part of
their diet. Reconstructed mammoth hunts are certainly more spectacular than
foraging for limpets on the sea-shore. Also the remains of small animals have
often been overlooked in the past, whereas it is hard to miss a mammoth bone.
Small bones are often lost during the selective processes of burial and
fossilization. However, a very interesting story has been revealed by some
recent detailed analyses of abundant small-animal remains from Palaeolithic
sites in Italy and Israel, which were occupied successively by Neanderthals and
Cro-Magnons.

The archaeological bone evidence shows that a variety of small animals
played an important part in the diet of the Palaeolithic peoples of the
Mediterranean region from around 200,000 years ago until about 10,000 years
ago. The total contribution to the overall diet stayed much the same at about
30–40 per cent of the animal remains found at the sites, but the types of small
game changed significantly. These changes are thought to reflect important
demographic shifts and may well provide some of the first independent dating
of the late Palaeolithic population explosion.

Small game can vary enormously in its biology and ecology. However,
the remains found at the Italian and Israeli sites are restricted to relatively few
species and reflect a mixture of what was most available in the surrounding
landscape and what had preservable hard parts that remain in the fossil record.
Again, the archaeologists have had to distinguish between remains that have
accumulated at sites through human activity and those remains introduced by
other animal predators and scavengers such as wolves. In this situation, the
presence of damage by burning, tool marks and certain breakage patterns can
distinguish human activity from the chew marks left by other animals.

The role of plants, which was also probably very important, is still largely
unknown but some intriguing evidence is emerging from some unlikely sources.
The lower levels of small-game remains in the Italian coastal sites are dominated
(over 90 per cent) by shoreline shellfish, especially limpets and clams such as
oysters, and a small percentage of tortoises. The larger game in these sites,
which comprise more than half the remains, is made up mostly of red deer,
aurochs, roe deer and, occasionally, ibex, wild ass and boar.

By comparison, the Israeli sites are inland and again the lower layers of
remains are dominated by tortoises and legless lizards, with minor amounts of
ostrich eggs, birds (such as chukar partridges) and hares. The accompanying
larger game is mostly mountain gazelle and fallow deer.

Most of the smaller creatures are relatively easy to catch without any special equipment; and, although small in size, they would nevertheless provide invaluable protein, fat and other rare nutrients for the diet. Importantly, much of this game could be caught by women and even children with minimal risk. The ready availability of such easily harvested creatures could significantly enhance the chances of survival of children and lead to population increase. This in turn would create greater predator pressure on the small-game resource, whose sustainability would depend on their reproduction rates.

As archaeologists traced the fossil evidence upwards through Palaeolithic time they found some marked changes in the relative proportions of the various animals. In the Italian sites the change happened around 30,000 years ago and is marked by a dramatic decrease in the proportion of shellfish being exploited (to less than 20 per cent of remains at any one level in the site), accompanied by an equally significant increase in the proportion of rabbit, hare and bird remains. In Israel, the change happened much earlier, over 100,000 years ago, and is marked by a decrease in the proportion of tortoises and increase in birds. Similar changes in small game have been recorded from Palaeolithic sites in Spain and Germany.

There is clearly something very interesting going on here. Birds, hares and rabbits are much more difficult to catch than tortoises and shellfish. So why should the people change their diets to include animals that required much more energy to catch, unless of course they had no option? Perhaps they had over-exploited the resource or there were significantly more mouths to feed, or maybe there was a combination of the two factors. If the latter were true, then perhaps these shifts in prey-species

abundance record important demographic shifts and tell us when they occurred in different parts of the Mediterranean. But how can such ideas be tested?

Alternatively, these changes could have been affected by climate change, but archaeologists have been able to discount this possibility. The relative size of the shellfish and tortoise remains, which are most commonly preserved, show a sudden decrease in size coincident with the shift in proportion of small-game animals. Both shellfish and tortoises are relatively long-living and slow-maturing organisms. Inevitably, the human predators would have preferentially selected the largest because these provide the best nutritional return for the effort spent on recovering them. However, if too many are taken over any one breeding season the populations cannot easily recover and only smaller immature individuals are left.

The suddenness of the change in small-animal size is significant. Between 36,000 and 24,000 years ago there was no change in the average size of limpet shells recovered from the Italian sites. Equally, from 200,000 to 100,000 years ago there was no change in average tortoise size recovered from the Israeli sites; but then the diminution is very marked in both areas. Such size changes have also been recorded in shellfish remains from South Africa and Spain.

The changes seem clearly to be the direct result of over-harvesting and therefore induced by humans. They reflect relatively sudden increases in population densities that happened much earlier in Israel than in Italy and elsewhere in northern Europe. The fact that a much greater proportion of birds and rabbits and hares were subsequently being taken must have signified much greater effort. Also, it probably required the development of much improved and perhaps innovatory hunting technology such as the use of nets and snares. Ecologically, this was an important breakthrough as well because birds and rabbits mature much more quickly than shellfish and tortoises. They can sustain much higher levels of predation on a year-to-year basis (between seven and ten times as great as shellfish and tortoises) and still recover.

The fact that the earlier Palaeolithic small-game patterns involve species that are particularly sensitive to over-predation suggests that the people who were exploiting them were very few in numbers and highly dispersed. This was sustainable hunting by small social groups of Neanderthals. The change in remains of prey seems to have been due to population explosions, and new technology and hunting practice. The new practices did not necessarily require great physical strength but rather attention to detail and small-scale technological innovation and perhaps the use of plant materials for nets.

Biodegradable materials like this are not normally preserved in the fossil record, but there may be indirect evidence for the technological development of fibre-based materials by Cro-Magnon people. The textured impressions of woven fabrics have been found on 27,000-year-old baked clay fragments found at Dolní Věstonice in Moravia. Several of the so-called 'Venus' figurines of Upper Palaeolithic Europe around 28,000 (26,000–23,000 radiocarbon) years old, have curious cap-like ornaments on their heads, which in some examples even obscure the face. The caps have been interpreted as evidence of hair styling, but a new interpretation suggests that their patterns indicate the use of woven material, with considerable sophistication in terms of their knotting techniques. It is further speculated that such techniques would also have allowed the manufacture of nets for trapping small game

– and would have been the province of women and children. For the women the provision of such small but relatively abundant dietary supplements could have made all the difference to the survival of their children, especially in times of environmental deterioration.

The Neanderthals' basic armoury of wooden spears and stone tools must have been adequate for survival in Europe as the only human occupants for nearly 200,000 years – much longer than the occupation by modern humans so far. They survived despite the changing climate as small bands of fairly isolated hunters living a very rough and ready existence in the Ice Age 'game park' surrounded by plentiful animal prey and predators. But from around 40,000 years ago, the Neanderthals faced a new challenge: greater than any they had previously encountered. Bands of people from the south and east began to appear. They were strange-looking, and better armed. What use would the weapons of the Neanderthals be against the technological skills of these Cro-Magnon incomers?

Neanderworld was about to change irrevocably.

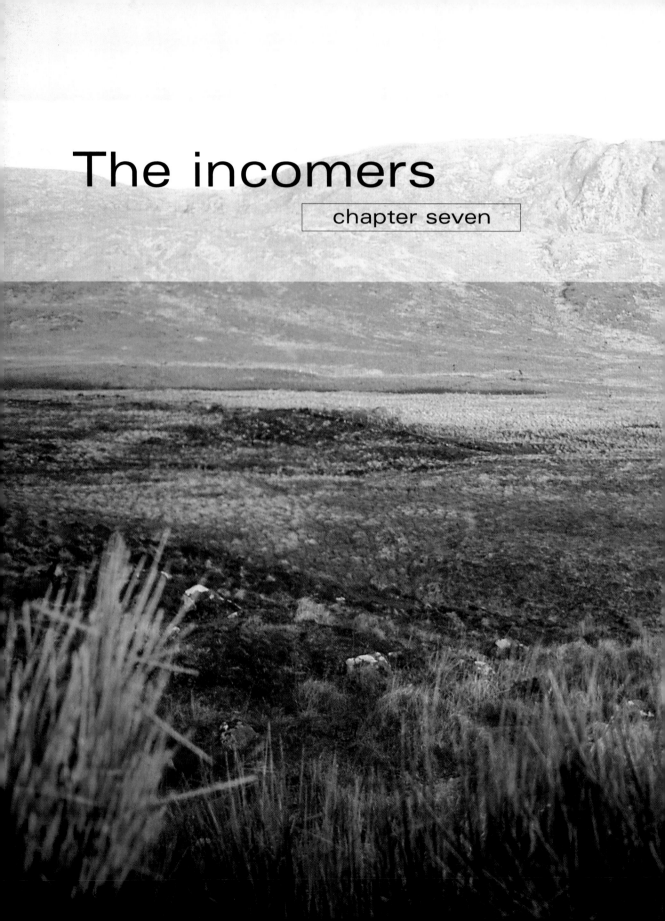

The incomers

chapter seven

NOTHING COULD HAVE PREPARED THE NEANDERTHALS FOR THE shock of their first encounter with the Cro-Magnons. It might even have had the same kind of impact on them as the arrival of extra-terrestrials would have on us. Individually, they would have known that there were other people in their world but until that moment all of them had been recognizable as other Neanderthals. These new people looked different, and behaved in alien ways.

The physical differences would have been striking. Cro-Magnons were taller and more slender, and possibly darker-skinned. While Neanderthals had the squarish heavy build of weightlifters or wrestlers of today, the Cro-Magnons looked like middle-distance runners. The average height of an adult male incomer was 178cm (5ft 10in) and a female 168cm (5ft 6in), some 75–100cm (3–4in) taller than Neanderthal men and women. Most noticeable was the difference in their body proportions, especially the limbs. As we have seen, the Neanderthal body proportions were cold-adapted with relatively short limb extremities. The relative length of the Cro-Magnon shin was about 85 per cent of the thigh, whereas the Neanderthal proportion was about 79 per cent. And the overall length ratios of the Cro-Magnons' arms to their legs were as different. The incomers had the more extended stature of peoples from much warmer climates far to the south. Their bones were less heavily built and less robust, better suited for faster travelling over greater distances but less well suited for close-encounter killing. Their more lightly built pelvis and slightly different hip joints allowed them to walk and run more efficiently.

Face to face, the incomers were different as well. The Cro-Magnon face was distinctly smaller, with finer features and a more prominent chin, which made the mouth look smaller. The nose was also much smaller and the brow-ridge so reduced as to be practically non-existent, while the forehead was much higher. Overall there was little or no difference in brain size between the Cro-Magnons and Neanderthals, but both had a greater capacity than the modern human average. The Cro-Magnon skull was higher domed than the flatter, wider Neanderthal skull.

It was not just the bodies of the new people that were different. They wore more elaborate and 'sophisticated' skin clothing, which was tailored with rough stitching. They were decked out with personal adornments – perforated shells and teeth – and, significantly, they carried a new generation of hunting hardware: more advanced hunting spears.

The Neanderthals would have been at a complete loss to comprehend what was happening. They would have no way of knowing where these strange new people had come from or why they had come. Only now, tens of thousands

THIS SPREAD For 200,000 years or so, the Neanderthals were the only human inhabitants of Europe. Then about 40,000 years ago their dominion faltered as they found themselves face to face with strange humans with a different life-style. We shall never know what went through the minds of these two peoples when they met for the first time.

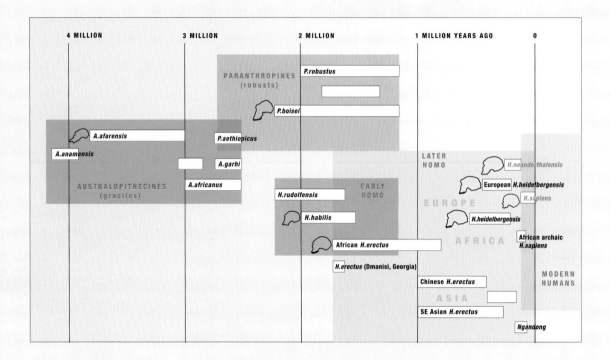

| 4 MILLION | 3 MILLION | 2 MILLION | 1 MILLION YEARS AGO | 0 |

PARANTHROPINES
(robusts)

P.robustus

P.boisei

P.aethiopicus

A.afarensis

A.anamensis

A.garhi

AUSTRALOPITHECINES
(graciles)

A.africanus

H.rudolfensis

EARLY
HOMO

H.habilis

African H.erectus

H.erectus (Dmanisi, Georgia)

Chinese H.erectus

SE Asian H.erectus

LATER
HOMO

H.neanderthalensis

European H.heidelbergensis

H.sapiens

H.heidelbergensis

EUROPE

AFRICA

African archaic
H.sapiens

MODERN
HUMANS

ASIA

Ngandong

THE FAMILY BACKGROUND

The Neanderthals were humans (*Homo neanderthalensis*) but different from us (*Homo sapiens*). We belong to a separate species but share common ancestors who lived between 853,000 and 365,000 years ago. We also share common ancestry with the chimps over 5 million years ago.

The human 'family' (members of the genus Homo) originated in Africa around 2 million years ago from ancient relatives (like *Homo rudolfensis*) who in turn evolved from ape-like but still human relatives: the southern apes or 'australopithecines'. The old idea of a straight evolutionary line of 'ascent' through time has been abandoned. At times, different australopithecines and members of the human genus have coexisted in the same continent.

The so-called human family 'tree' is more of a 'bush' with at least twenty 'branches', whose connections are far from clear. The first humans (*Homo erectus*) left Africa around 2 million years ago and by 1.8 million years ago had reached Georgia and the Far East. It has been established that others got to Spain around 800,000 years ago but there are still vast gaps in our knowledge. In Europe these people eventually evolved into the Neanderthals, *Homo neanderthalensis*.

Meanwhile, in Africa they continued to evolve separately into modern humans and by 125,000 years ago had begun the long march northwards, spreading out in all directions to Asia, the Far East, Australasia and, later, into North America (over 20,000 years ago). They had reached south-west Europe 40,000 years ago, where they are known as Cro-Magnons, and found it already occupied by bands of tough hunters – the Neanderthals.

of years later, are we modern humans able, for the first time, to try to piece together our own ancient history. Such interests are among the few attributes that distinguish us from our immediate human ancestors. But as we have seen, the relatively recent discovery and realization of the significance of our fossil ancestry has not been immediately acceptable. There is still no universally accepted version. To outline the story of Neanderthal and Cro-Magnon ancestry, it is necessary to reach back in time and move geographically south into Africa.

A common ancestry

Despite their differences, the Neanderthals and Cro-Magnons shared a common but deep ancestry in Africa. The process of unravelling this ancestry is ongoing, and new finds can make significant changes to the prevailing view of human evolution. A few decades ago, the most recent part of the story seemed to be fairly straightforward, with a single evolutionary line from 2-million-year-old African ancestors known as *Homo erectus*, who trekked northwards and fanned out into Asia. Then around 500,000 years ago, a more modern but still robust human evolved from *Homo erectus*. These people, called archaic *Homo sapiens* to distinguish them from anatomically modern *Homo sapiens*, were thought to have given rise to the Neanderthals and then later on to anatomically modern *Homo sapiens* – our immediate modern human ancestors. Newer finds have thrown doubts on several aspects of this story; furthermore, there is a fundamental schism in the way the evidence of the bones is interpreted.

Out of Africa

The underlying theory of human evolution which is most widely accepted at the moment is that known as the 'Out of Africa' theory. According to this, the fossil evidence shows that there were two major successive waves of human 'innovation' and replacement. Firstly, from around 2 million years ago, *Homo erectus* swept northwards into Eurasia and beyond. Secondly, around 200,000 years ago and again from Africa, more evolved *Homo sapiens* people moved northwards. In Europe these are the people we know as Cro-Magnons. They encountered the resident Neanderthals and eventually replaced them, just as they replaced the remnant populations of *Homo erectus* in Asia and the Far East. From here, modern humans eventually spread into Australasia and North America. One major implication is that there was no significant, widespread or lasting mixture of Neanderthal and Cro-Magnon features as a result of interbreeding. However, there is an alternative theory.

Multi-regionalism

Essentially, this theory claims that there was only one move out of Africa and that was made by *Homo erectus*. From this single ancient human diaspora, all

RIGHT Two rival theories give alternative explanations for the origin and distribution of modern humans. The 'Multi-regional' idea envisages evolution, extensive interbreeding and gene flow (shown by green arrows) from widely distributed populations of *Homo erectus* to produce today's variety of modern humans. The 'Out of Africa' idea claims a much more recent African origin for *Homo sapiens* and is most in favour. The lack of significant genetic difference between living humans, and existence of interbreeding and gene flow (green arrows), suggest that modern humans share a recent common ancestry. The sold black bars denote the extinction of a species.

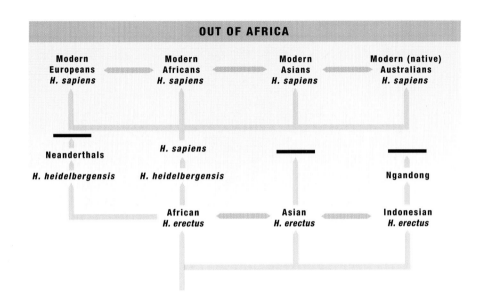

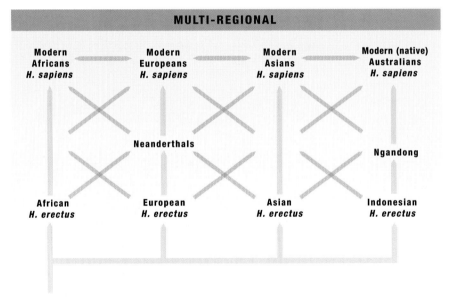

subsequent humans are thought to have evolved (see the box on page 159). According to this theory, modern Europeans have evolved partly from the Neanderthals through the Cro-Magnons. In Asia and the Far East, *Homo erectus* also evolved into *Homo sapiens*. To explain the widespread similarity in the modern human gene pool, the multi-regionalists argue that there was constant interbreeding and gene flow between the evolving populations across Europe and Asia. Consequently, the constant muddying of the gene pool by interbreeding kept the global population on a more or less similar track towards modern humans.

Multi-regionalism

One of the founding fathers of 'Multi-regionalism' was the German-born, Jewish anthropologist Franz Weidenreich, who moved to America in 1934 to avoid growing Nazi persecution. He had studied human evolution from an Asian perspective and believed that the ancestry of modern humans in the Orient could be traced back to an oriental *Homo erectus* stock. Likewise, he thought that a similar stock gave rise to 'Java man' and along a parallel line to living native Australians. As for Neanderthals, Weidenreich claimed them to be 'a widely spread evolutionary phase which may well have perished in one circumscribed territory, but had flourished, expanded and been transmuted somewhere else, and so have given origin to *Homo sapiens*'.

Weidenreich's ideas were taken up by Carleton Coon, an American anthropologist, who in 1962 published a very detailed comparison of the fossil record of human ancestry. Coon proposed that each of the five 'races' of modern humankind that he recognized, those of Asia, Europe, the Americas, Australasia and Central and Southern Africa, had evolved from a 'pre-sapient' population. Each group had separately and at different times crossed the 'critical threshold from a more brutal to a more sapient state'. But added to this analysis was a distinct whiff of white supremacism, with white and oriental populations being more advanced than those of Africa and Australia. According to Coon, 'If Africa was the cradle of mankind, it was only an indifferent kindergarten. Europe and Asia were our principal schools.'

Coon left his interpretation open to abuse by racists, compounding the problem by refusing to openly distance himself from them and being severely criticized as a result. On the purely biological aspect of his ideas, he was particularly taken to task by Theodosius Dobzhansky, an American geneticist who was one of the founders of modern genetics. Dobzhansky pointed out just how unlikely it is, from the biological point of view, that *Homo sapiens* should have evolved on five separate occasions from *Homo erectus*.

But the idea was not yet dead in the water. A group of anthropologists resurrected it with an important modification designed to try and overcome the problem of how such separate development could produce the underlying similarities in modern humans. They invoked regular gene flow between the five 'racial' groups, through interbreeding. They now tend to emphasize how modern features 'coalesced' from different sources around the world.

However, as another scholar of human prehistory, Philip Rightmire, points out, 'Lumping distinctive populations like Neanderthals … together with *Homo erectus* … is not going to help us explore the patterns of evolutionary change that ultimately produced populations like us.'

The trouble with fossils

One of the major problems with trying to put together the human story is that there are so few fossil clues as to what might have happened. Human remains do not preserve very well unless buried in the right conditions. Most early human remains were preserved only by accident; purposeful burial does not appear to have become common until the first appearance of people such as the Cro-Magnons – although some Neanderthals and early modern humans who lived in the Middle East (at the Skhūl and Qafzeh sites, for example) were also intentionally buried. In addition, the increase in human numbers that accompanied the Cro-Magnon incursion and takeover in Europe greatly increased the chances of their remains being fossilized, either accidentally or as a result of ceremonial burial.

The fossil record of human ancestry is incredibly gappy, with so few remains scattered over continents and a vast timescale that challenges the imagination.

New views on human ancestry

The jigsaw put together twenty or so years ago, to explain the distribution in time and space of human fossil remains then known, has had to be extensively revised. The old neat explanation was based on a picture that had more gaps than pieces. We still do not have the final picture – far from it – which is one of the reasons why the study of our human ancestry is so continuously fascinating. An outline of the human story so far gives some idea of its emerging complexity.

Palaeontologists trace our beginnings back to the first upright walking group of primates (hominids) to emerge from the forests of Africa, over 4.4 million years ago. The oldest of these hominids (*Ardipithecus ramidus*) is known only from fragmentary remains found in Ethiopia, but seems to have been distinctly ape-like. Better known is the slightly younger *Australopithecus anamensis* from northern Kenya, which is about 4.2–3.9 million years old. This australopithecine (literally meaning 'southern ape') was quite small, standing about 120cm (3ft 11in) high and weighing 50–55kg (8st–8st 10lb); an upright walker (biped), it was small-brained (350–500ml capacity), with a relatively big face that still retained a prominent ape-like muzzle and flat nose. It also retained some anatomical features that suggest it was still capable of knuckle walking and climbing trees, very much like its arboreal ape ancestors.

Australopithecus anamensis was rather like the somewhat younger *A. afarensis* (3.8–3.0 million years ago), to which the famous 'Lucy' (the first partial skeleton of an ancient human relative to be found, see page 65–66) belonged. Lucy and her relatives were widely spread over East Africa but they were not alone. The distinctive jawbone of another contemporary australopithecine (*A. bahrelghazali*) was recently found in Chad, far to the west of the East African 'Eden' of the Great Rift Valley, and alerts us to the fact that these australopithecines were already diverging into a number of different kinds; we have found only a very small sample of their populations so far. Indeed, another new and as yet unnamed australopithecine relative, some 3.3 million years old, has recently been found in southern Africa.

Around 3 million years ago, southern Africa saw the emergence of yet another australopithecine (*A. africanus*). This was the first of the southern apes to be found in modern times (1924) and described to an incredulous scientific community back in 1925 by Raymond Dart. Still not much more than 140cm (4ft 7in) in height, weighing up to 60kg (9st 7lb) and with a similar brain size to the earlier australopithecines, these hominids were no longer capable of knuckle walking. But a recent analysis suggests that some of them may still have been adept climbers. They appear to have survived for a million years.

About 2.5 million years ago there was a further splitting up of these hominids into new groups with the appearance of the first of the robust australopithecines (*Paranthropus aethiopicus*), and not long after this the first members of the human genus *Homo*. For well over a million years (from 2.5 to 1.2 million years ago) several of the heavily built 'robusts' evolved in eastern and southern Africa. They were slightly taller and brainier than the earlier australopithecines, but they were also more heavily built and, like the more advanced australopithecine species, these 'robusts' did not knuckle walk.

The tree-living habit had well and truly been left behind by this time, but the plant-eating habits of their ancestors had not and they still had very ape-like faces with powerful muscular jaws. Although their brain capacity was slightly larger at 410–530ml, this was mainly related to their increased body weight (up to 80kg/12st 8lb), which correlates with brain size. They seem to have been a successful group but nevertheless an evolutionary cul-de-sac. Further evolution in the hominids seems to have originated from the more slenderly built (so-called gracile) australopithecines such as *A. garhi*, another newly named and imperfectly known species from Ethiopia which has been dated at about 2.5 million years old and must have lived alongside the 'robusts'.

The next big change, as identified from the fossil record, is the first appearance of the human genus *Homo* around 2.3 million years ago. There is considerable diversity within the fossil remains of these most ancient of humans and many of the fossils are extremely fragmentary.

Inevitably, there is disagreement among experts over which genus some of these new species belonged to. Two of the earliest species, *rudolfensis* and *habilis*, are shuffled about between the genus *Homo* and the genus *Australopithecus*. Around 2 million years ago, East Africa was a hotbed of hominid evolution with at least four species belonging to robust and gracile australopithecines, and the emerging humans sharing the same landscapes.

These earliest human relatives were anatomically still quite similar to australopithecines such as *A. africanus* and *A. garhi*. *Homo habilis* (2.0–1.6 million years ago) was the first to be found in the late 1950s by Mary and Louis Leakey at Olduvai in Tanzania. It was thought to have been the first hominid to make and use basic stone tools, but it still retained a rather small brain, large

Atapuerca

In 1994, reworking of the nineteenth-century site of Gran Dolina on Atapuerca Hill in Spain revealed an ancient fissure in the limestone rock, filled with an astonishing jumble of human bones: the remains of over thirty men, women and children. The dating of these remains as more than 780,000 years old surprised and excited the experts because they fell right in the middle of a gap in the fossil record.

Just to add to the excitement, stone tools and animal remains were found. The face, possibly of a boy, was particularly interesting because it showed some familiar, modern-looking features – sunken cheekbones, a projecting nose and midface. Also, there is a distinct horizontal rather than vertical ridge where the upper teeth attach to the upper jaw. Mixed with these modern features are some more archaic ones, such as a prominent brow-ridge and multiple-rooted premolar teeth. The Spanish scientists tried to 'shoehorn' these features into a match with those known from archaic humans, otherwise known as *Homo heidelbergensis*. They concluded that the size of the misfit was sufficiently great to require the establishment of a new species of human, which they have called *Homo antecessor*, meaning 'one who goes first'.

The next problem was to see where the new human fitted into the prevailing evolutionary scheme. The pre-existing scheme would predict that it fell into line between *Homo erectus* and archaic modern humans. But instead, the Spanish team argue that the new contender actually has closer affinities with a much older African human species, *Homo ergaster*, who lived between 1.9 and 1.4 million years ago. Furthermore, they argue that their 'new human' has 'exactly the morphology we would imagine in the common ancestor of modern humans and Neanderthals'.

Such big claims, if correct, give the Atapuerca human a pivotal role in human evolution over the last 1.8 million years. The new Spanish version would run thus: well over a million years ago, *H. ergaster* gave rise to *Homo antecessor* in Africa. *H. antecessor* then spread out of Africa around a million years ago, reaching Spain by 800,000 years ago. Some of them evolved into *H. heidelbergensis* and headed further north into Europe where they evolved into Neanderthals. Meanwhile, southern *H. antecessor*, still in Africa, gave rise to modern humans via some as yet unknown intermediary. A few bones can make a surprising difference.

The implications for the position and role of *H. erectus* and *H. heidelbergensis* are drastic: both are effectively sidelined from the ancestry of modern humans. Needless to say, such revolutionary drafting of the storyboard, on the basis of such fragmentary skeletal evidence, does not tend to be accepted overnight by other experts. One of the most worrying aspects is that the whole new interpretation hinges on facial characters of a child. It is well known that juvenile traits can be deceptive; for the story to be more acceptable, comparison with an adult of the same kind is needed.

Conversely, the *H. erectus–heidelbergensis–sapiens* linkage is now pretty well established with supporting fossil evidence, even if it is far from being watertight. We will have to wait and see if Atapuerca's new human is truly 'one who went first' or is itself another evolutionary cul-de-sac.

teeth, a big projecting face and flat nose, which is why some experts still place it in the genus *Australopithecus*. The number of species of early human relatives is also a matter of considerable argument. The more recent recognition of *Homo rudolfensis* (2.3–1.7 million years ago) is based largely on a distinctive skull with a somewhat larger brain capacity (averaging 700ml).

The first of the human relatives that we know to have had a basically modern body form was *Homo ergaster* (1.9–1.4 million years ago). The discovery of the so-called 'Nariokotome' or 'Turkana boy', dated at about 1.5 million years old, has greatly improved understanding of these ancient human relatives. Analysis of the almost complete skeleton has shown that he was an adolescent, about 11 years old, stood some 160cm (5ft 3in) tall and would have grown to an imposing 185cm (6ft 1in) when adult. His skull has a smaller jaw and chewing teeth than earlier hominids. Small cheek teeth are more suited to eating meat than tough plant material. Some experts have argued that this change in diet from plant to meat eating was a crucial factor in promoting the dispersal of humans because, as carnivores, they would have needed larger territories than their plant-eating ancestors. Others have argued that it was the possession of tools and larger brains that prompted the first major dispersal.

The first evidence that there must have been a major dispersal event quite early in human evolution came from Eugene Dubois's discovery of 'Java Man' in 1891 (see page 27). The dating of what is now known as an Asian *Homo erectus* is still disputed and ranges between 1.8 and 1.0 million years ago. The famous Beijing fossils (previously called Peking Man), found in the 1920s and subsequently lost, are estimated to be even younger at around 400,000 years old. Nevertheless, the evidence suggests that ancient, stone-tool-using bipeds had migrated out of Africa and had reached as far away as south-east Asia. There are similarly problematic and ancient teeth and jaw fragments from Longgupo cave in China, which have been dated at 1.9 million years old, but some experts are not convinced they are human. However, a startling new find from Dmanisi, just east of the Black Sea in Georgia, and re-evaluation of an earlier find has provided some really convincing evidence for an early dispersal of archaic humans out of Africa.

The first European humans

Two remarkably primitive-looking human skulls and over 1000 stone tools have been excavated from Ice Age deposits at Dmanisi. The site forms a natural defensive prominence above the confluence of the Masavera and Pinezouari Rivers, and is around 1.7 million years old. The simple form of the 'tool-kit' closely resembles those of similar age found in Africa, where they are known as Oldowan (originally named after Olduvai Gorge in Tanzania where they were first found). And the skulls are like those of similar age from Africa.

This is the oldest Eurasian site with tools of this primitive kind, and the discovery has doubled the age of the oldest-known Eurasian humans. The implications for the story of this part of human evolution is still being worked out.

Until this Georgian discovery and other recent finds in Spain and Italy, the European hominid record did not begin until about half a million years ago.

The Dmanisi excavation has been ongoing since the 1980s; quite early in the proceedings a lower jaw was found, but its provisional dating of 1.8 million years was not generally accepted. Independent dating of a volcanic lava layer and associated fossils of the extinct rodent *Mimomys*, which lived between 2 million and 1.6 million years ago, now confirm the antiquity of the site. One of the human skulls is that of an adult male with a braincase capacity of about 780ml, and the smaller skull, which may be that of an adolescent girl, is 650ml in volume. The skulls have prominent brow-ridges like those of the Neanderthals and other early humans, but here they also retain another primitive feature. Behind the brow-ridge there is an abrupt narrowing of the skull before it expands to form the main dome of the skull cap. The same feature is found in australopithecine and the earliest human relatives such as *Homo ergaster* and *Homo erectus* from Africa. The effect is to emphasize the brow-ridge, which looks almost like a visor.

The Dmanisi people had only simple stone tools – flakes, scrapers and various choppers. How they managed to survive, travelling over 6000 kilometres (around 3700 miles) with just simple tools like these, is quite astonishing. Perhaps we are getting only a tantalizing glimpse of a much more complex story. However, the picture we have so far does seem to reinforce the view that it was biology rather than technology that allowed them to migrate so far so quickly. Previously, it was thought that migration out of Africa had depended, at least in part, on the development of the more advanced stone technology of the Acheulian tradition, as is found at the 1.5-million-year-old site of 'Ubeidiya in Israel.

Now, as Ian Tattersall, a palaeoanthropologist at the American Museum of Natural History in New York, says, 'The story is looking strong that up until 1.9 million years ago the only hominids were archaic and restricted to the forest fringes of Africa. Somehow a modern body was acquired, then all hell broke loose and this strutting biped was mobile enough to set out of the forest fringes and walk out of Africa.'

How exactly the Dmanisi people got to Georgia and where they went from there is still unknown. The likelihood is that they would have taken an east African coastal route north through the Red Sea, or up the Nile valley then along the eastern Mediterranean coast and through the Aegean into the Black Sea. From there, they probably went east and gave rise to the Asian populations of *Homo erectus* – but this is highly speculative. The real puzzle now is the million-year European gap between the 1.7-million-year-old Dmanisi people and the next youngest evidence, which comes from Ceprano in Italy (800,000–900,000 years old but the dating is in doubt) and the oldest layers of Atapuerca in Spain (780,000 years old), both of which contain Oldowan-type stone tools.

The oldest Atapuercan remains have been distinguished as yet another human species, *Homo antecessor*, a very fragmentary and controversial one at that, which the Spanish archaeologists claim was the link between a lineage to both Neanderthals and modern humans (see the box on page 162). Then about

600,000 years ago there is fossil evidence in Africa for a new, more advanced human. Some experts refer to these humans as archaic *Homo sapiens*, while others prefer to distinguish them as a separate human species, *Homo heidelbergensis*. Their fossil remains are subsequently also found at sites in Europe and Asia between 500,000 and 200,000 years ago. This widespread group of ancient humans includes a diversity of forms and may well end up by being split into several species. It is generally thought that in Europe *H. heidelbergensis* was ancestral to the Neanderthals, while in Africa the remaining population of *H. heidelbergensis* evolved independently into another human species, *H. sapiens*, over 150,000 years ago.

Making modern 'man'

The actual origin of modern humans is not clear in detail. Most of the evidence points to an origin in Africa some time between 200,000 and 150,000 years ago, while the Neanderthals were becoming established in Europe. But there is a big gap before that African origin and no clear link, as yet, with any of the older human species. Nevertheless, it is now generally accepted that for modern humans, Africa is 'the Garden of Eden', the ancestral homeland. However, the question of when and why early *Homo sapiens* first left Africa is another highly contentious issue. Was there just one or several human diaspora and which way did they go?

A new discovery of stone tools at Abdur on the Eritrean shores of the Red Sea has provided some new clues that might help answer some of these questions. The tools were embedded with animal bones and shelly reef debris, which can be reliably dated to 125,000 years ago. The stone tools themselves include hand-axes and obsidian flakes, which characteristically belong within the Middle Stone Age of Africa (equivalent to the European Middle Palaeolithic, where such tools were made by Neanderthals). No human bones have yet been found but fossils of *Homo sapiens* belonging to this time span have been found in nearby Ethiopia (Omo Kibish) and Sudan (Singa), and further afield in Kenya (Guomde) and Israel (Skhūl and Qafzeh), so there is a reasonable chance that they were made by early modern humans.

This is the first well-dated evidence that early modern humans were living in this coastal area during the last interglacial and probably using the readily available marine food resources. If so, this implies a significant change in human adaptive ability at the time. It may also indicate that they were using the eastern coastal route for their exodus from Africa. Previously, it was thought that coastal food resources were not exploited until much later during the Eurasian Upper Palaeolithic, from around 40,000 years ago. But in recent years the origination of this mode of food gathering has been pushed further and further back.

Coastal resources are now known to have been exploited by both early modern humans in southern Africa (Klasies Cave and Herold's Bay Cave) and Neanderthals on the northern shores of the Mediterranean (Vanguard Cave, Gibraltar, and Moscerini Cave, Italy) during the Middle Palaeolithic. But unfortunately much of the evidence for seaside dwelling is now drowned

beneath today's high sea-levels, which started to rise around 12,000 years ago when the last glacial ended.

New evidence from Australia suggests that modern humans reached that continent at least by 50,000 years ago and before the main development of Upper Palaeolithic bladed stone tools. It could have been significantly earlier since a south-eastern Australian site where there was symbolic use of red ochre has just been redated at 60,000 years old. Their colonization of Australasia must have happened by boat because sea-levels were high at the time and there were no land bridges. If this important Australian evidence is correctly dated then it implies that the elements of modern human behaviour were in place by well before 60,000 years ago.

The Red Sea find supports this idea and fills in another piece of the jigsaw. The exodus of early-modern, Middle Palaeolithic, people from Africa might have followed the eastern coastal route along the shorelines of Arabia, around the Indian peninsula to south-east Asia and on to Australia. There were several advantages to taking the coastal route. Passage was generally easier and there was less danger from predators. Nutritious food was readily available from shellfish and small game. Coastal climates were ameliorated by the sea and not so subject to the wide fluctuations of the latter part of the Ice Age. Also, such coastal migration might explain why the modern humans did not immediately replace older populations living inland in Indonesia.

The same coastal route explanation can probably be applied to the movement of modern humans along the eastern and northern Mediterranean coast before moving into the continental heartlands of the Neanderthals in western Europe.

The cause for the movement out of Africa most likely relates to climate change. Between 190,000 and 140,000 years ago, during the penultimate glaciation, the North African climate became increasingly dry. There was renewed aridity at the peak of the last interglacial around 120,000 years ago. The phases of hyper-aridity may well have destabilized the ecology and communities of the continental interior. The lakes and rivers of East Africa would have shrunk considerably and there would have been fierce competition for dwindling resources, perhaps enough to have forced the early modern humans to the coast. Once there, they would be safe from competition by large terrestrial animals. However, at the peak of aridity, even the coast of the Red Sea itself would have been uninhabitable because of a lack of fresh water. The people would have had to move on.

When modern humans arrived in the Middle East it was already occupied by scattered bands of Neanderthals; the moderns may have been just as surprised by the encounter as the original inhabitants. As we have seen, the archaeological evidence from the Levant suggests that there was quite a lengthy overlap between the two peoples, much longer than occurred further to the north-west in Europe. One of these peoples was destined for extinction. Before that eclipse, was there a meeting of alien minds – and perhaps more?

Culture shocks

ARCHAEOLOGICAL EVIDENCE FROM THE 200,000 YEARS OF Neandertime – the sites, the people's stone tools and other artefacts – shows remarkably little change over most of this lengthy period. This stability might seem puzzling when the background climate was often changing rapidly, swinging back and forth between colder and warmer conditions. However, there were intriguing shifts and changes in tool production technology, site distribution and social patterns among the Neanderthals, especially in the latter part of the Middle Palaeolithic (Mousterian). Some of these appear to have been cyclical and may well have been responses to climate change. One of the great challenges to archaeologists over recent decades has been to match the greatly improving knowledge of climate change with evidence for change in environments, faunas and artefacts and their distribution through the latter part of the Ice Age.

However, none of these changes was as drastic as the 'big break' that occurred between 40,000 and 35,000 years ago, marking the end of the Middle Palaeolithic. There are a number of issues here that need to be clarified in order to assess the magnitude of the break. What were the behavioural changes and how reliably can they be interpreted from the archaeological record? Can they be linked to population change and specifically to the arrival of the Cro-Magnons? If such a link can be established, it is likely that there was some contact between the incomers and the resident Neanderthals. If so, what was the nature of that contact? Why did this encounter between the two peoples happen when it did, right in the middle of the last glaciation?

The rise of the 'chattering classes'

Symbolism, art and language are the most important pieces of technical equipment in the human repertoire. Symbolism and art have a greater permanence than language, and allow communication and identification to be extended over a greater distance than the immediacy and transience of the spoken word. The development of language has enabled more complex information and ideas to be communicated between individuals, and allowed modern humans to dominate much of the Earth. Unfortunately words do not fossilize, but art and material symbols can. Nevertheless, as we have seen, there is evidence from brain casts and rare fossilized parts of the vocal apparatus which tell us that Neanderthals possessed some ability to speak. But language is not just about physiology or neurology; it is about understanding, thought abstraction and

80,000
years ago

70,000
years ago

60,000
years ago

50,000
years ago

40,00
years a

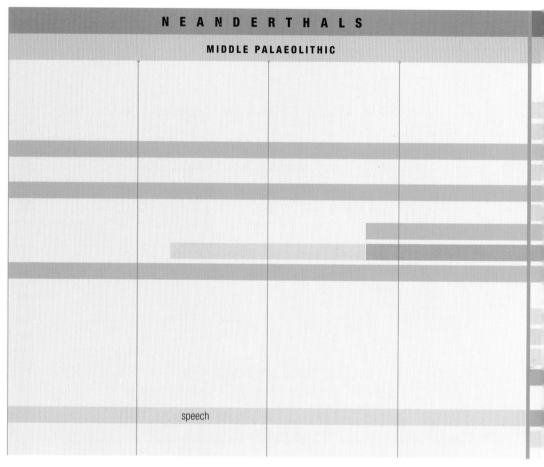

culture, and there are considerable questions about the extent to which the Neanderthals were capable of these.

Abstract thought and complex language are inextricably linked to planning, survival and productivity in humans. The manufacture of artefacts requires certain cognitive skills, conceptualization and the ability to communicate these skills from generation to generation primarily by example but also by language. Tools talk, if only indirectly, and the existence of increasingly sophisticated tools is probably indicative of increased language skills. The fossil evidence from sophisticated stone tools and other artefacts such as jewellery and art suggests abstract thought. There is a general absence of these artefacts from Neanderthal sites before 40,000 years ago, whereas when the Cro-Magnons appear in Europe they seem to have arrived already equipped with more sophisticated tools and personal accoutrements.

The basic tool-kit of the Neanderthals changed very little and does not

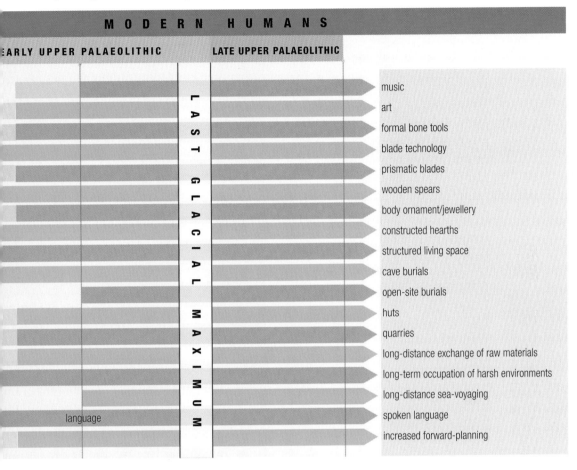

30,000 years ago	20,000 years ago	10,000 years ago

MODERN HUMANS

EARLY UPPER PALAEOLITHIC | LATE UPPER PALAEOLITHIC

LAST GLACIAL MAXIMUM

- music
- art
- formal bone tools
- blade technology
- prismatic blades
- wooden spears
- body ornament/jewellery
- constructed hearths
- structured living space
- cave burials
- open-site burials
- huts
- quarries
- long-distance exchange of raw materials
- long-term occupation of harsh environments
- long-distance sea-voyaging
- spoken language
- increased forward-planning

language

appear to have been developed technically until around the time they came into contact with the Cro-Magnons. This technical conservatism suggests that they were unable to introduce or sustain radical new ideas such as those associated with the development of new technology. For example, they appear not to have fully realized the potential uses of bone as a material for tools, although there are now some well-documented examples of simple bone tools made by Neanderthals. The problem seems to have been that the Neanderthals treated bone as if it were a brittle stone material rather than as a more plastic medium that in fact can be fashioned into a wide variety of forms. The prevailing argument at the moment is that, as with their technology, the language of the Neanderthals was probably fairly basic and did not develop to any great extent. But as we shall see, not all experts accord with this view.

Neanderthal social groupings also support the idea that their language was strictly limited. Social relationships would have been easy to maintain within

ABOVE Archaeological evidence for cultural, technological and behavioural developments in Europe show a marked change between 40,000 and 35,000 years ago when the Cro-Magnons first appeared. The archaeological record reflects the developmental differences between these two peoples.

the small Neanderthal groups. In such tight-knit bands gesture, body-language, social grooming and a limited functional language are all that is necessary to achieve the necessary social cohesion. Only where experience is very wide-ranging and diverse is it necessary to have an extended vocabulary and complex sentence structure.

Some experts claim that Neanderthal language would have been very limited in vocabulary and grammar, with a concentration on the present tense. It may well have been like that of young children or the pidgin language of tourists in a foreign country, allowing communication about basic needs and the 'here and now' but not much more. However, research has shown that even chimps can in fact make generalizations about the past. The implication is that if chimps have this capacity then it is likely the Neanderthals did too, and probably to a more developed extent. So perhaps the Neanderthal language capacity is being underestimated.

As the sole human occupants of Europe for so much time, and operating in small independent bands within fairly constrained territories, there was not much need for a complex language to engage with the world at large. However, the Neanderthal world was suddenly turned upside-down with the arrival of the Cro-Magnons. There is clear evidence from their use of art and symbolism that the incomers did have complex language. Whether either side ever got to communicate in words, we shall never know – but coping with the contact probably would have been a much greater problem for the Neanderthals.

Nature or nurture?

One of the longest-running arguments in the study of language is whether its structure is learned or innate. Noam Chomsky rekindled the debate back in the 1950s, when he claimed that children's ability to master complex language with ease suggests that the skill must be 'hard-wired' into the human brain. In other words, language and grammar might have a genetic basis. This would explain why there appear to be some universal grammatical constructs, and why there are not more types of language in the world. Linguists have been trying to test out these ideas ever since. There developed a widespread agreement that at least some grammar, such as the constructs for framing questions, is universal and therefore innate. But there are bitter academic arguments about the exact nature of this universal grammar and questions over how extensive it is.

One of the most basic attributes of any primitive language would relate to spatial concepts. Thinking spatially is a necessity for higher animals, especially social hunters, and is perhaps the one basic attribute that is most likely to be hard-wired into the brain. If this is so, then perhaps there should be a basic common mode of expression of spatial concepts in all human languages. In trying to explore this possibility, linguists have been surprised to find significant cultural variation.

Many languages express spatial concepts with reference to body orientation, such as left/right, front/back. However, there are languages in remote parts of the world, especially Australia and South America, which express spatial concepts very differently. For instance, there is an Australian aboriginal language, Guugu Yimithirr, spoken by fewer than 800 people, which uses external fixed reference points in the surrounding landscape, perhaps because orientation within a difficult environment can be a matter of life and death for them. Here, even when a part of the body is being mentioned, it is referred to the nearest fixed point in the landscape. Rather than saying, 'There is an ant on your left knee,' they would say, 'There is an ant on your leg near the river.'

The use of such a system is difficult to learn for young children with limited experience of their local environment, but they learn remarkably quickly. Indeed, there is evidence that all very young children can master the system used by their own culture. This suggests that spatial thinking is learned rather than innate and again raises questions about the existence of any universal grammar.

Another basic feature of language has to deal with the concept of time. As we have seen, there is evidence that chimps have some generalized concept of the recent past and it is certain that Neanderthals would have significantly more aware of temporal concepts than chimps. But we have no idea of just how developed their awareness of time might have been since there are no convincing artefacts with representations of repeated units of space or time. All the evidence, both anatomical and cultural, suggests that the Cro-Magnons were linguistically more able.

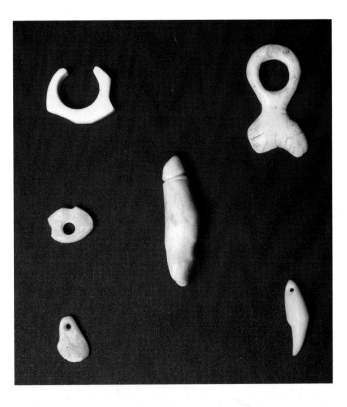

ABOVE There are very few bone and animal tooth pendants found in Châtelperronian levels associated with the Neanderthals. Jewellery such as this, found at Arcy-sur-Cure in central France, suggests that Neanderthals were mimicking Cro-Magnon body ornaments.

Cultured Cro-Magnons

Analysis of the movement of Cro-Magnon tools and artefacts in Europe shows that there was trade between groups, which would have promoted the development of language. Such trade connections would also have provided a vehicle for other kinds of exchange such as information and ideas. The Cro-Magnon world was more complex, their horizons wider than those of the

Neanderthals. Perhaps most important of all for hunter-gatherers, the tool-kits and weaponry of the Cro-Magnons were technically more advanced and still developing. The global arms race was under way.

These radical developments in technology, with their increasing use of new materials, and the culturally associated innovations in terms of ornament and symbolic products almost certainly reflect profound changes in the social, cognitive and probably language patterns of the Cro-Magnons.

Cro-Magnon tools

The incomers brought a new stone technology with them. Their ancestors had discovered the technique of making longer and thinner blades. These had several advantages: more blades could be produced from a single core and they were lighter but just as effective as earlier tools and in some instances more so. There were new forms of scrapers and bladelets, and blades with heavily retouched edges that improved their cutting ability. More dramatic was the burst in technical and cultural development by the incomers through working of more plastic materials such as antler, bone and ivory into a new generation of tools, weapons and other kinds of cultural artefacts of symbolic and ornamental use and value. Overall, this new technology is characterized as Aurignacian throughout Europe.

Points, tubes and perforated batons were made by cutting and grooving as well as by new techniques such as fine sawing and grinding. Despite the rare occurrence of bone tools in Middle Palaeolithic sites, such as the pointed mammoth rib bones found at the open-air site of Salzgitter-Lebenstedt in northern Germany, this Aurignacian industry represented a radical technical innovation.

BELOW The base of this reindeer antler, from the Upper Palaeolithic (Magdalenian) site of Bruniquel in France, has been grooved by the sawing action of a stone tool. The antler may have been used by Cro-Magnons as a portable lap bench or rest for cutting other materials on.

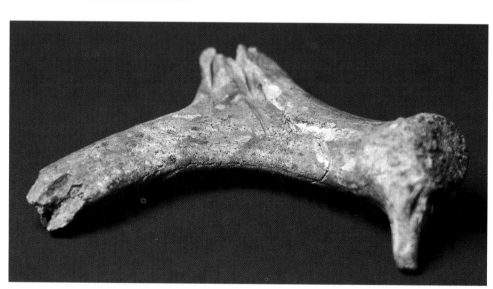

Creative expression

The same animal-derived materials were used for another completely innovative purpose. Hand-in-hand with the new tools appears a variety of perforated beads and pendant-like ornaments made from teeth, bone and shells. For instance, over 1000 ivory and stone beads have been found at three adjacent early Aurignacian sites in south-west France.

Perforated seashells and imitations of them, made from mammoth ivory, have also been found at sites in the same region. Their occurrence is particularly remarkable because their origin can be reliably traced. Some have come from the Atlantic coast, some 200 kilometres (125 miles) to the west, and others are Mediterranean species that have been carried some 300 kilometres (185 miles) from the south-east. This reflects a major change in social habit; there is no evidence of Neanderthals transporting such apparently non-functional goods over such distances.

The dramatic appearance of carved and engraved animalistic figures in the archaeological record is essentially linked to the early Aurignacian, and has been dated to around 32,000 to 30,000 years ago. Even some of the spectacular painted images on cave walls, such as Chauvet in Ardeche, which is dated to around 32,000–31,000 years ago, can now be linked to the Aurignacian. The technical mastery of the images suggests that they must have come from a more ancient tradition of which we know nothing as yet. Our modern term 'art' is all too easily applied to such work but it is probably quite inappropriate. It is very difficult to know exactly why such objects were being made – certainly not for sale. On the other hand, neither were they the equivalent of today's amateur 'dabbler'.

The nearest modern equivalent is the manufacture of the few remaining, truly aboriginal or tribal works of symbolic expression. Like the most powerful examples of tribal work, many of these often sophisticated and beautifully executed ancient works are impressive by any standards. Found more or less simultaneously throughout Aurignacian sites in western and central Europe, they signify an intriguing burst of symbolic expression.

The caves of southern Germany have provided some of the most famous carvings, such as the animal figures from the Vogelherd, carved in mammoth ivory, and the figure from the Höhlenstein-Stadel which combines human and animal features in the shape of a lion-headed man. The figures clearly represent contemporary megafauna animals of the Ice Age: plant-eating prey animals such as horse, mammoth and bison, but also including images of carnivorous predators such as big cats.

The depictions are also evidently much more than simple attempts at realism. The image is simplified without being caricatured; there seems to be an aura of reverence about them. The objects are clearly designed to be handled and most probably had some symbolic function. There is also a range of abstract symbols and carvings, some of which have been interpreted as sexual symbols and linked to fertility magic. But the dating is often highly problematic and experts on Ice Age art, such as Paul Bahn, question whether they are indeed sexual symbols. Even more puzzling is the proliferation of abstract motifs across Europe. At their most simple they can consist of notches on pieces of bone or ivory, which may be simple tally devices. But there are other more complex patterns of dots and lines carefully carved on to relatively soft but otherwise durable surfaces where they persist. It has been speculated that they might be calendars or number systems.

There is no comparable material found in the older Middle Palaeolithic sites occupied by the Neanderthals. The marked change in type and variety of such artefacts signifies a major shift in personal and more general cultural expression.

Trading places?

Crossing the Middle into Upper Palaeolithic boundary sees evidence for a considerable expansion of distribution and 'commercial' or trading networks. With regard to stone materials for tools, the expansion is largely one of degree. As we have seen, in the Middle Palaeolithic, the Neanderthals were developing some long-range supply routes for certain materials, although these comprise a very small proportion (1–2 per cent) of tools recovered by archaeologists. By comparison, Aurignacian sites across Europe from south-western France to northern Spain, southern Germany and Bulgaria preserve evidence of a marked increase in the magnitude (20–25 per cent in some sites) of high quality stone imports from considerable distances.

The most impressive evidence for marked change in distribution networks and perhaps trade between groups of Cro-Magnons comes from the marine shells found hundreds of kilometres inland from their original coastal sites. The movement of such small objects over such distances suggests the existence of exchange or barter between groups. It may be concluded that although changes do occur in the patterning of Middle Palaeolithic artefacts and hence the concepts behind them, the changes are much simpler and less extensive than those encountered in the Upper Palaeolithic. According to Paul Mellars, such changes may well 'reflect significant social, demographic or cultural divisions within Middle Palaeolithic populations'. But the further implication is that the 'jump' into Upper Palaeolithic tool patterns reflects even greater social changes.

Tool technology

The Neanderthals cannot but have been aware of the superiority of the incomers' tool-kits and the improved hunting techniques that went with them. There is intriguing evidence to suggest that from 38,000 (36,000 radiocarbon) years ago the Neanderthals began to make some advances themselves. Several Neanderthal sites in south-western France and the adjacent Pyrenees preserve evidence of a new kind of tool tradition, which has been called the Châtelperronian after one of these sites.

ABOVE Châtelperronian tools from the original site of Châtelperron from where they were first found and described.

FOLLOWING SPREAD From what is known so far of the fossil distribution of the first humans (*Homo erectus*) to leave Africa, their route took them as far as the Far East and into western Europe. Some of the sites of more ancient human occupation are also shown.

Here, more slender blades, scrapers, burins (elongated blades with a narrow end or point, probably used for boring or making grooves) and tools made of animal bones and antlers have been found along with simple ornamental pieces, such as perforated shells and animal teeth. When they were first found it was, not surprisingly, assumed that they had been made by the Cro-Magnon incomers. However, one of the most distinctive of these Châtelperronian tool types is a curved, pointed and blunt-backed blade, which is conspicuously absent from Aurignacian sites in the same region. But there are some possible precursors within the older Mousterian tradition of the Neanderthals, and this has led to some interesting speculation and not a little argument among archaeologists.

However, there is evidence from France which supports the association of the Châtelperronian with the Neanderthals. In 1979 a partial skeleton and skull of an undoubted Neanderthal (36,000 years old), along with some well-formed flint blades, were found at the rock shelter site of Saint-Césaire. The bones and blades were found all together in the upper of two Châtelperronian layers of sediment.

There is an obvious but highly important question to be asked. Were the Neanderthals making a great leap in development and consciousness, or simply copying ideas from the Cro-Magnons?

EUROPE

Caspian Sea

Black Sea

H.erectus 0.8 MYA

Ceprano

Atapuerca

H.erectus 0.7 MYA

H.erectus 1.7 MYA   Dmanisi

GEORGIA

Mediterranean Sea

'Ubeidiya

1.5 MYA

AFRICA

Bahr al Ghazal

Hadar

Aramis

ETHIOPIA

2.0 MYA

Omo

Kanapoi

Nariokotome   Koobi Fora (*H.erectus* 1.8 MYA)

H.erectus 1.5 MYA   *L. Turkana*

KENYA

Olduvai Gorge

Laetoli

1.8–1.2 MYA

ATLANTIC
OCEAN

IND

O C

H.erectus 1.5 MYA   Swartkrans

Sterkfontein 2.0 MYA

Taung

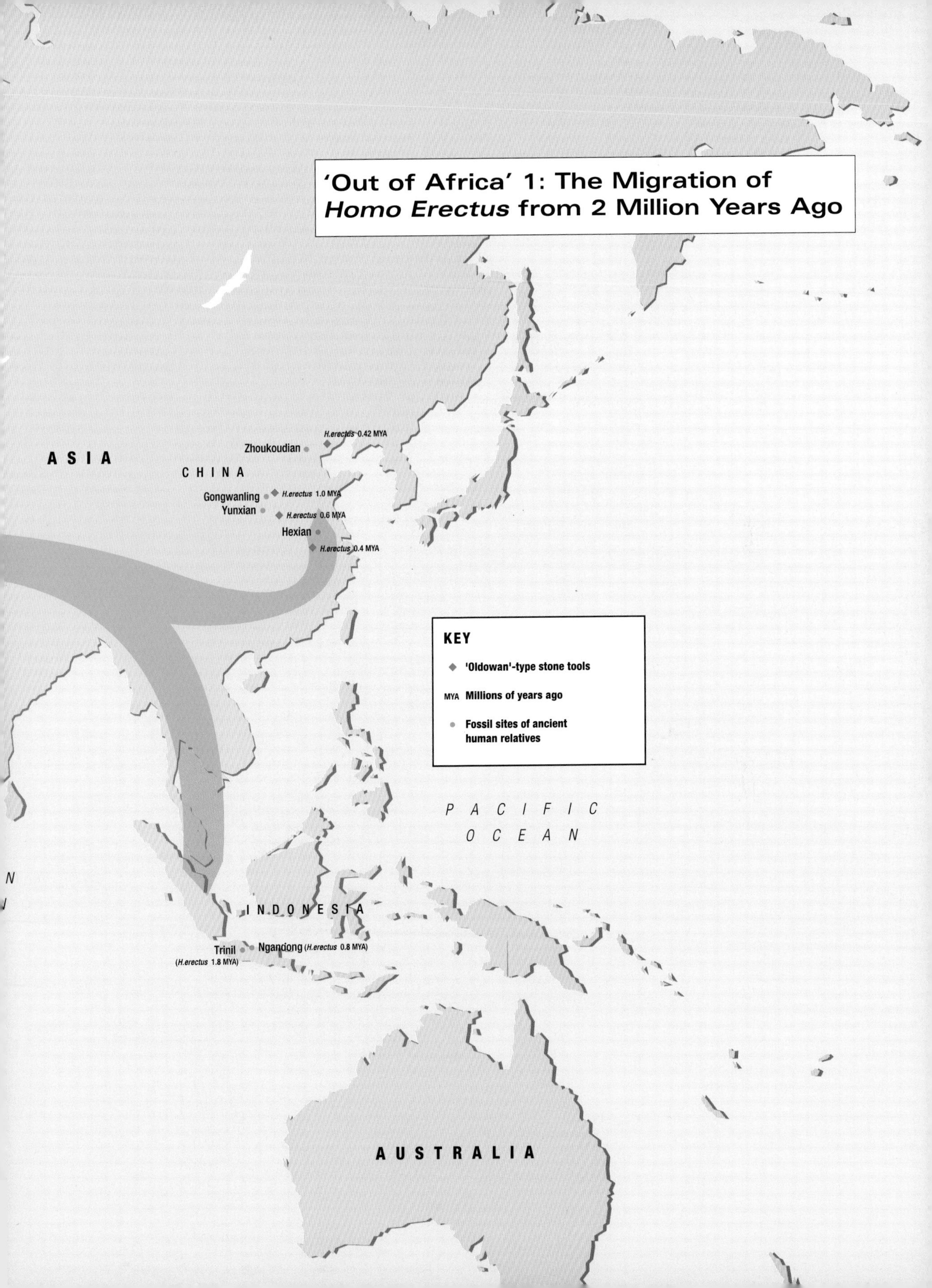

'Out of Africa' 1: The Migration of *Homo Erectus* from 2 Million Years Ago

ASIA

CHINA

Zhoukoudian ◆ *H.erectus* 0.42 MYA

Gongwanling ◆ *H.erectus* 1.0 MYA
Yunxian ● ◆ *H.erectus* 0.6 MYA

Hexian ● ◆ *H.erectus* 0.4 MYA

KEY

◆ 'Oldowan'-type stone tools

MYA Millions of years ago

● Fossil sites of ancient human relatives

P A C I F I C O C E A N

I N D O N E S I A

Trinil ● ● Ngandong (*H.erectus* 0.8 MYA)
(*H.erectus* 1.8 MYA)

N

U

AUSTRALIA

ICE CAP

MAMMO

CENTRA

EUROPE
40,000

Moscerini
60,000

Vanguard
50,000

Qafzeh
• 90,000

AFRICA

Abdu
125,000

I

INDIAN
OCEAN

ATLANTIC
OCEAN

ANCESTRAL MODERN HUMANS
150,000–100,000

Klasies River mouth

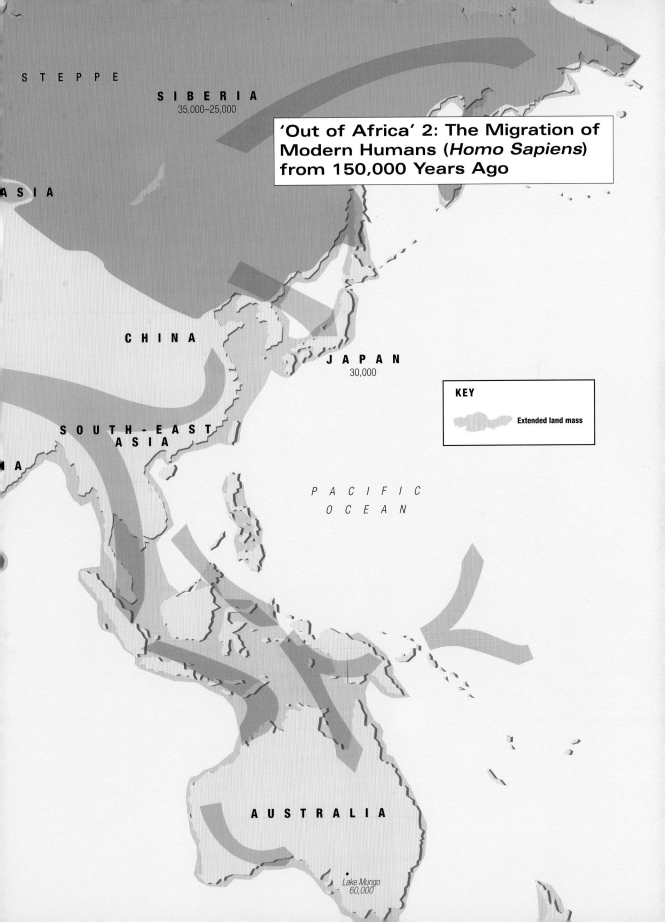

STEPPE

SIBERIA
35,000–25,000

ASIA

'Out of Africa' 2: The Migration of
Modern Humans (*Homo Sapiens*)
from 150,000 Years Ago

CHINA

JAPAN
30,000

KEY

Extended land mass

SOUTH-EAST
ASIA

A

PACIFIC
OCEAN

AUSTRALIA

Lake Mungo
60,000

Evolving tool technology

Understanding the sequence of changes in the developing technology of stone-tool manufacture has turned out to be very difficult. The original hopes of establishing fairly straightforward evolutionary patterns have not been fulfilled. Distinctions between, for instance, points and blades are still purely formal but there is hope that microscopic examination of wear patterns may eventually reveal connections between some shapes and specific uses.

Nevertheless, these different tool types are thought to reflect distinct and separate concepts in the minds of the people who made them. Paul Mellars cites the case of the so-called 'backed-knife' tool, a distinctive stone-tool type in which one side of the blade is used for cutting and is often serrated or scalloped by retouching for better cutting, while the other side has a more steeply angled surface to which pressure can be more easily applied in the cutting process. (The latter form was achieved by more intensive retouching of flake 'blanks' rather than blades.) Mellars argues that there is a clear difference in the form of this tool between the somewhat irregular examples of the older Mousterian tradition and the much more regularly developed Châtelperronian examples from the beginning of Upper Palaeolithic times. There was also a rapid increase in the scale of blade production. The difference between Mousterian and Châtelperronian backed-knife blades, as we shall see, is one of the critical points in a major argument about the potential of the Neanderthals and the nature of their contact with the Cro-Magnons.

Shifting populations

At the heart of arguments over the origins of modern humans in Europe lies the big issue of population dispersal and replacement. It is one thing to show that the appearance of Cro-Magnon modern humans coincided with a revolution in culture and behaviour; it is quite another to argue that this revolution is the result of the dispersal of these incomers throughout Europe.

Behind all this is the argument over how modern people arose and dispersed in the first place. Was there a localized and gradual evolutionary development from ancient to modern humans in each of the main regions of the world, without any significant geographical dispersal? Or was there one main point of origination for modern humans and then widespread dispersal? Since we know that ancient humans (*Homo erectus*) already had a widespread distribution from Africa through Europe and Asia, the first, 'multi-regional', idea would seem reasonable and perhaps even the most plausible. By comparison, the second, 'Out of Africa', idea that requires global migration might seem less persuasive.

However, over the last couple of decades the 'Out of Africa' idea has dominated. Genetic 'fingerprinting' of modern humans around the world has shown a remarkably close degree of similarity – so close that there must have been a single point of origin, a mere 200,000–300,000 years ago and, most importantly, in Africa.

The revolution in dating techniques has allowed accurate dating of skeletal materials which are beyond the temporal range of the old established method of radiocarbon dating. Most important has been the dating of anatomically modern human bones from Israel, which surprisingly turn out to be around 90–110,000 years old. They indicate that modern humans were well established in the Middle East in Middle Palaeolithic times, some 50–60,000 years before their first appearances in the more northern regions of Europe and Asia.

The further implication that particularly concerns us here is the evidence that modern humans must have coexisted with the Neanderthals in Europe and indeed with other ancient human populations in Asia. Another critical piece of archaeological evidence comes from the discovery and dating of Neanderthal skeletal remains from Saint-Césaire in western France, at about 36,000 years old.

These bones with their classic Neanderthal features are very close in age to the earliest recorded remains of modern humans in western Europe as represented by the original Cro-Magnon find and that of Vogelherd in Germany. It is not possible for the Neanderthals of Saint-Césaire to have evolved into Cro-Magnon modern humans in the available time gap. The existence of modern humans in western France at such an early date points to a major population dispersal of modern people into Europe.

Supporters of the multi-regional idea argue that these examples are just extreme end members of populations and do not take into account the anatomical variability that would have existed at the time. They also argue that outside western Europe, eastern Europe, the Middle East, Asia and Australasia there is strong anatomical evidence for continuity between ancient and modern humans.

The archaeological evidence

The material archaeological evidence for the rapid dispersal of new populations of modern humans across Europe is based on the establishment of a crucial link between the Aurignacian stone industry and Cro-Magnon peoples as its manufacturers. In recent decades a number of critical sites have emerged across Europe from Germany to France, in which Aurignacian stone tools have been found associated with Cro-Magnon remains.

The next question is whether the Aurignacian industries of the different parts of Europe were generated by the Cro-Magnon incomers, or whether they could have developed independently and locally from older Neanderthal patterns of the Middle Palaeolithic age. Most experts, except for the American archaeologist Milford Wolpoff, one of the chief proponents of multi-regionalism, now agree that the Aurignacian tools were not made by Neanderthals. If the 'multi-regional' hypothesis were true and the Cro-Magnons evolved in Europe from the Neanderthals, we might reasonably expect to find some blending or gradual development and transmission of the older Mousterian patterns through into the Aurignacian tools.

However, the diversity of Middle Palaeolithic tool industries across Europe is replaced by both the marked uniformity of the Aurignacian tools and their greater sophistication. From Israel to the Atlantic, across some 4000 kilometres (2500 miles) of Cro-Magnon territory, Aurignacian tools are virtually indistinguishable. Even some of the more idiosyncratic bone and antler tool designs are widespread. Nowhere is a gradational change from Middle Palaeolithic tool technology seen. It is very difficult to imagine how such widespread uniformity of design could have arisen from such diverse original patterns so quickly.

However, Paul Mellars claims that dating of the first appearance of Aurignacian tools shows an interesting geographical distinction, but other experts such as Paul Pettitt are not so sure. Sites in northern Spain, such as L'Arbreda and El Castillo, have been dated to between 41,000–37,000 radiocarbon years ago. By comparison, the earliest Aurignacian sites in south-west France, such as La Ferrassie and Roc-de-Combe, cluster around 36,000–35,000 radiocarbon years ago, that is, some 4–5,000 years later than in northern Spain. These dates do not necessarily preclude some earlier short-lived incursions into France in response to brief intervals of improved climate. Indeed, there may be evidence for such incursions from a couple of sites in the Lot region of south-western France (Roc-de-Combe and Le Piage) and El Pendo in Cantabria, which some experts claim shows interlayering of Châtelperronian and early Aurignacian levels. But the main phase of colonization of south-west France does seem to have been significantly later than along the adjacent Mediterranean coast and in northern Spain. The question is: why the delay, especially since the regions are not that geographically distant?

Paul Mellars argues that while climate might have played a role in delaying the colonization of south-west France, the main reason may well have been a continued presence of substantial Neanderthal populations in this region. From the large number of Neanderthal sites here, the region certainly does seem to have supported a high Neanderthal population density. The implication is that Neanderthals and Cro-Magnons coexisted in adjacent territories for several thousand years.

Conflict?

One of the questions that fascinates us is how the Neanderthals and Cro-Magnons faced up to one another. Should we assume that antagonism would have been the 'normal' response of a meeting between them? Or are we biased by the confrontational violence that seems to be endemic in our own societies today? The question inspired the Nobel Prize-winning author William Golding, who portrayed the interaction of these two peoples with great sensitivity and insight. The novel is not a romance, so the Cro-Magnons do not emerge in a particularly good light. Golding's sympathies clearly lie with the Neanderthals – 'victims' of their own limitations and Cro-Magnon territorial aggression.

Would these people actually have engaged in combat, whether physically or ritualistically? With their everyday experience of killing medium-sized and occasionally big game, both groups certainly knew how to kill at close quarters. The Neanderthals were individually stronger but the Cro-Magnons might have been better strategists and better armed. Nevertheless, as long as the Neanderthals continued to be present in significant numbers, they would not have been easy to beat – quite the reverse.

The archaeological evidence

What we do not find are Palaeolithic versions of Flanders fields, where farmers still plough up the skeletal remains and artefacts of First World War conflict – bones with bullet holes and empty cartridge cases. No one has yet found any direct evidence of hand-to-hand combat or conflict between Neanderthal and Cro-Magnon people. Neanderthal skeletal remains are not found with Aurignacian stone weapons embedded in them or even lying around them nor, for that matter, are Cro-Magnon bones associated with any artefacts from Neanderthal tool industries.

What is found, however, at some sites on the western fringes of Neanderworld, in south-west France and northern Spain, is the close physical proximity of Aurignacian tools to Châtelperronian artefacts but their proximity in time is not clear. Excavation of the sequence of layers in these sites reveals that layers with Aurignacian tools lie above and are therefore younger than tools of the older tradition which are found lower in the sequence at the same site. Most archaeologists argue that the two tool industries and traditions are the products of two quite separate human populations.

THIS SPREAD Competition for game may have led to territorial conflict between the Neanderthals and Cro-Magnons, but as yet there is no unequivocal archaeological evidence for mortal combat between the two peoples.

Throughout Europe Neanderthal industries show considerable local variation, reflecting their social isolation and parochialism and the lack of significant interchange between Neanderthal groups. By contrast, the younger Aurignacian products of the Cro-Magnons are much more uniform across a vast stretch of Europe. But, as we have also seen, the incoming of the Aurignacian tradition varied in time, especially in the far western reaches of Neanderworld. Along the Mediterranean coast and in Cantabria, Aurignacian tools were being produced 41,000–38,000 (34–28,000 radiocarbon) years ago, while to the north in south-west France tools of the Neanderthal Châtelperronian tradition were still being manufactured and continued to be so for another 4–5000 years. It is the Châtelperronian stone industry of western and central France that provides evidence of the nature of the interaction during that period of overlap. And it is the interpretation of this tradition which is so vehemently disputed.

The trouble with the Châtelperronian

The distribution of Châtelperronian stone tools has a well-defined and constrained geographical range centred on south-western France and the adjacent Pyrenees. There are a few outposts in the surrounding areas of Cantabria, Catalonia and northern Burgundy but none is found east of the Rhône river valley. Experts such as Paul Mellars argue that while the roots of the Châtelperronian industry are in the older Mousterian tradition of the Neanderthals, many of the specific characteristics of the Châtelperronian tools are of a distinctly Upper Palaeolithic (Aurignacian) type. Moreover, Châtelperronian tools appear in the record only at a very late stage, from 38,000 (36,000 radiocarbon) years ago, after Aurignacian tools are first found in northern Spain 41,000 years ago. The first signs of the Aurignacian do not appear in south-west France until around 36,000 (34,000 radiocarbon) years ago.

Mellars claims that the development of Châtelperronian tools by the Neanderthals, just in the western reaches of Neanderworld, can be best explained as a result of their contact with Cro-Magnons – so-called acculturation – rather than by spontaneous invention. This scenario envisages the Neanderthals of the region building on the older Mousterian tradition, but essentially borrowing or copying the more advanced technology of the Cro-Magnons during their several thousand years of overlap and contact.

However, a few experts, notably the Italian archaeologist Francesco d'Errico and the Portuguese João Zilhão, disagree, especially with Mellars's chronology for the Châtelperronian, and argue that neither acculturation nor coexistence happened. Instead, they claim that the Neanderthals developed the Châtelperronian tool industry in south-western France and northern Spain quite independently of the Cro-Magnons. They also believe that the Neanderthals 'were capable of manufacturing the kinds of lithic [stone] and bone tools which have been found in Aurignacian levels'. They do concede, though, that so far all skeletal remains from Aurignacian levels have been those of Cro-Magnons.

At the conceptual level, the argument is about the ability and intent of the Neanderthals compared with the Cro-Magnons. Were they really quite limited in their cognitive skills as Mellars and others argue? Or did their brains evolve to give them more potential than they are normally credited with, bringing them closer in ability to the Cro-Magnons? To support their argument, d'Errico and Zilhão point out that there are Châtelperronian tools, especially some awls for perforating skins, from the Grotte du Renne, which are 'decorated' with sets of carefully made and regularly spaced notches and also heavily worn by intensive use. The wear indicates that the decoration would have been hidden by the user's hand during work. From this d'Errico and Zilhão conclude that the decoration was therefore part of an everyday and normal use of symbolism by the Neanderthals. Furthermore, it was an integral part of a late cultural development by them and not just something borrowed from the Cro-Magnons.

An alternative view, proposed by Mellars, is that there must have been some substantial barrier between the two peoples that prevented their integration and assimilation over 5–6,000 years of coexistence. He argues that if there had been greater integration, there should not be such a distinction between the Châtelperronian and Aurignacian technologies; the former would have graded into the other at some point, but this does not happen. Mellars points out that there is no known instance of modern contact between European and indigenous populations of other modern humans where separate development has been maintained for more than a few centuries. The fact that there was only limited acculturation between the Neanderthals and Cro-Magnons suggests to Mellars that there must have been some fundamental barrier between these two peoples, probably at the biological level, which had significant repercussions at the behaviour level. As we shall see, this line of argument is supported by the new DNA evidence.

However, d'Errico and colleagues insist that the production of complex Châtelperronian bone tools and various items of personal adornment, and the use of red ochre, provides strong evidence for relatively advanced cognitive and social skills in the Neanderthals. To some extent the argument here is one of degree. Just how advanced and close to the Cro-Magnons' level of development did the Neanderthals get?

Mellars draws an analogy with a child threading beads. The child is simply copying its mother. But in anthropological terms a mature woman threads beads to attract a mate or as a symbol of her family's wealth. But the child is not

ABOVE Seashells and other personal ornaments were commonly worn by Cro-Magnon people, and adopted by some of the last Neanderthals – perhaps in imitation of the newcomers.

aware of this deeper significance when it threads beads. Another modern example is seen in the cargo cults of New Guinea, where the aboriginal inhabitants make small models of aeroplanes. This activity does not imply an understanding of aeronautics, but symbolizes for the people the extraordinary arrival of strangers from the sky. Mellars's purpose is to illustrate how simplistic correlations between particular behavioural patterns and their underlying motivation can be misconstrued. He thinks that in the social climate of late Neanderworld, the ability to copy the novelties of the incomers might have given additional status and possibly mating success to those individuals with the necessary skills to imitate them. As with the child and the beads, the Neanderthals would not necessarily have understood the symbolic meaning attached to the artefacts by the Cro-Magnons. (As an aside, we might reflect that similar kinds of motivation relating to copying novelty by children and some adults who are unaware of their symbolic value are still very much with us modern humans, and are profitably exploited by the fashion and advertising industry today.)

ABOVE The ability to learn from others is a common human trait that the Neanderthals undoubtedly possessed. The Neanderthals may have learned new hunting techniques from the Cro-Magnons and copied their jewellery but whether they understood the symbolic significance of Cro-Magnon ornaments is more debatable.

There is a question here about the very origin of symbolic behaviour and its pattern of development that falls into a familiar evolutionary debate. The question is whether such developments are gradual, as Darwin originally envisaged, or sudden (or 'punctuated', as the American evolutionary palaeontologist Steve Gould calls it). D'Errico and others have argued that generally there have been many symbolic and technological innovations in the evolution of humans that appear suddenly. Moreover, innovations may be developed independently by different peoples at different times, such as writing and agriculture. Just as there was no gradual transition to writing, d'Errico argues that the adoption of body ornaments was 'sudden or punctuated among Neanderthals as well as among moderns'. Such arguments will run and run without much conclusion until better data is available.

Peaceful coexistence?

At present there is considerable support for the idea that the Neanderthals and the Cro-Magnon incomers did come into contact, especially in south-west

France and northern Spain over a considerable period of time – at least 5000 years. But the exact nature of this contact is almost entirely speculative. It has been thought that the two peoples had very different survival strategies, with the Neanderthals being more locked into subsistence and opportunistic foraging, partly dependent on scavenging rather than strategic hunting.

This analysis is based on the generalized remains of a variety of prey in south-western France, with a mixture of wild cattle, horse, red deer and reindeer. The Cro-Magnons have been envisaged as broad spectrum hunters, preying on a variety of game; they may have been more mobile and locked into seasonal hunting patterns. Because of these different subsistence strategies, there may have been relatively little competition between the two groups. But as we have seen, the evidence from elsewhere, such as northern Germany, suggests that older Neanderthal groups were perfectly capable of more targeted medium-sized game hunting, specifically of reindeer.

It is a very interesting problem of interpretation. A simple explanation would be that if the Neanderthals were splintered and operating as very separate groups in both space and time, then there was little reason why specific hunting strategies should have been communicated throughout Neanderworld. However, if there was not much contiguity between Neanderthal groups, why should there be any between the Neanderthals and Cro-Magnons?

There may be one very good reason: the build-up of Cro-Magnon population density in the middle and later part of the Aurignacian. Such increased population pressure would have occurred mainly in the best hunting grounds, which were the most ecologically favoured landscapes such as the south-west of France. The archaeological evidence suggests that by this time the Neanderthals had already been marginalized and pushed into western and central France. The replacement of the Neanderthals may have been more a matter of gradual replacement with a slow movement of populations and occupation of territories rather than any face-to-face confrontation.

From the scant evidence available so far, the situation was similar elsewhere in Europe. More sophisticated industries, equivalent to the Châtelperronian, have developed locally from older Mousterian ones in eastern Europe (Szeletian industry), southern Russia (Streletskaya industry) and in Italy (Uluzzian industry). They coexisted with more uniform Aurignacian industry but so far cannot be directly and specifically linked by skeletal evidence to Neanderthals or Cro-Magnons.

Pressure point

Why the Cro-Magnon colonization of Europe happened when it did, progressively from around 45,000 years ago in the east to around 35,000 years ago in the west and 28,000 years ago in the British Isles, is a particularly interesting and important question. Dating of anatomically modern human skeletal remains from the Levant, at around 100,000 years old, shows that in the

Middle East the moderns coexisted with Neanderthals for more than 50,000 years, a much longer period than their coexistence in the far west. That these modern people stayed around in the Middle East for so long before pushing north is perhaps not surprising. They were essentially people from the tropics and subtropics of Africa and were consequently basically adapted to hot climates rather than the cold ones of Ice Age Europe. Not surprisingly, they would take some time to acclimatize.

The Neanderthals, by comparison, had adapted to the harsher conditions of northern Europe over 100,000 years and more. In these terms, it is quite hard to see why the moderns pushed north and how they were able to compete effectively with the Neanderthals who were more used to the cold. There must have been a pretty strong incentive and adaptive advantage for the moderns to have achieved what they did. The answer almost certainly lies in their more advanced cultural and technological equipment, which allowed them to colonize a whole new range of territories and cold environments.

It is still not clear exactly what precise pre-adaptive mechanism allowed this initiative. Was it primarily the improved technology of the moderns, changes in their social organization or the emergence of more complex and effective language, or a combination of all these factors? It is quite likely that new developments in language and linked cognition systems provided the original source, because any organizational changes would have been predicated by them and so might the technological changes.

Behind the final prompt, when push became shove, there probably lay increasing population expansion and overcrowding in the favoured areas of the Middle East. Then, between 60,000 and 40,000 years ago a relatively warm spell in the last glaciation opened a window of opportunity. A series of rapid climate fluctuations produced an overall increase in average annual temperatures in many regions of western Europe, with temperatures rising by 5–6° C (9–11° F). The warmer conditions allowed temperate woodland to invade landscapes that had previously been periglacial tundra and steppe grassland. This environmental change may finally have opened the way for the dispersal into northern and western Europe of the moderns.

The two most readily available and open routes would have been along the Mediterranean coast and from the Black Sea along the Danube river valley. The coastal route was much longer and slower but had the advantage of readily available food supplies of shellfish and small game. It took at least 10,000 years for the moderns to reach south-west France by this route. The inland route from the Black Sea along the lush and productive Danube waterway eventually led directly into central and northern Europe. There would have been plenty of game, but negotiating the marshes and powerful river must have had its share of hazards from seasonal flooding.

The Cro-Magnons' 12,000-year-long march through Europe possibly brought them progressively into contact with more and more Neanderthal bands. There is no direct evidence of exactly when and where contact was made nor what happened when they did meet. The view of the Neanderthals that has been built up from various sources is that they operated in small groups and would most likely have been highly territorial. Most models of territorial groups suggest that they would have been hostile to strangers who threatened their land and food resources. However, there is no direct evidence for any conflict.

Cro-Magnon cave art certainly portrays the violence of the hunt and in times of shortage of game it is likely that the two peoples may have come into direct conflict. But there are no piles of bones with signs of mortal conflict. The scenario is rather like trying to prove a murder without a body – which can be done, given circumstantial evidence and modern technology. But there has been plenty of speculation, some fanciful, some more informed. The fossil record gives some clues but there is no single clear outcome in the short term. However, we do know what happened in the long term.

As we have seen, there appears to have been quite long periods of coexistence, maybe as much as 6000 years. The Ebro Valley in northern Spain preserves evidence of a stand-off between the two peoples which seems to have lasted for at least 5000 years. But it is not possible to tell from the data whether these groups were tacitly interacting but keeping their distance or simply ignoring one another. Again, there is considerable argument between experts as to what may or may not have happened.

ABOVE Better developed communication, organisational and hunting skills were probably essential ingredients of the incomers' success.

The same environmental changes that may have been advantageous to the moderns may have had the opposite effect on the Neanderthals. Some experts have speculated that environmental change would have destabilized the ecology and culture of local Neanderthal groups and upset their well-established behavioural patterns. Such perturbation may have promoted fragmentation of the groups and/or population decline. This is a very debatable issue and has many parallels with what happened to many other non-human Ice Age populations such as the mammoth. It is also happening today to most of the remaining higher primates and other animals such as elephant and tiger. Populations of most mammals with low rates of reproduction, relatively few offspring and considerable parental investment, such as elephants, chimps and humans, can easily be pushed into a negative feedback of spiralling decline in numbers. Mathematical modelling has shown that it only takes slight shifts in relative birth and death rates to precipitate such a decline. Evidently an opposite shift promoted the expansion of the Cro-Magnons.

If this scenario is correct, then the 200,000-year-long reign of the Neanderthals was coming to an end. The people were literally dying out. But was their extinction total, or did they leave a trace of their existence in the European gene pool?

The beginning of the end

chapter nine

FORTY THOUSAND YEARS AGO, THE NEANDERTHALS WERE ON THE brink of extinction. The icy cold of another glacial was creeping southwards into Neanderworld, while from the south and east the colonizing Cro-Magnons kept coming. Caught in the middle, the Neanderthals moved slowly but inexorably towards final oblivion. They had endured extremes of climate many times before, but now the pressure was compounded by increasing competition from alien people for land, for food – for life.

Neanderworld did not survive. But for many years, in our modern world, there has been speculation that the Neanderthals may have left a legacy of their existence, in our genes.

Exile

For around 200,000 years, fertile valleys such as the Dordogne in southern France had been favoured Neanderthal homelands. But by 35,000 years ago, the Neanderthals were pushed out of the valleys and moved up on to the surrounding uplands. Life on the open limestone plateaux was harsher, with less vegetation and little water or protection against the elements. The assumption is that direct competition from the Cro-Magnons for the vital resources of everyday sustenance – their game food – had driven them out. Under pressure, the Neanderthal bands may not have been able to retain their cohesiveness. Isolated remains of individual Neanderthals suggest that perhaps they no longer moved around the landscape in groups.

Generally in Europe, once the Cro-Magnons occupied the cave sites there was no return of the Neanderthals – they were ousted once and for all. A number of factors could have worked in the Cro-Magnons' favour. Sheer numbers and more co-operation between groups could have helped them dominate hunting along the migratory routes of the game animals. Superior planning, prediction and communication of game movements through more highly developed language skills may have kept them always one step ahead of the Neanderthals. And finally, their better hunting techniques and superior weaponry could well have increased their kill rate.

Out on the upland plateaux, game resources were more thinly stretched; the tougher vegetation was not able to sustain the same density of animals as the lusher valleys. The Neanderthal groups could have been forced to operate over larger regions to gain a living from the land. Dwindling in numbers and more isolated one from another, the fragmentation of their populations would have been a recipe for disaster. As with many of the endangered mammals of today, there are clear thresholds for populations below which they cannot maintain themselves but go into a spiral of decline towards extinction.

Not surprisingly, the Neanderthals lasted longest in the most out-of-the-way places where competition from the Cro-Magnons was least. Like most 'endangered species', they held out in a few isolated retreats, some of the most marginal parts of their territory, rather than in any of the areas rich in game resources. It is quite possible that they had previously retreated here during earlier climate deterioration. In those earlier times, however, they were able to recover and reoccupy their old territories as the climate improved. But not this time.

In western Europe it was the peripheral areas of mountainous terrain and rocky coasts where they hung on longest. With their cold-adapted physique, the Neanderthals were better equipped to survive more extreme conditions than the Cro-Magnon incomers from the south. But even these inhospitable and marginal areas were gradually becoming less habitable as Europe's climate worsened.

Some of the last known Neanderthals hung on in a coastal and rocky region of southern Spain, eventually dying out 31,000 years or so ago. Dating by Paul Pettitt of Oxford University has shown that other isolated groups hung on in Croatia, Crimea and further to the east in the Caucasus until 29,000 years ago. Pettitt reckons that some of the stragglers may have survived at least this long in Britain, but their remains have not yet been found. Certainly several other creatures of the Ice Age managed to hang on, such as mammoths and giant deer, which survived longest on offshore islands.

Extinction

The delicate balance between the Neanderthal clans, their European territories and the game they hunted was disturbed first by the competition from Cro-Magnons for the same prey animals and land. Then around 35,000 years ago, any hope of readjustment and accommodation between the two groups was destroyed. The rapidly fluctuating climate applied the *coup de grâce*.

We can speculate that if Neanderthal birth rates had been that much higher or if the climate had improved, then perhaps they would not have become extinct. (Of course, some fringe cryptozoologists have claimed that they did not become extinct but survive as the Yeti of the Himalayas or the Big Foot of North America.) There may not have been bloodshed and bodies on the ground at the end but, either directly or indirectly, the Cro-Magnons were probably behind this extinction event, especially in the best hunting grounds. Elsewhere the knock-on effects of climate change may have played a more significant role. Paul Pettitt interprets Cro-Magnon art, with its depiction of carnivores and lion-headed figures, as symbolizing aggression – which may have been directed towards the Neanderthals.

In much the same way, the descendants of the Cro-Magnons and other modern humans who colonized the world have been behind the extinction of most of the other members of the Ice Age megafauna. From the giant ground sloth of South America to the Australian giant marsupial diprotodont (rather like a large bear), and perhaps the mammoths of Eurasia and North America, some thirty-five large mammal species were driven to extinction in a relatively short time. And of course, more recently, modern humans have turned on minority peoples such as the Caribs in the West Indies, the original Fuegian Indians of Tierra del Fuego and native peoples of Tasmania and wiped them out.

ABOVE The Neanderthals may have tried to walk away from the incoming Cro-Magnons, but with another glacial advancing from the north, there were not too many refuges left for them.

The Neanderthals were out-manoeuvred, out-'gunned', out-bred and ousted from their territories. They seem to have gone with more of a whimper than a bang, pushed into oblivion to become yet another extinct human species. The distinctive anatomical features of the Neanderthals are not found in the fossil remains of later Cro-Magnons except, as we shall see, perhaps in the fossil skeleton of a child found recently in Portugal.

Hybrid species?

Inevitably, there has been much speculation about whether the interactions between Neanderthal and Cro-Magnon people involved sexual relations. Both peoples were human. Although some clear differences of emphasis can be seen in their skeletal structures, they were nevertheless biologically very close.

Thirty-five thousand years ago, however, when they first met in western Europe, both Neanderthals and Cro-Magnons would have been only too well aware of their differences. But, in places, they did live alongside one another for protracted periods of time. Although there were fundamental differences of language, behaviour and culture between them, there is the question of whether these differences were great enough to have always kept them apart, especially when it came to sex. Some scientists find it hard to believe that these two peoples co-existed for thousands of years without there being some sexual encounters between them.

If, for the sake of argument, we assume that there was, then we can consider what the outcome might have been. The primary factor here is genetic similarity. The definition of a biological species is that its members can interbreed to produce fertile offspring that in turn can reproduce. For many years now, the consensus has been that Neanderthals were a separate species from Cro-

Magnons and their descendants – European modern humans. But the separateness of the Neanderthals was based on morphological features of their skeletal remains; as such they are a *fossil* species. While the morphological evidence of their separateness is convincing to palaeontologists, there is still a lingering doubt about their validity as separate *biological* species. However, as we shall see, the remarkable innovation of fossil DNA analysis suggests that they were a species in their own right.

Only a few closely related mammal species can interbreed. The lack of gene flow between any pair of closely related species may be due to a number of different reproductive barriers, such as hybrid sterility. The best-known domesticated example is the mule, which humans have artificially bred in Asia since the seventh century BC by crossing the horse and ass. The interbreeding produces live young – mules – but they are sterile. In some other closely related species such as goats and sheep, fertilization can occur but the embryos die early on in their development.

Among mammals in the wild, hybridization is not particularly common, although it does occur in some of the many cattle species, and dog relatives such as coyotes and wolves. Part of the reason for the problems of hybridization is the different number of chromosomes in separate species. In normal interspecies reproduction, exchange of genetic material is facilitated by the basic similarity of the chromosomes from the two parents. However, in hybrids, where there is a considerable difference between chromosomes, it is more difficult for the successful exchange of genetic material (crossing over) to take place. The horse has sixty-four chromosomes and the ass sixty-two, so that the mule has sixty-three and cannot pair them all off during the exchange of genetic material.

Fact or fiction?

The idea of a hybrid born of sex between Neanderthals and Cro-Magnons was used to telling effect in a novel by the late Björn Kurtén, a Finnish palaeontologist. He was an authority on the Ice Age and its inhabitants, and in his 1980 *Dance of the Tiger* he portrays a convincing if ultimately tragic story of the end of the Neanderthals. In Kurtén's version, there is sex between Neanderthal and Cro-Magnon and many children are born. But these children are unable to produce offspring themselves because they are infertile hybrids – not that they could have had any idea of this themselves.

Kurtén's vision seemed prophetic when, in November 1998, the fossilized remains of a child were discovered buried at the base of a cliff at Abrigo do Lagar Velho in the Lapedo Valley, near the famous modern religious shrine of Fatima in Portugal. A local landowner was cutting a road with a bulldozer when he exposed the base of a rock face. Two Portuguese archaeologists, João Maurício and Pedro Souto, were in the area, following up reports of rock art. They examined the rock and found bits of bone, stone tools and charcoal from an ancient hearth. Another Portuguese archaeologist, João Zilhão, was called in and led a team who excavated the site during the bitter December rains. They were rewarded for their efforts by finding a burial with the skeleton of a child that was nearly complete – but for the skull which, frustratingly, had been crushed by the bulldozer.

The American archaeologist and expert on Neanderthals, Erik Trinkaus of Washington University in St Louis, has become a major collaborator on the project. Trinkaus and Zilhão think that the child was a four-year-old boy who had been buried with ceremony. He was wearing either clothing or a burial shroud covered with red ochre, with a pierced periwinkle shell around his neck as a pendant. Three pierced deer teeth lay near his shattered skull. The ceremonial style of burial is similar to the 28–30,000 (26,000 radiocarbon)-year-old Cro-Magnon burial at Paviland in the Gower Peninsula, Wales, and others in Moravia, Italy and Russia.

The archaeologists claim that the skeleton has a strange mosaic of characteristics, with the chin and teeth of a modern human but the robust limb bones and limb proportions of a Neanderthal. Because of this mixture of characteristics, it is further claimed that the child is a hybrid and provides evidence for interbreeding between Neanderthals and Cro-Magnons. But for other experts, it is just a robust modern human child. Since the details have not yet been published, the wider community of scientific experts has not had a chance to give a critical judgement on the evidence.

An intriguing piece of information about the find has been its age. Experts in radiocarbon dating by the

OPPOSITE
Archaeological evidence shows that Cro-Magnons took over Neanderthal campsites, although it is unclear just how close the encounter was. If there was a close encounter between these two groups of people, it is hard to imagine that it did not at times involve sex.

BELOW A child's skeleton, some 27,000 (25,000 radiocarbon) years old, uncovered by a bulldozer in Portugal is claimed by some experts to be a hybrid, showing a mixture of Neanderthal and modern human features.

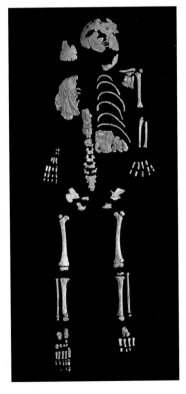

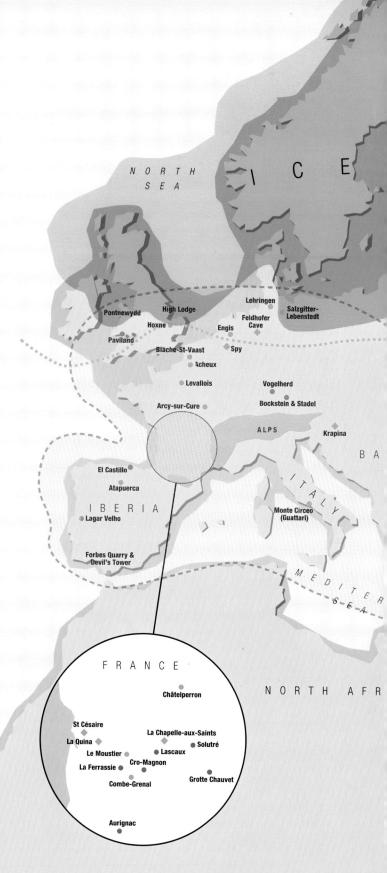
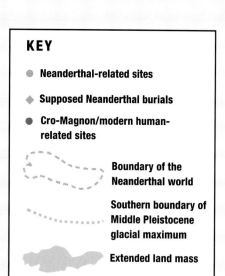

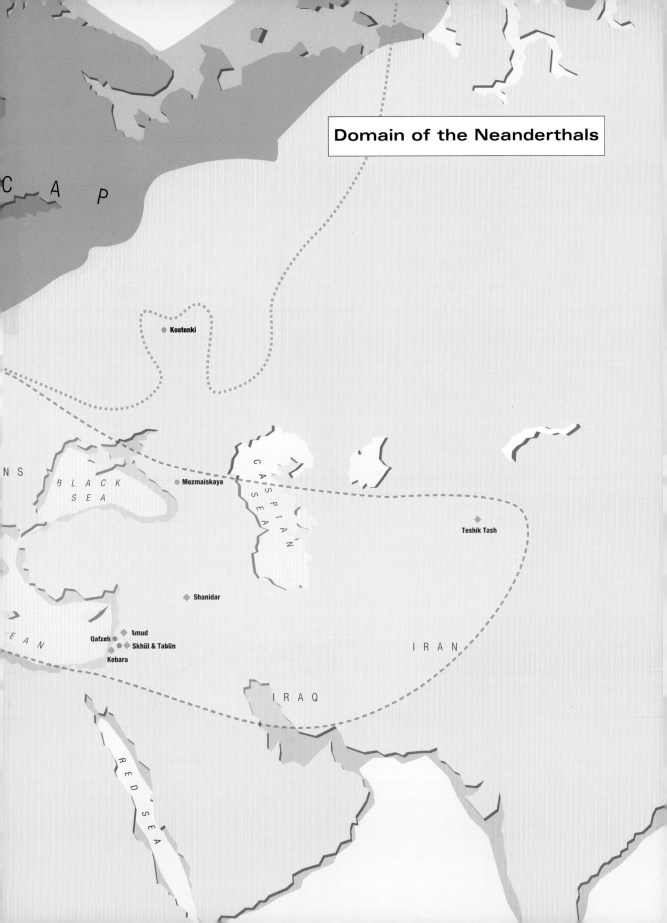

Domain of the Neanderthals

C A P

Kostenki

N S

BLACK
SEA

Mezmaiskaya

C
A
S
P
I
A
N

S
E
A

Teshik Tash

Shanidar

E A N

Amud
Qafzeh
Skhūl & Tabūn
Kebara

I R A N

I R A Q

R
E
D

S
E
A

PREVIOUS PAGE
The distribution
of Neanderthal remains
showing the considerable
extent of their territory in
relation to glacial
environments and the
distribution of early
Cro-Magnon sites.

accelerator mass spectrometry technique, such as Paul Pettitt, have radiocarbon-dated cultural objects from above the burial level to around 21,000 years ago. They have also dated the red deer remains in the grave to between 25,000 and 24,000 (about 27,000 chronological) years ago, and the backbone of a rabbit placed intriguingly on his leg is 24,000 years old. Their conclusion is that the boy died somewhere between 25,000 and 24,000 radiocarbon years ago – some 5000 years after the Neanderthals died out in Iberia. If the skeleton does truly retain a mixture of Neanderthal and Cro-Magnon features, it would imply that hybridization had in fact happened, at least within this group living in the farflung, most south-western coast of Europe.

The acid test would be to check the boy's DNA against that recently recovered from other undoubted Neanderthal remains, but unfortunately the bones are not well enough preserved. So although the consensus is that the Neanderthals did die out, for some there is still that nagging, lingering doubt and the possibility that behind the face in the mirror is the ghostly vestige of a Neanderthal in everyone of Eurasian origin. But the story is far from over: new advances in sampling and analysing fossil DNA have opened up the possibility of investigating just how close or distant we are to our ancient relatives.

Genetic analysis

The remarkable techniques of biomolecular analysis have enormous potential in the study of human evolution. There have been two main drives: first, to make detailed comparisons between the variety of living humans, other primates and other organisms in general; secondly, to try and recover fossil DNA.

We have known since the 1960s what Linnaeus and Darwin had suspected – that chimps are our nearest living relatives; 98 per cent of their DNA is identical with ours. The analysis was based on certain genes such as those of the haemoglobin family which were among the first to be detailed. From a stretch of some 11,000 base pairs, there will be some fifty or so differences between two humans, who will then differ by over 200 base pairs with the chimps. The two chimp species (the common and bonobo chimps) differ by over 100 base pairs.

By this measure it is clear that the human global population is very closely linked genetically, with about 0.5 per cent difference in haemoglobin. The two chimp species have about a 1 per cent difference, and there is a 5 per cent difference between chimps and humans. Although this percentage difference between us and the chimps might seem to some uncomfortably small, it is important to remember that the human and chimp genome is enormous – about 3000 million base pairs – and 2 per cent of that is not insignificant.

Gene trees can be constructed to illustrate the relationships between animals on the basis of similarities of particular genetic components such as the haemoglobin gene family. This comparison clearly highlights the greater closeness of humans to monkeys from the Old World compared with lemurs and New World monkeys. The most up-to-date comparison places chimps as our nearest living relative with gorillas next closest and then the orang-utans. It is no accident that there is an association between us, the chimps, gorillas and the continent of Africa.

With a knowledge of the rates of genetic mutation for particular genes, a measure of genetic distance can be turned into an estimate of when two groups of organisms diverged from one another in the past. For instance, the chimp–human distance translates into a shared ancestor about 4 million years ago and most probably in Africa.

In the 1980s there was a very well-publicized claim that the mitochondrial DNA of all living people could be traced back to a single female who lived in Africa around 200,000 years ago – the so-called 'mitochondrial Eve hypothesis'. Unlike nuclear DNA, which consists of a combination of genes from both

parents, mitochondrial DNA is inherited only from the mother. In addition, it was claimed that 'African Eve' was a member of a population, estimated at around 10,000, whose descendants spread around the world displacing all older ancient humans and human relatives such as *Homo erectus*.

The theory was more consistent with the single-origin 'out of Africa' hypothesis than the 'multi-regional' model. But it turns out that the analysis was in many ways over-ambitious for the relatively small global number of individuals sampled, as were the claims being made for it at the time. The trouble was that when other investigators tried to improve the sample size, their computational problems became unwieldy. As a result, new approaches using other elements of the genome and other techniques such as population history have been applied to the problem.

ABOVE Even the cold-adapted woolly mammoths were vulnerable to the dangers of life in the Ice Age freezer. This emaciated baby mammoth, found still frozen in the permafrost of a Siberian gold-mine in 1977 had apparently starved to death. It was originally covered in hair.

More recently, the 'molecular clock' has been used to try and track back to ancestral populations. In 1997 the convergence times for some fourteen genetic loci in modern populations were measured. They gave significant dates of around 200,000 years ago. Another analysis using what are called micro-satellites of DNA – short, rapidly evolving stretches of DNA – gives a shorter coalescence time of 156,000 years ago. Both these measures support the recent-origin model for modern humans.

Forensic and fossil DNA

The sophisticated techniques pioneered in the 1980s for amplification of fragments of DNA have been widely used in forensic science, securing headline-hitting convictions for murder and other serious crimes based on DNA recovered from specks of blood, spit or semen. But it also opened up the possibility of recovering and amplifying fragmentary fossil DNA, stimulating equally spectacular news stories and speculation about fossil DNA being used to clone dinosaurs or mammoths. Nobody has suggested cloning a Neanderthal yet, but perhaps it is just a matter of time. There have been some hiccups and spectacular failures in the fossil DNA story but also some remarkable successes.

Analysis of mitochondrial DNA has also been used recently to try and answer one of the biggest questions of human ancestry. Can genetic analysis determine whether the ancestors of modern humans interbred with the Neanderthals before they 'died' out?

This intriguing question was unanswerable until the recent advent of forensic DNA testing which essentially allows DNA to be recovered from dead tissue. It was less than fifty years ago that Francis Crick and James Watson first worked out the double helix structure of DNA, the so-called genetic 'fingerprint' or code that is contained in all living cells. It then took many years, until the 1980s, before the very difficult technology was developed for the extraction, amplification and sequencing of the DNA molecule which encodes genetic information. Even more difficult has been the recovery of fossil DNA (see the box on page 211).

Over the last three or four years, scientists have realized just how tricky the sequencing of fossil DNA can be, and how easily contamination can occur. Most claims for the recovery of fossil DNA that is millions of years old cannot be replicated and are the result of contamination. However, now that the necessarily fastidious protocols for producing and replicating results in scrupulously clean dedicated labs have been established, some remarkable fossil DNA sequences have been recovered.

One of the most recent successes has been the recovery of fragments of Neanderthal DNA and their amplification, enough to compare with the DNA of modern humans and answer that final question: did they or did they not interbreed with the Cro-Magnons?

In 1997 a bone sample was taken from the 'original' Neanderthal, the 40,000-year-old skeleton found in 1856, lying within the Feldhofer cave in Germany. Analysis of the quality of bone preservation and the degree of

Ancient DNA

The perennial allure of dinosaurs and the huge success of *Jurassic Park* created great interest and excitement at the possibility of recovering fossil DNA. As a result, many scientists rushed to cash in on the publicity potential of such work. Claims were subsequently made in the early 1990s that fossil DNA had been recovered from insects embedded in amber, which superficially look as if they are perfectly preserved. Then there was a claim that DNA had been extracted from a dinosaur bone. But when other scientists tried to replicate their results in the late 1990s – replication of results being one of the foundation stones of science – they found that they could not do so. These claims for very ancient DNA, many millions of years old, were unfounded and the result of contamination or mistakes. As many DNA specialists had been warning for some time, DNA is fairly ephemeral stuff, a complex molecule that readily deteriorates, especially in the presence of water or oxygen and generally within hours or days of a cell's death.

Rapid dehydration after the death of the animal seems to provide the most favourable circumstances, but even so only tiny amounts of the original DNA can be recovered. The DNA fragments stand the best chance of preservation in tissues such as skin and bone. But only when the sophisticated technique of amplifying these fragments by the polymerase chain reaction (PCR) method became available in the 1980s could fossil material be tackled.

Theoretically, with PCR a single DNA molecule can be amplified to provide enough material for sequencing. The problem is that it is so sensitive that contamination can very easily occur, as happened with the attempts to recover fossil DNA from material that is millions of years old. Unfortunately, most bone is very porous and especially susceptible to post-mortem contamination by 'foreign' biomolecules from microbes such as fungi and bacteria.

In the 1980s, a Finnish biologist, Svaante Pääbo, was able to extract fragmentary DNA from dried tissue such as the skin of a mummified Egyptian and that of a quagga, a recently extinct horse-like animal. But this DNA was only hundreds or a few thousand years old at most. It was Pääbo's success at sequencing fossil DNA that had encouraged others to try their hands on the more ancient material. However, Pääbo is a particularly meticulous researcher who always used the strictest protocols and replication to check his results. He had warned about the limits of the material and the method, showing that so far the upper limit to the successful retrieval of fossil DNA is, at the moment, about 100,000 years.

The whole basis of the *Jurassic Park* story had been founded on the idea of resurrecting dinosaurs using their DNA, extracted from blood-sucking insects preserved in amber. A nice idea and a good story, but science fiction. Even if dinosaur DNA could be sequenced, it would be so fragmentary as to form a very small part of the dinosaur genome and quite inadequate for cloning the beasts. More recently, the prospect of cloning an extinct animal has taken a step closer to reality with the idea of trying to resurrect a mammoth.

Mammoth DNA from cadavers frozen in the Siberian permafrost was first recovered in 1994. Even this genetic material from the Arctic deep freeze is still fragmentary and, while it certainly proves the relationships between mammoths and living elephants, it is still not nearly complete enough to allow a mammoth to be cloned. Yet there is a possibility of recovering better mammoth DNA, and so the resurrection of the mammoth is rather more realistic than trying to bring dinosaurs back to life.

breakdown and deterioration of biomolecular structure showed that it might just be possible to recover some fragmentary DNA. The process did indeed work and, once the fragments were amplified, the resulting sequences showed a distinctive pattern that was tentatively identified as a Neanderthal one. The problem was that it was not possible to say for sure that the distinct sequence was purely Neanderthal, or whether the sample had been contaminated by some unknown source.

Independent replication of the result by a different lab showed that it was certainly not contamination and was most likely Neanderthal. If this is truly so, the sequence was sufficiently different from that of modern humans to suggest that the two groups of humans had diverged some time between 317,000 and 741,000 years ago.

Even more important has been the more recent (March 2000) analysis of another Neanderthal from the other end of their territory. These newly found skeletal remains were recovered over 4000 kilometres (about 2500 miles) away

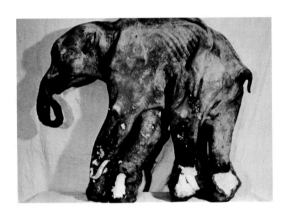

in the Mezmaiskaya Cave, in the northern Caucasus. The region is one of the areas through which humans entered Europe from the Near East and Africa. It is not known exactly when the Neanderthals invaded the area, but they may have lived alongside modern humans from around 40,000 years ago. Recent excavation at the Mezmaiskaya Cave uncovered some bones of a Neanderthal infant. Although the skeleton is fragmentary, the 29,000-year-old bone material is beautifully preserved and gives us a more detailed insight into the perplexing question of the Neanderthal genetic legacy.

Importantly, the Caucasus Neanderthal DNA results are closely related but not identical to those from the Feldhofer Neanderthal. The closeness of the match removes many of the lingering doubts about the Feldhofer data. Also, neither set of Neanderthal DNA is more closely related to DNA from modern Europeans than to DNA from any other modern population, such as the !Kung people of southern Africa. Or, to put it another way, these Eurasian Neanderthals are just as distant genetically from modern Europeans as from any other group of modern humans.

And so these new results reinforce the argument against any gene flow between Neanderthals and modern Europeans and support the 'out of Africa' theory for the origin of modern humans. They do not entirely rule out the possibility of some gene flow, because just two individuals make a very small sample, but they make it less likely. The data also show that there was a common gene pool for the Neanderthals, which had no more or less variation within it than the gene pool of modern humans has. The genetic difference between these two geographically separated Neanderthals indicates that they

ABOVE The body tissue from the frozen corpses of the Siberian permafrost is well enough preserved to still retain fragmentary strands of the animals' DNA.

shared a common ancestor between 151,000 and 352,000 years ago. Their difference from modern humans indicates a divergence for the Neanderthals as a whole between 365,000 and 853,000 years ago, a measure very close to that obtained from the Feldhofer data.

Both samples are from late Neanderthals, indeed the Mezmaiskaya infant is one of the most recent known. What would be really interesting to find out now is how early Neanderthal DNA from around 200,000 or more years ago compares. Equally, it would be wonderful to be able to get fossil DNA from the other ancestral humans to clarify where exactly the Neanderthals came from. Did they originate from *Homo heidelbergensis* or from *Homo erectus*? The difficulty will be to find fossil bone of that age with well-enough preserved DNA, but it could happen and then it will be possible to get a better understanding of Neanderthal origins and population genetics.

European genes today

Support for the Neanderthal DNA analysis comes from a recent genetic survey of present-day European populations. Bryan Sykes and colleagues of Oxford University's Institute of Molecular Medicine have examined over 2000 samples of European mitochondrial DNA without finding any that are sufficiently distinctive to suggest any Neanderthal heritage.

Other classic ideas of European genetic heritage have also been upset by some of this new genetic information. What has surprised many experts is a claim that 10 per cent of the European gene pool still has a signature coming from the earliest of the Cro-Magnon incomers of the Upper Palaeolithic, originating some 50,000 years ago when they first arrived in Neanderworld.

Previously it had been thought that the incoming of much later Neolithic farmers around 8500 years ago had swamped the European gene pool. But it seems that the major contribution (70 per cent) has come from Late Upper Palaeolithic modern humans from between 14,000 and 11,000 years ago, and that the Neolithic contribution has been no more than 20 per cent.

A major problem is a lack of information from between 20,000 and 14,000 years ago, because of the effects of the last glacial when even the Cro-Magnons were nearly wiped out in Europe because of the extreme conditions. They probably survived only in refuges in south-west France, Cantabria and Ukraine. Only when the glaciers retreated and climate improved again did they venture forth across northern Europe along with the revived herds of surviving and initially prospering Ice Age animals. It was this dispersal event that probably created the basis for the modern gene pool of Europe.

Blood, spit and words

Bones, even when we have them as evidence, do not always help resolve the picturing of the deep prehistoric past of humanity. Fortunately they are not the only sources of information. In recent decades some surprising new areas of study have shown promise, especially the language and genes of modern populations. Both are like fossil shells in that they still retain and preserve traces of their historical development. But recovering the data and understanding that story can be difficult.

As an example, consider the English language and its distribution today. The greatest number of native English speakers are at present located in North America, with smaller isolated populations in Australasia and the British Isles. But an analysis of English shows that it is one of a group of 144 languages of Indo-European origin, which are mostly confined to Europe and western Asia. Within that language cluster, English is closest to the Germanic tongues of northern Europe. Peeling away the next layer of the language 'onion' reveals a closer affinity between English and west German, rather than Scandinavian languages. And it is possible to take off another layer and reveal a small group of 'Low' German languages in the north German region, differing slightly from those of southern 'High' German.

The kernel links English and Frisian of the North Sea coast from Holland to south Denmark. This is where English originated from when the Angles, Jutes and Saxons settled in Britain in the fifth century and brought their language with them. Unlike so many invaders, they not only stayed on but were reinforced in number and pushed westwards to dominate the heartlands of England.

The Basque core

The most intriguing aspect of European languages has been the role of the Basque language and peoples of northern Spain and south-west France in the prehistory of Europe. Their language is unique in Europe and they have the world's highest frequency (more than 50 per cent) of a very particular genetic marker, the Rhesus-negative blood group. Superficially the Basques seem to stand out from the general mélange of the European crowd and the question is, how did they get there?

An interesting and informative possibility is that the Basques might represent the last survivors of the original Cro-Magnon incomers, who were replaced by a wave of Rhesus-positive invaders from the east and south-east who brought Indo-European languages with them.

Cro-Magnon gene maps

Studies of the general genetic variation, derived from analysis of blood, saliva and hair from the peoples of Europe, reveals an overall match with the archaeological evidence and radiocarbon dating of the north-westwards spread of agriculture from the Middle East over 9000 years ago. The interesting question concerns what it was that spread: the technology or the farmers. Did the idea of farming spread with hunter-gatherers learning how to change their ways, or were the Cro-Magnon hunter-gatherers pushed out of the way by an influx of farmers, just as they displaced the Neanderthals?

The coincidence of genetic patterns and the prehistoric arrival of farming strongly indicates that it was the farmers themselves who spread. Their genes are diluted from south-east to north-west just as the hunter–gatherer genes are diluted in the opposite direction. Considering the subsequent tumultuous history of Europe, it is surprising that such patterns from 5000 and more years ago should persist down to the present. The answer lies in the remarkable efficacy of farming and herding compared with hunter–gathering, especially when the game is getting scarcer, perhaps as a result of over-hunting. Farming produces so many more calories per acre that farmers can afford to breed and survive at population densities between ten and a hundred times that of hunter–gatherers. Farming produced an enormous population explosion that just swamped the old genes.

None of Europe's subsequent historic upheavals – even the catastrophic wars and famines – has seriously dented the old pattern set by the influx of farmers. The Goths, Huns and Romans have come and gone without any significant impact on the ancient gene map of Europe.

It is deeply ironic that the Cro-Magnon ancestors of modern Europeans seem to have experienced the same displacement as they meted out to the Neanderthals. It is particularly interesting that it seems to have been a mixture of the linked cultural, economic and reproductive advantages of the Neolithic farmers that displaced them. Again, despite their apparent intelligence, communication skills and technology, the Cro-Magnons were still, on the whole, not able to change their ways in order to survive. Even though there is no doubt that they could and did interbreed with the Neolithic incomers, still 5000 years later the pattern is clear.

The lesson seems to be the old and familiar one of 'adapt or perish'. We would do well to remember the Neanderthals when climate change next accelerates. There might be human-induced global climate warming at the moment, but we are still living within a warm interglacial. One day, perhaps thousands of years in the future, this will end and the climate will descend inexorably into another glacial.

The image of the Neanderthals has come a long way since they were first thought of as rickety horsemen, savages or ape-like and hairy cavemen. They may not have been the ancestors of modern Europeans but they were human beings. Just as we now have to reassess our concern for our nearest living relatives, the great apes, to prevent them from becoming extinct, perhaps we should revise our opinions about the Neanderthals. As we have seen, some of the evidence from the stones and bones about their nature may be uncomfortable for us, but no more so than our own recent history. The ghosts of the Neanderthals may not in fact have any material existence today, but perhaps they are a salutary reminder that humans have a long and troubled history, and an ever-changing relationship with the natural world.

Glossary

Acheulian: an ancient tradition of tool-making characterised by hand-axes usually worked on both sides and known as bifaces. First found at St Acheul in Picardy but since discovered in Africa dating back more than a million years and lasting until about 150,000 years ago.

Alluvium: old name for surface deposits lying above the Diluvium, subsequently joined together with it to form the Quaternary (see below).

anatomically modern humans: those humans whose anatomy is very similar to that of living humans and who first appeared around 130,000 years ago. There are significant differences between them and 'archaic' modern humans who lived between about 300,000 and 100,000 years ago.

anthropoids: a group of higher primates which include the Old and New World monkeys, apes and humans, and which originated some 40 million years ago.

archaic modern humans: early modern humans who lived between about 300,000 and 100,000 years ago and are neither *Homo erectus* nor *Homo sapiens* but perhaps an evolutionary link between the two.

Ardipithecus ramidus: a very ancient, possible biped found in Ethiopia, dating from around 4.4 million years ago and thought to have been more ape- than hominid-like but still perhaps a distant human relative.

artefact: any object made, modified or used by humans and ancient human relatives.

Aurignacian: the first major tool industry of early Upper Palaeolithic age in Europe, from ?40/37,000–31,000 (34–28,000 radiocarbon) years ago, characterized by steep-sided scrapers, long retouched blades, bone points and occasionally jewellery and art. First found at Aurignac in southern France by Edouard Lartet with anatomically modern human remains and bones of extinct animals.

aurochs/aurochsen: extinct wild cattle (*Bos primigenius*) which were often illustrated by Cro-Magnon artists on cave walls and carvings and only died out in 1627. Ancestor of today's cattle and were first domesticated about 8000 (6000 radiocarbon) years ago.

australopithecines: meaning southern ape, a group of early hominids (of the genus *Australopithecus*) including at least 7 species that lived in Africa between about 4 and 1 million years ago, some of which had very robust jaws and teeth and others which were more gracile in form.

bifaces: see **hand-axe**.

bovids: a grouping of cattle, sheep, antelope, etc., which are hoofed mammals with even-toes.

brow-ridge: a ridge of bone above the eyes.

Châtelperronian: a tool industry found in central and south-west France and northern Spain between the end of the Middle and beginning of the Upper Palaeolithic between about 38–34,000 (36–32,000 radiocarbon) years ago. It shows some features of both Mousterian and Upper Palaeolithic traditions, including some of the earliest bone, antler and ivory objects and is associated with the late Neanderthals. Named after Châtelperron in central France.

Cro-Magnons: the first anatomically modern humans in Europe, named after a rock shelter near the town of Les Eyzies in the Dordogne.

culture: an archaeological term based on very large or widespread collections of material objects, such as stone and bone tools, that show some common characteristics and belong to the same space-time continuum, such as Magdalenian. Now broadened to include behavioural traits, belief systems, etc., and is a more embracing term than industry (see below).

Diluvium: deposits thought to have been laid down by the Biblical flood, found above Tertiary deposits and below the Alluvium (see **Quaternary**).

DNA: deoxyribonucleic acid, the self-replicating genetic material present in every cell.

endocast: a cast of the internal space of the skull, closely approximating the shape of the brain.

flint: a natural, crypto-crystalline silica mineral which occurs as irregularly shaped nodules in certain limestone strata, especially the Cretaceous age Chalk rock (100–65 million years old) in Europe. Hard and brittle like glass, it can be fashioned into a variety of shapes with very sharp edges and was a favoured material for stone tools.

glacial period: a cold period during an ice age when ice sheets and glaciers grow and sea-level falls (see **interglacial**).

grooming: the cleaning of hair by hand or teeth to remove parasites, often practised between individuals to reinforce social bonds.

hand-axe: a stone tool of varied shape from oval to triangular, with both faces worked (also called a biface) to give a sharp edge, characteristic of the Acheulian tradition of the Lower Palaeolithic but also found in some Mousterian industries.

Holocene: the second and present epoch of the Quaternary period which began 12,000 (10,000 radiocarbon) years ago and is climatically the interglacial in which we are now living.

hominids: members of the extended human family which includes all the species of *Australopithecus*, *Homo* and the great apes.

hominines: members of the human family, including the extinct fossil members, the australopithecines.

Homo: the genus to which all humans, living and extinct, belong, of which between 5 and 8 species of humans have so far been found. They lived over the last 2.5 million or so years and ranged from *Homo rudolfensis* to *Homo sapiens*.

Ice Age: a colloquial term for the most recent of nine or more prolonged cold phases in the history of the Earth most of which have lasted 20–100 million years. The recent Pleistocene Ice Age has, so far, consisted of some 24 stages of global climate change oscillating between relatively long, cold phases (glacials) and slightly warmer and shorter phases (interglacials) which last tens of thousands of years. Altogether, the recent Ice Age has lasted some 2 million years.

interglacial: a relatively warm climate phase during an ice age when ice sheets and glaciers retreat and subsequently sea-level rises. Global climates are at present in an interglacial phase.

industry, stone tool: tools with certain forms repeated and found within a limited geographical region and timespan, which may be a single site or specific region, suggesting that they were made by a single group of people. More narrowly defined than the broader term culture (see above).

Levallois: an advanced stone-tool technology which appears in the Lower Palaeolithic by 400,000 years ago or earlier and becomes increasingly used from 350,000 years ago, i.e. the beginings of the Middle Palaeolithic of which it is a characteristic feature. It required the preparation of a stone core from which thin flakes were then struck, and allowed a certain degree of predetermination of the ultimate form of the flakes detached. Named after the Levallois site, now in the Paris suburbs and associated with the Neanderthals.

Lower Palaeolithic: earliest part of the Old Stone Age, beginning around 2.4 million years ago with the Oldowan stone tool tradition in Africa and includes the Acheulian, ending with the development of Middle Palaeolithic flake tools from 350,000 years ago. Some experts link the start of the Middle Palaeolithic with the beginning of the Levallois technique.

Magdalenian: the main late Upper Palaeolithic tool tradition in western Europe, dating from about 21–14,000 (18–12,000 radiocarbon) years ago, which includes stone, bone and antler tools, decorative items and many painted caves, e.g., Lascaux. Associated with anatomically modern humans, it is named after the rock shelter of La Madeleine in the Dordogne.

Middle Palaeolithic: characterized by the flake tools of the Mousterian tradition between around 350,000 and 35,000 (33,000 radiocarbon) years ago; separates the Lower and Upper Palaeolithic.

Mousterian: a stone tool industry characterized by certain technologies such as the Levallois technology as well as the production of small hand-axes, triangular points and side-scrapers. Mainly associated with the Neanderthals and lasting from over 350,000 to around 35,000 (33,000 radiocarbon) years ago. Named after Le Moustier in the Dordogne.

Neanderthals: the most recently extinct human species (*Homo neanderthalensis*) who lived in Europe and Eurasia between about 200,000 and 30,000 (28,000 radiocarbon) years ago and share a common ancestor with modern humans about 400,000 years ago. Recent DNA analysis reinforces their separateness from modern humans and suggests that they did not interbreed with the Cro-Magnons, with whom they overlapped for some thousands of years.

Neolithic: (New Stone Age) prehistorical phase, succeeding the Mesolithic in Europe, associated with the beginnings of cereal cultivation, cattle and sheep domestication, ceramic pottery and increasing sedentism and village life in the Old World, starting around 12,000 (10,000 radiocarbon) years ago in western Asia.

Oldowan: the oldest known tradition of tool-making which began in Africa at least 2.4 million years ago and consists of mainly choppers, flakes and hammer stones. These types of tools were generally made from cobbles from which flakes had been struck. Named after Olduvai Gorge in Tanzania where they were first recognized but they have since been found as far away as China and Georgia.

Palaeolithic: (Old Stone Age) the first long period of the Stone Age which began around 2.4 million years ago in Africa with the beginnings of the Oldowan tool tradition and which in Europe was followed by the Mesolithic around 12,000 (10,000 radiocarbon) years ago. (See **Lower**, **Middle** and **Upper Palaeolithic**).

permafrost: ground in polar and alpine regions which is permanently frozen to depths of up to several hundred metres throughout the year, apart from the surface which may unfreeze during the short summer. At present some 20 per cent of the Earth's surface is permafrost.

Pleistocene: the first epoch of the Quaternary period, dating from about 1.8 million years ago until 12,000 years ago, which includes the most recent Ice Age and is characterized by a series of glacial and interglacials (see **Holocene**). The epoch is divided into Lower, Middle and Upper with the boundary between the Middle and Upper dated at around 128,000 years ago.

point: a category of stone tools consisting of pointed tools flaked on one or both sides, used as knives and, from Middle Palaeolithic times, to tip spears.

primates: a group of mammals with features in common that includes all humans, apes, monkeys, lemurs, lorises, tarsiers and their fossil representatives who originated at least 65 million years ago.

Quaternary: the youngest system of geological deposits comprising the old divisions of Diluvium and Alluvium which are now known respectively as the Pleistocene and Holocene and laid down over the last 1.8 million years.

radiocarbon dating: a method of dating organic materials such as wood and bone, based on the rate of decay of radioactive carbon isotopes but only effective over the last 55,000 years. Radiocarbon years are not exactly calendar years and so significant adjustments have to be made in converting one to the other, as shown throughout this book.

Solutrean: a late Upper Palaeolithic stone industry found in Spain and France between 23,000 and 21,000 (21–18,000 radiocarbon) years ago, named after the open-air site of Solutré in eastern France. The tools are characterized by thin and flat 'laurel-leafed' points, often with considerable surface retouching.

Tertiary: a grouping of relatively young geological strata first recognized in the eighteenth century and now largely replaced by the Paleogene and Neogene. Preceded by the Cretaceous, the last period of the Mesozoic era, and succeeded by the Quaternary. The Tertiary is subdivided into a number of epochs from the Palaeocene to the Pliocene and is now known to have lasted from 65–1.8 million years ago.

tool industry: see **industry, stone tool**.

Upper Palaeolithic: the last epoch of the Palaeolithic in Europe, North Africa and parts of Asia, lasting from about ?40/35–12,000 (33,000–10,000 radiocarbon) years ago and characterized by diversified blade industries, diverse working of bone, antler and ivory, decoration, art and sophisticated hunting, gathering and fishing.

Further Reading

Neanderthals and Cro-Magnons
Gamble, Clive, *The Palaeolithic Settlement of Europe*. Cambridge University Press, Cambridge, 1986
Jordan, Paul, *Neanderthal*. Sutton Publishing, Stroud, 1999
Mellars, Paul, *The Neanderthal Legacy*. Princeton University Press, Princeton, New Jersey, 1996
Shreeve, James, *The Neanderthal Enigma*. Penguin Books, London, 1995
Stringer, Christopher and Clive Gamble, *In Search of the Neanderthals*. Thames and Hudson, London, 1993
Tattersall, Ian, *The Last Neanderthal*. Westview Press, Boulder, Colorado, 1999

Primate Evolution and Biology
Bodmer, William and Robin McKie,*The Book of Man*. Abacus, London, 1994
Caird, Rod, *Ape Man*. Boxtree, London, 1994
Cartwright, John, *Evolution and Human Behaviour*. Macmillan Press Ltd, Basingstoke, 2000
Changeux, Jean-Pierre and Jean Chavaillon (eds), *Origins of the Human Brain*. Clarendon Press, Oxford, 1995
Diamond, Jared M., *The Rise and Fall of the Third Chimpanzee*. Vintage, London, 1991
Fleagle, John G., *Primate Adaptation & Evolution*. Academic Press, San Diego, California, 1988
Foley, Robert, *Humans Before Humanity*. Blackwell Publishers, Oxford, 1995
Gibson, Kathleen R. and Tim Ingold, *Tools, Language and Cognition in Human Evolution*. Cambridge
    University Press, Cambridge, 1993
Harrison, G.A., J.M. Tanner, D.R. Pilbeam and P.T. Baker, *Human Biology* 3rd ed., Oxford University Press,
    Oxford, 1992
Johanson, Donald C. and Maitland A. Edey, *Lucy: The Beginnings of Humankind*. Penguin Books, London, 1990
Jones, Steve, Robert Martin and David Pilbeam (eds), The Cambridge Encyclopedia of Human Evolution.
    Cambridge University Press, Cambridge, 1992
Klein, Richard G., *The Human Career*. Chicago University Press, Chicago, 1989
Lewin, Roger, *Principles of Human Evolution*. Blackwell Science, Oxford, 1998
McKie, Robin, *Apeman*. BBC Worldwide Ltd, London, 2000
Mithen, Steven, *The Prehistory of the Mind*. Phoenix, London, 1996
Oxnard, Charles E., *Fossils, Teeth and Sex*. University of Washington Press, Seattle, 1987
Rightmire, G. Philip, *The Evolution of Homo erectus*. Cambridge University Press, Cambridge, 1990
Stringer, Christopher and Robin McKie, *African Exodus*. Pimlico, London, 1996
Tattersall, Ian, Eric Delson and John Van Couvering (eds), *Encyclopedia of Human Evolution and Prehistory*.
    St James Press, London, 1988
Trinkaus, Eric, and Pat Shipman, *The Neanderthals*. Knopf, New York, 1993
Tudge, Colin, *The Day Before Yesterday*. Jonathan Cape, London, 1995
Vrba, Elisabeth S., George H. Denton, Timothy C. Partridge and Lloyd H. Burckle (eds), *Paleoclimate and
    Evolution with Emphasis on Human Origins*. Yale University Press, New Haven, 1995
Walker, Alan and Pat Shipman, *The Wisdom of the Bones*. Phoenix, London, 1997

General
Bahn, Paul G., *The Cambridge Illustrated History of Prehistoric Art*, Cambridge University Press,
    Cambridge, 1998
Bahn, Paul G. and Jean Vertut, *Journey Through the Ice Age*, Weidenfeld & Nicolson, London, 1997
Palmer, Douglas, *The Atlas of the Prehistoric World*, Marshall Editions, London, 2000
Patterson, Colin, *Evolution*, The Natural History Museum, London, 1999

Fiction
Auel, Jean, *The Clan of the Cave Bear*, Bantam Books, New York, 1980
Golding, William, *The Inheritors*, Faber, London, 1955
Kurtén, Björn, *Dance of the Tiger*, Abacus, London, 1982

Web sites with information on Neanderthals:

- www.mc.maricopa.edu/academic/cult_sci/anthro/exploratorium/hominid_journey/
- Neanderthals: a cyber perspective. **thunder.indstate.edu/~ramanank/index.html** An excellent general site with good links section.
- The Neanderthal Museum (Germany): **www.neanderthal.de/** (English version available.)
- Smithsonian Museum: human evolution pages. **web1.si.edu/harcourt/nmnh/human/default.htm**
- 'The Latest Neanderthal': *Scientific American* article. **www.sciam.com/explorations/1999/110899nean/index.html** Also has links to other *Scientific American* articles.
- 'Neanderthal Noses': – *Discover* magazine article **208.245.156.153/archive/output.cfm?ID=1076**
- 'Possible Hybrid Child': – *Discover* magazine article **www.discover.com/july_99/featneander.html**
- Chauvet Cave (earliest cave art – Cro-Magnon) **www.culture.fr/culture/arcnat/chauvet/fr/** (English version available.)

Academic Web sites with information on Neanderthals:

- Mediterranean Prehistory Online (academic journal) **www.med.abaco-mac.it/home.htm**
- Article on the Portugese possible hybrid child (academic) **www.med.abaco-mac.it/articles/doc/013.htm#A1**

Web sites on more general aspects of human origins and evolution:

- *National Geographic* **www.nationalgeographic.com** Several articles over the last few years dealing with human evolution.
- Indiana State University **www.indiana.edu/~origins/index.html** Academic site aimed at students. Many good links from here.
- Institute of Archaeology: University College London home page **www.ucl.ac.uk/archaeology/**

Museums

- American Museum of Natural History: **www.amnh.org**
- National Museum of Natural History, Smithsonian Institution: **www.nmnh.si.edu/paleo/links.html**
- Natural History Museum, London: **www.nhm.ac.uk**
- University of California Museum of Paleontology, Berkeley: **www.ucmp.berkeley.edu**

Societies and organisations

- Discovery Channel: **www.discovery.com**
- Natural Environment Research Council, UK: **www.nerc.ac.uk**
- The Wellcome Trust: **www.wellcome.ac.uk**
- The Sanger Centre Human Chromosome 22 project: **www.sanger.ac.uk/hgp/chr22**
- The Palaeontological Association, UK: **www.palass.org**
- Geological Society of London: **www.geolsoc.org.uk**

Science journals

- American Scientist: **www.amsci.org/amsci/**
- Discover: **www.discover.com**
- National Geographic: **www.nationalgeographic.com**
- Nature: **www.nature.com**
- New Scientist: **www.newscientist.com**
- Trends in Ecology & Evolution: **www.trends.com**
- Scientific American: **www.sciam.com**

Index

Page numbers in *italics* refer to photographs, tables and illustrations.

Picture Acknowledgements:

DW Design: 16, 32, 43, 156, 158 (top and bottom), 172–3, 180–1, 182–3, 206–7;

Eammon Egerton/Emma Armstrong-Evans: 102–3 (main), 166;

Illustrated London News: 29;

Instituto Português de Arqueologia: 205;

Japan–Syria Joint Excavation Team: 117 (top);

Lascaux Project/Eurelios/Science Photo Library: 177;

Dinosaurs and Prehistoric Animals/Marshall Editions: 49 (bottom), 53, 55;

Stephen Morley: 2–3, 10–11 (main), 12, 15, 35, 38–9 (main), 50, 56–7, 59, 60–1 (main), 61 (inset), 67, 71, 72 (sequence), 73 (top and bottom), 76, 77, 79 (inset), 80, 82, 83, 84, 86, 87, 90, 92, 93, 97, 100, 103 (inset), 104, 106, 110 (top and bottom), 117 (bottom), 119, 126–7 (main), 128, 138–9, 140, 143 (sequence), 145, 148–9, 150–1 (main), 164–5, 170, 174, 191 (top and bottom), 198–9 (main and inset), 200, 203;

Natural History Museum/Jay Maidment: 14, 19, 26, 30, 62, 99, 113, 116, 118 (top and bottom), 133, 175, 176, 179, 184;

Novosti (London): 209;

Douglas Palmer: 58;

John Reader/Science Photo Library: 11 (inset), 22, 28, 64, 69, 72 (top);

Royal Geographical Society: 75;

Society of Antiquaries: 20;

N.K. Vereshchagin: 212;

Wall to Wall Television: 89 (top and bottom), 91, 96 (top and bottom), 108–9, 111 (sequence), 112, 115 (sequence), 120 (sequence), 127 (inset), 136 (top and bottom), 141 (sequence), 142, 147 (sequence), 151 (inset), 152, 154–5, 169 (inset), 188–9, 192 (top and bottom), 194–5 (main), 195, 204 (sequence);

Dr Ian Willis, University of Cambridge: 4–5, 16, 24–5, 39 (inset), 40, 47, 48–9 (top), 78–9 (main), 168–9 (main).

Acknowledgements

Two academic consultants for the television series, Professor Chris Stringer, of the Natural History Museum, London and Dr Paul Pettitt of the University of Oxford have been generous with their time and extremely helpful in commenting on the text and diagrams. Any remaining errors are mine. Dr Ian Willis of the University of Cambridge and Professor Martin Sharp of the University of Alberta have generously supplied photographs of glacial landscapes. Robert Kruszynski of the Natural History Museum in London was particularly helpful in arranging archaeological specimens for photography.

I owe special thanks to Katy Carrington and Christine King. Katy as my editor at Channel 4 Books, was particularly encouraging and spared no effort to see the book through production. As text editor, Christine was indefatigable in improving the text. Ailsa Orr, Emma Fenton and Dan Kendall at Wall to Wall provided helpful information and comments on the text and Nerys Morgan, of DW Design, has been instrumental in achieving the high standard of design and illustration.